W.E.B. Du Bois

ON SOCIOLOGY AND THE
BLACK COMMUNITY

THE HERITAGE OF SOCIOLOGY

A Series Edited by Morris Janowitz

W.E.B. Du Bois

ON

SOCIOLOGY AND THE

BLACK COMMUNITY

Edited and with an Introduction by
DAN S. GREEN AND EDWIN D. DRIVER

THE UNIVERSITY OF CHICAGO PRESS

CHICAGO AND LONDON

The University of Chicago Press, Chicago 60637
The University of Chicago Press, Ltd., London

Library of Congress Cataloging in Publication Data

Du Bois, William Edward Burghardt, 1868–1963.
   W. E. B. Du Bois on sociology and the Black community.

   (Heritage of sociology)
   Bibliography: p.
   Includes index.
   1. Afro-Americans—Social conditions—to 1964—Collected
works.   I. Green, Dan S.   II. Driver, Edwin D.   III. Title.
E185.86.D845   301.45′19′6073   78-770
ISBN 0-226-16762-3

Contents

Preface and Acknowledgments   vii
Introduction by Dan S. Green and Edwin D. Driver   1

I. THE TASKS OF SOCIOLOGY   49

  1. The Atlanta Conferences   53
  2. The Laboratory in Sociology at Atlanta University   61
  3. The Twelfth Census and the Negro Problems   65
  4. The Study of the Negro Problems   70
  5. The Negro Race in the United States of America   85

II. COMMUNITY STUDIES   113

  6. The Philadelphia Negro   115
  7. The Black North in 1901: New York   140
  8. The Negroes of Dougherty County, Georgia   154
  9. The Negroes of Farmville, Virginia   165

III. BLACK CULTURE AND CREATIVITY   197

  10. The Negro American Family   199
  11. The Religion of the American Negro   214
  12. The Problem of Amusement   226
  13. The Conservation of Races   238

IV. CHANGING PATTERNS OF RACIAL RELATIONS   251

    14. The Relations of the Negroes to the Whites
        in the South   253
    15. The Social Evolution of the Black South   271
    16. The Problem of the Twentieth Century Is the
        Problem of the Color Line   281
    17. Prospect of a World without Race Conflict   290

Notes   303
Selected Bibliography of W.E.B. Du Bois   311
Index   317

Preface and Acknowledgments

The purpose of this volume is to make available to sociologists and other interested scholars a wide selection of the sociological writings of W.E.B. Du Bois. Special effort was made to include contributions which are out of print and very difficult to obtain. The selections which are included demonstrate Du Bois' concentration on black Americans and black community life in the United States. This collection of Du Bois' sociological writings is also of interest since it highlights Du Bois as an early American sociologist.

Throughout a lengthy and active life, W.E.B. Du Bois excelled in numerous occupations. Important above all, however, was his initial and, to him, most significant occupation—sociologist. Du Bois embarked on a career as a sociologist prior to the turn of the century; his goal was to ameliorate the race problem in the United States through a careful, scientific, sociological analysis of black Americans.

From 1896 to 1910 Du Bois was an extremely productive sociologist. His credits include a major monograph on black urban life, numerous other studies, published and unpublished, on various aspects of black American life and culture. In 1897, following his research in Philadelphia, he joined the faculty at Atlanta University; his primary responsibilities were to teach sociology and to take charge of the newly created program of sociological studies on the American Negro. In 1910 he left Atlanta for a career as a journalist and propagandist. He was somewhat disheartened about abandoning his goal of ameliorating the race problem through scientific analysis but felt that he might be more effective toward this end in his new career. Most of Du Bois' sociological writings were done between 1896 and 1910, although as this collection of his sociological writings shows, they continued after he left the academic world. In this sense, W.E.B. Du Bois remained a sociologist throughout his life.

We are deeply appreciative to the Ford Foundation for supporting the research on W.E.B. Du Bois which led to this volume. We would also like to express our gratitude to the many libraries and librarians who were helpful in supplying us with Du Bois' writings and pertinent background material.

Credit is given to the original publisher of each of Du Bois' essays at the beginning of each chapter. We are grateful for their generous permission to reprint them in this volume.

DAN S. GREEN and EDWIN D. DRIVER

INTRODUCTION

I

William Edward Burghardt (W.E.B.) Du Bois engraved his name in the annals of American history during a lifetime that spanned ninety-five years, from shortly before the Emancipation Proclamation to the eve of the 1963 civil rights protest demonstration in Washington, D.C. During a life filled with creativity and controversy, Du Bois had a varied occupational history; he was a historian, editor, writer, educator, civil rights activist, propagandist, and sociologist. Known primarily for his propagandistic activities and leadership on behalf of his race, Du Bois began his career as an empirical sociologist committed to the sociological study of the condition and problems of black Americans.

Du Bois was born in Great Barrington, Massachusetts, in 1868, shortly after the legal emancipation of enslaved black Americans. He was the only child born to Alfred and Mary Burghardt Du Bois. He later, partly humorously, remarked that he was born "with a flood of Negro blood, a strain of French, a bit of Dutch, but thank God! no 'Anglo-Saxon.'" Although from a poor family, he recalled that even with his brown face and frizzled hair, he was accepted by his peers and was, at times, even a leader among the town gang of boys. His color did not seem to interfere with his early social life. Generally, his childhood was idyllic in the small New England community where the color line was not sharply drawn, and social class and town roots seemed to be more important than skin color. The youngster grew up adhering to the local Protestant, Yankee values; he later wrote that he was taught to cordially despise the poor Irish and South Germans who worked in the local mills.

1

As he grew up, although still generally socially accepted, he began to realize that he was different from the other children. First, he was aware of an intellectual difference that allowed him to excel in his school work and to recite in a manner which he referred to as a "happy, almost taunting glibness." He also slowly began to become cognizant that some people considered his color a misfortune or even a crime. This realization brought "days of secret tears," but it also compelled him to try harder and to perform better.

His competitiveness and perseverance are indicative of the Yankee heritage with which he was thoroughly indoctrinated. He learned to guard his emotions, to be sparing in his daily greetings with others, and generally to be restrained in his social interaction. Most of his behavioral patterns were thoroughly New England. In retrospect Du Bois noted that, later on, Southern Negroes were troubled by his reticence and his reluctance to greet them casually and warmly on the streets. His aloofness and coldness has been noted by others, and he has been criticized for being unable to identify or appear comfortable with common men.[1] Though this aloofness was in part due to his New England social heritage, some was undoubtedly engendered by his race, and some by his unusually keen intellect. Du Bois was by no means a common man.

Will Du Bois, as he was known as a youth, was the only black student in his graduating high school class. He took a standard college preparatory course which he completed with high honors. One racial incident occurred during this time, when the students proudly exchanged visiting cards. A girl, a newcomer to the community, refused his card. It occurred to him that her refusal was based on his color.

By this time Du Bois had already demonstrated a unique talent for writing. He had written for the *New York Globe* and as a local agent had sent weekly letters to the *New York Age*, both black newspapers. He was also the Great Barrington correspondent for the Springfield, Massachusetts, *Republican*. Even at this early age, his writing frequently tended toward social criticism.

When Du Bois graduated from high school in 1884, he hoped to continue his education at Harvard. His mother died the same year, and without either financial resources or a relative who could assume the costs of a college education, he could not then attend Harvard. However, his high school principal and several local clergymen were able to offer the talented graduate a scholarship to Fisk University, a school for black students which was affiliated with the Congregational church. Although disappointed that he was not going to Harvard, Du Bois was pleased to have the opportunity of continuing his education and also of interacting with blacks.

As a high school youth, he had taken his first trip away from the tranquility and seclusion of Great Barrington. He had been invited to visit his paternal grandfather, a boat steward in New Bedford. It was, he claimed later, his "greatest boyhood trip," and his "first great excursion into the world." On his return home, he stopped in Providence at the house of a friend of his grandmother's and had what he called "another stirring experience." He went to an annual picnic on Narrangansett Bay attended by black people from three states; here he "viewed with astonishment" thousands of black people "of every hue and bearing." In open-mouthed astonishment, he saw "The whole gorgeous gamut of the American Negro world; the swaggering men, the beautiful girls, the laughter and gaiety, the unhampered self-expression. I was astonished and inspired. I apparently noted nothing of poverty or degradation, but only extraordinary beauty of skin-color and utter equality of mien, with absence so far as I could see of even the shadow of the line of race."[2]

II

Du Bois left the sheltered tranquility of Great Barrington in 1885 for the "real world." With him he took his hardy Yankee morality, a flair for writing, a developing social consciousness, and an eager thirst for learning. In retrospect, he noted that his disappointment at not going to Harvard was partially balanced by the excitement of going South, where he could again meet blacks of his own age, education, and ambitions. In looking back, Du Bois wrote that he leapt into this world with enthusiasm and discovered a loyalty and allegiance to his race which took precedence over his nationality: "Henceforward I was a Negro."

As it turned out, this new world of racial prejudice, discrimination, and color consciousness was wholly unlike anything that Du Bois had ever experienced. He quickly learned the role of the black man in Tennessee. One day while he was walking through the streets of Nashville, a white woman suddenly came around a corner and brushed against him. He tipped his hat, and manifesting his customary politeness, said, "I beg your pardon, madam!" She adamantly responded: "How dare you speak to me, you impudent nigger!"

Du Bois found the Fisk curriculum excellent but limited. His education at Fisk is perhaps best described as a mixture of traditional classical training and liberal arts. He seems to have been highly regarded by his teachers, and he, in turn, returned the compliment, claiming that he had been inspired by them. He furthered his literary skills by editing the school paper. In that capacity he wrote perhaps his first statement on the race problem, "An Open Letter to the Southern People." Here he noted the arbitrary distinction made between black and white, and pointed out that while whites justified black disfranchisement on grounds of ignorance, little was done to provide blacks with equal opportunities in education. During summer vacations, he gained first-hand knowledge of the rural South by teaching in black country schools. Du Bois graduated from Fisk in 1888.

The yearning to attend Harvard continued while Du Bois was at Fisk. The opportunity occurred when Harvard decided to become more of a national institution by attempting to enroll qualified students from the South and West. The young scholar applied, feeling that his New England background, his race, and the fact that he was studying in the South would work in his favor. He was accepted with a scholarship and matriculated at Harvard in 1888 as a junior. Although he had already received a bachelor's degree, Harvard required him to enroll as an advanced undergraduate because of the supposed academic deficiencies of Fisk.

At Fisk he had learned about race and the two worlds of the South; in contrast, at Harvard he experienced the loneliness of a black man in a white university. As an undergraduate from 1888 to 1890, he took courses in the "hard sciences," social sciences, and philosophy. In 1890 he was awarded a second B.A. degree, with honors in philosophy, and along with another black graduate, he gave the class oration. He could not, however, readily identify with the institution and did not consider himself a part of it. He sought only the "tutelage of teachers" and the use of the laboratory and library facilities. He later wrote, "I do not doubt that I was voted a somewhat selfish and self-centered 'grind' with a chip on my shoulder and a sharp tongue."[3] Commenting elsewhere, he said, "I was desperately afraid of not being wanted; of intruding without invitation; of appearing to desire the company of those who had no desire for me."[4] He insulated himself as far as possible in a completely colored world. He said that, while he was in Harvard, he was not part of Harvard.

Du Bois applied for a graduate fellowship at Harvard, writing in his application that he desired to obtain a Ph.D. in social science, "with a view to the ultimate application of its principles to the social and economic rise of the Negro people."[5] He received a stipend for the study of ethics in relation to jurisprudence or sociology. "From 1890 to 1892," he wrote "I was a fellow at Harvard University, studying in history and political science and what would have been sociology if Harvard . . . recognized such a field."[6] Thus Du Bois was taking his initial steps toward the new discipline of sociology, feeling that it was the science of social action. He commented that in his quest "for basic knowledge with which to help guide the American Negro I came to the study of sociology, by way of philosophy and history rather than by physics and biology. After hesitating between history and economics, I chose history."[7]

His first research effort was begun during his first year of graduate study in a history seminar taught by Albert Bushnell Hart, his advisor. He methodically checked the United States statutes, colonial and state laws, the *Congressional Record*, executive documents, and other relevant sources for information about the African slave trade. Upon Hart's suggestion, the suppression of the African slave trade later became his thesis topic. He presented the initial results of his research to the American Historical Association in 1891. Apparently his presentation was well-received; the New York *Independent* mentioned it as one of the best three papers presented.[8]

Harvard granted Du Bois a master's degree in 1891, and he was reappointed a fellow for the following year. During the 1891-92 academic year, he spent most of his time working on his dissertation. Most of his graduate study was in history and political economy. One of the later courses is noteworthy since it was the only sociology course that Du Bois took. It was entitled "Principles of Sociology: Development of the Modern State and Its Social Functions."[9] The course was taught by Edward Cummings, who apparently did not greatly impress Du Bois, because while Du Bois mentions many of his Harvard mentors in his writings, he does not mention Cummings.

With two bachelor's degrees and a master's degree, and being well on his way toward his doctorate, Du Bois was, by any standard, a highly educated person. Even so, he wanted at least a year of "careful training" at a European university to properly complete his education. Harvard had already turned down a request for financial aid toward this goal, so he looked elsewhere. He was fortunate in receiving a grant from the Slater Fund, half gift-half loan, for a year's study at the University of Berlin, with the possibility of a renewal for a second year.

From 1892 to 1894, at Berlin, Du Bois studied economics, history, and sociology under many of the recognized scholars of the developing social sciences, and used his vacations to travel and observe extensively throughout Europe. In his first semester he sat in a seminar taught by the renowned Gustav Schmoller, who, probably more than any other teacher, influenced his career as a sociologist. Broderick has noted that "Schmoller ... drew Du Bois away from history into a type of political economy which could easily be converted into sociology, and, at a more general level, encouraged him to a career devoted to scholarship."[10]

Schmoller's methodological approach favored the use of induction to accumulate historical and descriptive material. He saw the goal of social science as the systematic, causal explanation of social phenomena, and he believed that social scientific facts, based on careful, inductive analysis, could be used as a guide to formulate social policy. He has been called a conservative social reformer who was deeply involved with the social question, remaining open to any kind of reform that would bring about social justice.[11] Even though Schmoller was interested in social reform, he taught his young

American student the difference between scientific issues and moral issues. Du Bois quoted his mentor as having said in a seminar: "My school tries as far as possible to leave the *Sollen* [should be] for a later stage and study the *Geschehen* [is] as other sciences have done."[12]

Du Bois' early sociological studies, until around 1910, manifest in many details Schmoller's tutelage: an emphasis on empirical data collection and the use of the inductive method, the collection of facts as a basis for formulating social policy, an underlying interest in social justice, and an emphasis on a historical approach. Speaking of his later research in Philadelphia, Du Bois seemed to be echoing Schmoller: "We simply collect the facts: others may use them as they will."[13]

The youthful scholar celebrated his twenty-fifth birthday in Europe. In a diary entry on his birthday he wrote that he dedicated "himself as the Moses of his people." Wondering about his future career and how he might best serve his race, he wrote: "These are my plans; to make a name in science, to make a name in literature and thus to raise my race. Or perhaps to raise a visible empire in Africa thro' England, France, or Germany ... I wonder what will be the outcome? Who knows?"[14] There can be little doubt that his first two goals were fulfilled; and against insurmountable odds, he spent much of his life working toward the third goal of an independent Africa, which he was instrumental in helping to establish.

The European experience broadened Du Bois socially as well as intellectually. He noted that as a result of his contact with Europeans, he began to perceive the color issue in the United States more broadly: "I began to see the race problem in America, the problem of the peoples of Africa and Asia, and the political development of Europe as one. I began to unite my economics and politics; but I still assumed that in these groups of activities and forces, the political realm was dominant."[15]

Prior to Du Bois' stay in Europe, and with the exception of his childhood, social distance between blacks and whites had functioned to separate him from whites; the racial social distance of Nashville and Harvard had undoubtedly hardened his convictions toward whites. In Europe, however, he discovered that he was readily accepted socially and that racial barriers were not what he had anticipated. He began to realize that not all whites were color conscious, and he began to feel "more human." Regarding his unencumbered social interaction with educated and mannered Europeans, he wrote:

> I emerged from the extremes of my racial provincialism. I became more human; learned the place in life of 'Wine, Women, and Song'; I ceased to hate or suspect people simply because they belonged to one race or color; and above all I began to understand the real meaning of scientific research and the dim outline of methods of employing its technique and its results in the new social sciences for the settlement of Negro problems in America.[16]

Du Bois left the United States in 1892 as a Harvard-trained historian with a background in philosophy; two years later he returned as an empirically oriented sociologist ready to use his experience for the uplift of his people. Du Bois did not obtain his Ph.D. from Berlin, because the Slater Fund was unable to provide the monies needed to complete another year there. The outstanding quality of his course work and thesis is evidenced by Schmoller's petitioning the university to admit Du Bois to candidacy in just one-half of the minimum time (6 semesters) established by the university. The petition was not honored because such a precedent would have meant acting on several other but less exceptional students.[17] After his return and while teaching at Wilberforce, he was awarded a Ph.D. from Harvard from the Department of History and Government. His dissertation, *The Suppression of the African Slave Trade to the United States of America, 1638-1870*, was published as the first volume in the Harvard Historical Series.

During the nine years from 1885 to 1894, Du Bois had received his formal academic instruction. Much of his undergraduate instruction had emphasized science, and what he referred to as "the scientific attitude." He was fairly well-trained in mathematics, language, psychology, philosophy, and economics, and was well-trained in history.[18] His overall training in social science and his instruction in courses with a sociological orientation provided him with a relatively solid foundation in the developing discipline of sociology. His later work would adequately demonstrate both his training and his sociological competence.

The young savant had discovered the value of education. He must have reflected upon how his education had shaped and influenced his opportunities and raised his status in a racist society. His essay "The Talented Tenth," which speaks of a certain selected few black youths receiving a college education so that they could lead the masses, is indicative of the value that he placed on a college education.[19]

III

Although his education had taught him what he must do to alleviate the Negro problem, his immediate concern was to earn a living. He began a systematic writing campaign to find a teaching position: "I wrote to no White institution—I knew there were no openings there."[20] He finally received an offer to teach classics at Wilberforce University, a small, black, Methodist school in Ohio; he immediately accepted. There were four other offers, including one from Booker T. Washington at Tuskegee Institute; he later speculated about the course his life might have taken had he accepted Washington's offer.

At Wilberforce, Du Bois taught Latin, Greek, German, and English. To his already busy teaching load he wanted to add a course in sociology, which he offered to teach on his own time; however, the administration did not see a need for such a course. This occurred in 1895, which means that if Du Bois had been allowed to teach the course, it would have been among the first sociology courses taught in the United States. The religious orientation of the school, the administration, and the fact that he was neither engaged in the teaching of social science nor pursuing any research made his position at Wilberforce less than satisfactory. His writings indicate that he became increasingly unhappy, and at age twenty-eight he was concerned about fulfilling his pledge to help his people through sociological research.

An unexpected opportunity arose in 1896 when he was offered a temporary appointment at the University of Pennsylvania as an assistant instructor. There is some dispute regarding the title; Rudwick has claimed that the actual title designated by the provost was "Investigator of the Social Conditions of the Colored Race in This City."[21] Ordinarily, the matter of an academic label would be of little concern, but Du Bois later accused the university and the faculty of not wanting a "colored instructor"—the rank which he claimed the department head might have offered him on the basis of his academic background.[22] According to Du Bois, he was hired for only a year, was given no real academic standing, no office at the university, and no official recognition of any kind; there was no mention of his name in the university catalog, he had no contact with students, and very little contact with the faculty, including the sociology department.[23]

Du Bois claimed that Philadelphia was one of the worst governed of our nation's ill-governed cities and was going through the throes of a periodic mood of reform and, as a consequence, desired a study of the "cause" of the urban problems. A scientific investigation backed by the prestigious university would provide empirical support to the already formed opinion of most white Philadelphians that the "underlying cause was ... the corrupt, semi-criminal vote of the Negro Seventh Ward."[24]

The young sociologist arrived in Philadelphia in 1896 to begin his first effort at sociological research. Performing the research as a participant observer, he wrote: "With my bride ..., I settled in one room ... over a cafeteria run by a College Settlement, in the worst part of the Seventh Ward. We lived there a year, in the midst of an atmosphere of dirt, drunkeness, poverty, and crime. Murder sat on our doorsteps, police were our government, and philanthropy dropped in with periodic advice."[25]

Du Bois' resulting social study, *The Philadelphia Negro*, is a 400-page monograph on the plight of black Americans in Philadelphia, based on a survey and demographic data, much of which was collected by the author during his stay. Du Bois undoubtedly realized the significance of the study; it was not only his first research endeavor, but it was also a study of a city that at that time had the largest Northern black community in the nation. The general aim of his study was

To present the results of an inquiry ... into the condition of the four thousand or more people of Negro blood now living in the city of Philadelphia. This inquiry extended over a period of fifteen months and sought to ascertain something of the geographical distribution of this race, their occupations, and, above all, their relation to their million white fellow-citizens. The final design of the work is to lay before the public such a body of information as may be a safe guide for all efforts toward the solution of the many Negro problems of a great American city.[26]

His work in Philadelphia is one of the first community studies in the United States.

Du Bois remained in Philadelphia for fifteen months working on his study, except for two months in 1897, when he traveled to Virginia to collect data for related research.[27] He was disappointed, following the completion of his study, that the university did not at least offer him a temporary instructorship either in the university or at the Wharton School; white classmates of his from Harvard of "lower academic standing," he wrote, became full professors at Pennsylvania and Chicago. What bothered him was that the idea of retaining him never occurred to the academicians and administrators at Pennsylvania.[28]

IV

In 1897, following his fifteen month stay in Philadelphia, Du Bois was hired by Atlanta University as a professor of economics and history and as director of the Sociological Laboratory and the Atlanta University Conferences. The year before, Atlanta had initiated a series of annual conferences to study the effect of urban problems on black Americans, and the series had generated a heightened interest in sociology among the students and graduates. During 1897-1910, Du Bois took complete charge of the annual sociological conferences, edited the annual studies, and taught an upper division, three-term course entitled Sociology.

The young sociologist brought his training and research experience to the conferences. Under his firm guidance, the research became more rigorous, and he established a long-range program whereby one study, as reliable and valid as experience and funds would permit, would be completed annually. One scholar has observed that "*The Atlanta University Publications*, consisting of 18 monographs published between 1896 and 1914, were the first attempts to study scientifically the problems of the American Negro anywhere in the world; the first studies to make factual, empirical evidence the center of sociological work on the Negro."[29]

Regarding the need for such a research program, Du Bois wrote, "Atlanta University is situated within a few miles of the geographical centre of the Negro population of the nation, and is, therefore, near the centre of that congeries of human problems which cluster round the Black American." He further claimed that Atlanta University could not escape studying and teaching some of the conditions related to that mass of social questions. Du Bois envisioned the Atlanta Studies as "a comprehensive plan for studying a human group."[30] Rather than focusing on social reform, he chose to work toward "the collection of a basic body of fact concerning the social condition of American Negroes, endeavoring to reduce that condition to exact measurement whenever or wherever occasion permitted."[31]

In retrospect, Du Bois noted that his initial ideas about altering the program were modified by such variables as cost, the availability of suitable data, and tested methods of investigation.[32] In spite of these limitations and a reluctance to investigate such important but controversial topics as politics and miscegenation, he finished a ten-year study cycle, the first two studies of which were completed prior to his affiliation with Atlanta:

1896   *Morality among Negroes in Cities*
1897   *Social and Physical Conditions of Negroes in Cities*
1898   *Some Efforts of Negroes for Social Betterment*
1899   *The Negro in Business*
1900   *The College-Bred Negro*
1901   *The Negro Common School*
1902   *The Negro Artisan*
1903   *The Negro Church*
1904   *Some Notes on Negro Crime, Particularly in Georgia*
1905   *A Select Bibliography of the American Negro*

Begining in 1906 he desired to initiate a broader, more logical, and more inclusive research program "designed to bring the whole subject matter into a better integrated whole."[33] Factors such as cost and the availability of data and what he called "outside diversions" kept his research from attaining the logical design which he had planned. His eventual resignation from Atlanta University left his desires for the program unfulfilled. Between 1906 and 1914, the following eight studies were completed:

1906   *Health and Physique of the Negro American*
1907   *Economic Cooperation among Negro Americans*
1908   *The Negro American Family*
1909   *Efforts for Social Betterment among Negro Americans*
1910   *The College-Bred Negro American*
1911   *The Common School and the Negro American*
1912   *The Negro American Artisan*
1914   *Morals and Manners among Negro Americans*

Du Bois' relationship with the Atlanta Studies was formally severed in 1914; however, the publications continued in 1915 and 1918 and then ended because of the war.

In 1903 he wrote about his general plan for the Atlanta Studies:

A subject is chosen; it is always a definite, limited subject covering some phase of the general Negro problem, schedules are then prepared, and these with letters are sent to the voluntary correspondents, mostly graduates of this and other Negro institutions of higher training. They, by means of local inquiry, fill out and return the schedules; then other sources of information, depending on the question under discussion, are tried, until after six or eight months' work a body of material is gathered. Then a local meeting is held, at which speakers who are specially acquainted with the subject studied, discuss it. Finally, about a year after the beginning of the study, a printed report is issued, with full results of the study, digested and tabulated and enlarged by the addition of historical and other material.[34]

His plan ultimately was to outline ten topics and keep each going at various stages simultaneously while publishing only a single study per year. The ten areas of study were population distribution and growth, health and physique of blacks, socialization, cultural patterns of morals and manners, education, religion, crime, law and government, literature and art, and a bibliography and summary. Commenting on the potential value of such a program, after the fact, he stated, "If it could have been carried out even imperfectly . . . who can doubt its value today, not only to the Negro, but to America and to the still troubled science of sociology."[35]

The object of the Atlanta Studies, according to Du Bois, was "a careful search for truth conducted as thoroughly, broadly, and honestly as the material resources and mental equipment at command will allow."[36] Unhappy with some social scientists who still thought in terms of theoretical speculation and eternal laws, his program attempted to focus on limited empirical investigations of a real group of human beings who he claimed were so artificially set off from the white population that the study would approximate a laboratory experiment.

During his stay at Atlanta University, Du Bois' research and grandiose plans received inadequate funding. Any criticism of the Atlanta University Studies, therefore, must consider that fact. Noting that he spent $500 for each study, he commented sarcastically:

> We can go to the South Sea Islands half way around the world and beat and shoot a weak people longing for freedom into the slavery of American color prejudice at the cost of hundreds of millions, and yet at Atlanta University we beg annually and beg in vain for the paltry sum of $500 simply to aid us in replacing gross and vindictive ignorance of race conditions with enlightening knowledge and systematic observation.[37]

He made frequent appeals for money to whomever he thought would aid him; he thought that his research "would have thrived if Booker T. Washington had not blocked support for the project."[38] Later he stated that white philanthropy had starved the studies to an untimely death.[39] Despite the financial problems, and with the help of limited outside funding, Du Bois managed to continue the program. It is not difficult to find fault with certain aspects of Du Bois' Atlanta Studies, especially when judged by contemporary standards of investigation. One must not fail to consider certain inadequacies simply because of the era in which the studies were done, but it is our opinion that it is unfair to judge these early, empirical studies strictly by today's standards. The research and methodological techniques employed in the Atlanta Studies generally conformed to social scientific procedures acceptable during the era in which they were made.

Du Bois was aware of some of the problems involved with his work. In 1904 he wrote that he had been greatly hampered in his research because of his inability to convince a "considerable number of American people of the burning necessity of work of this sort and its deep scientific significance." He maintained that the work should be done, and he was correct when he claimed that "we are doing it better than anyone else."[40] It must be emphasized that this was Du Bois' initial attempt at directing a large-scale, on-going research project. The Atlanta Studies were an altogether different undertaking than the research that he did single-handedly in Philadelphia. It could be posited that his overzealousness in obtaining an empirical base of information about black Americans, which he felt would alleviate "the Negro problem," overshadowed his otherwise heightened methodological conscience. In short, while Du Bois was aware of the methodological deficiencies of his work, especially the lack of reliability and validity, he nevertheless felt that some information was better than none. Perhaps he also felt that he was doing the best he could given the limitations under which he was forced to conduct his research.

Although it is difficult to assess the impact of the Atlanta Studies, it can be safely said that they formed an impressive body of research which must have served to strengthen racial pride among a large number of black Americans. Perhaps the most significant effect of the studies was in destroying some of the many myths that had arisen about blacks by gathering empirical data. Rudwick has claimed that the studies provided blacks with appropriate arguments for their low status in society, which arguments carried the imprimature of social science.[41]

From 1897 to 1910, as professor of economics and history at Atlanta, Du Bois not only took charge of the annual sociological conferences, but also taught an upper division three-term course entitled Sociology. (Later, his title was professor of either history and sociology or economics and sociology.) Du Bois' students learned about the significance of economics in social life, the inductive method, comparative sociology, and of course, various aspects of black American life in a predominently white society. He had his students performing sociological studies which he noted were at times of real scientific value. One class, for example, published a report in the *Bulletin* of the U.S. Department of Labor; studies by several classes were used in the Atlanta Studies.[42]

In retrospect, Du Bois spoke about his thirteen years at Atlanta University as the beginning of his real life work:

> They were years of great spiritual upturning, of the making and unmaking of ideals, of hard work and hard play. Here I found myself. I lost most of my mannerisms, I grew more broadly human, made my closest and most holy friendships, and studied human beings. I became widely acquainted with the conditions of my people. I realized the terrific odds which faced them.[43]

During his early years at Atlanta, Du Bois wrote most of his sociological material. Still striving to maintain a scientific orientation, and still optimistic that black progress could be built upon a foundation of empirically based data, he wrote, among other articles, "A Program for a Sociological Society" (1897); "The Negroes of Farmville, Virginia: A Social Study" (1898); "The Study of the Negro Problem" (1898); "The Negro in the Black Belt" (1899); "The Negro and Crime" (1899); "The Negro Landholders of Georgia" (1901); "The Laboratory in Sociology at Atlanta" (1903); "The Negro Farmer" (1904); "Sociology Hesitant" (1904); "Die Negerfrage in den Vereinigten Staaten" (1906); "Sociology and Industry in Southern Education" (1907); "Race Friction between Black and White" (1908); and "The Economic Aspects of Race Prejudice" (1910). This selection of Du Bois' sociological writings is representative of the work he was doing during this period; a complete list of his sociological writings appears in the Bibliography.

Not only was he becoming a prolific sociologist, but shortly after the turn of the century he began to publish in popular magazines. He also began publishing a weekly paper called *The Moon*, which lasted from 1906 to 1907. This was the first of five publications which he founded and edited. In 1907, along with two friends, he initiated another publication, *The Horizon*, which was somewhat more successful than his first one, lasting until the middle of 1910.

V

In 1900 Du Bois was approached by a publisher, A. C. McClurg, who solicited material for a book. He apprised them of his work with the Atlanta Studies, but they sought material with wider appeal. He finally collected a group of his essays and wrote a new one about the program and philosophy of Booker T. Washington and submitted these to the publisher. The collection, entitled *The Souls of Black Folks*,[44] is his most widely read publication and has been said to have "had a greater effect upon and within the Negro race in America than any other single book published in this country since *Uncle Tom's Cabin.*"[45] Broderick has remarked that "it is Du Bois' best statement of the Negro's case to white America, and despite a looseness of imagery which clouds meaning, it is a minor American classic."[46]

The essay about Washington, "Of Mr. Booker T. Washington and Others," established Du Bois as a critic of Washington's program of compromise between blacks and whites. It is important to note that Du Bois did not argue *ad hominem* but argued that Washington's program was not in the best interests of black Americans. Washington had become a national figure, hailed by both blacks and whites for establishing a foundation of rapprochement between races. Du Bois was not opposed to rapprochement or to Washington's proposals of thrift, hard work, patience, or industrial training. In fact, Du Bois had long praised Washington's efforts in reconciling blacks and whites, and the progress he had gained for blacks, but Du Bois feared that the Tuskegee leader's program would make it difficult, if not impossible, to win equal rights.

Du Bois was unequivocal in insisting that blacks not desert, even temporarily, efforts toward increasing political power, gaining first-class citizenship, and attaining higher education for their most promising youth. In contrast with Washington, Du Bois held that black Americans would be advanced by the leadership of their exceptional men; he regarded a college-educated cadre of leaders, later to be referred to as the "Talented Tenth," as a necessary condition for racial advancement. This concept had been formulated as early as 1891, while Du Bois was at Harvard.

The Washington–Du Bois dispute, which began in 1903, continued with growing intensity until 1908. Generally, Du Bois' position was that equal social and economic opportunity could not be expected or achieved without first gaining political rights. He was not opposed to industrial training, but he argued eloquently that higher education was also necessary. Washington, of course, countered by asserting that Du Bois was primarily interested in the progress of a small elite.

Du Bois was not actively or publicly anti-Washington. He only argued against those parts of his program which were antithetical to his own. He had long admired Washington's accomplishments and agreed with his ideas of black nationalism and self-help.

Washington had what seemed to Du Bois nearly complete power over national black and many local black political appointments, the black press, and philanthropic aid to black causes. Du Bois believed that he could have gained more financial support for the Atlanta Studies with Washington's support; in fact, Du Bois felt that his adversary was thwarting the Atlanta program because of his criticism of the Tuskegee leader. The controversy with Washington was a major factor in leading Du Bois away from his sociological studies and eventually steering him into actions beyond the academy.

A related issue which also led Du Bois away from sociology was his involvement in the Niagara Movement. In 1905 he was elected secretary of this "first black organization which aggressively and unconditionally demanded civil rights."[47] The Niagara Movement, which began in 1905, formulated a program for gaining civil rights for blacks, sought to call attention to the complaints of blacks, and offered dissident blacks a medium for opposition to the policies and programs of Booker T. Washington. The organization struggled through six annual meetings, from 1905 to 1910, with Du Bois leading the group. Initially it gained momentum and strength, but then it faltered because of differences of opinion and ideology, lack of finances, and organizational disputes. The Niagara Movement is significant in American history and in the life of Du Bois in that it foreshadowed future civil-rights organizations and provided blacks a choice between the melioristic and conservative program of Washington and the more radical and forceful policy of legal protest espoused by Du Bois and his followers. A record of how Du Bois' involvement hastened his evolution from the academy to community leadership is contained in his correspondence. [48]

Du Bois' program of continued agitation to end discriminatory practices, waged from 1903 to 1910, although seemingly diverse, was possessed with remarkable unity—civil rights and first-class citizenship for blacks. His Niagara involvement and the related controversy with Washington had publicly branded Du Bois a "radical" and a racial agitator. Without question, he was the greatest "race man" of the era; this role, however, whether he desired it or not, interferred with and compromised his role as an academic sociologist.

The early years at Atlanta, from around 1897 to 1900, found the young scholar intensely involved with the Atlanta Studies and other sociological research efforts. Beginning in 1901 and continuing until his public split with Washington in 1903, he was apparently moving through a transition period away from academic science and sociology toward action, agitation, and writing for popular magazines. By 1910 he could claim that he had stepped "out of my ivory tower of statistics and investigation . . . [and] sought with bare hands to lift the earth and put it in the path in which I conceived it ought to go." [49]

During the decade ending in 1910, he became convinced that scientific investigation was not sufficient to solve the problems of black Americans. The problems were not, as he had initially and idealistically assumed, those of ignorance, but were instead based on the conscious determination of one group to suppress and persecute another. "Not simply knowledge," he wrote, "not simply direct repression of evil, will reform the world. In long, indirect pressure and action of various and intricate sorts, the actions of men which are not due to lack of knowledge nor to evil intent, must be changed by influencing folkways, habits, customs, and subconscious deeds." [50] Reinforcing this viewpoint, he also noted that, "first, one could not be a calm, cool, and detached scientist while Negroes were lynched, murdered and starved; and secondly, there was no such definite demand for scientific work of the sort that I was doing, as I had confidently assumed would be easily forthcoming." [51] For these reasons, among others, Du Bois, the young, brilliant, scientific sociologist, evolved into a master of direct action.

Du Bois reluctantly resigned from Atlanta University in 1910, after coming to the uneasy realization that the difficulties the university was having in obtaining general financial support, and particularly money for the Atlanta Studies, was in part a personal issue attributable to the controversy with Washington. As long as he remained on the faculty, he perceived, Atlanta, already under financial strain, would continue to have difficulties obtaining funds. He resigned, under no pressure, to become an executive of the newly formed NAACP.

Although he had officially resigned from Atlanta, Du Bois continued to coedit, in absentia, volumes 15 through 18 of the Atlanta Studies. He was assisted in this effort by his successor and former student, Augustus G. Dill. Later he wrote that from 1910 to 1920 he followed "the path of sociology as an inseparable part of social reform," but that it was not the same type of sociology or detached investigation that he had formerly pursued. [52] He would never again, as he had during the early Atlanta years, pursue detached research.

VI

Until as late as 1911, Du Bois had remained optimistic that the Niagara Movement would continue as an annual conference, but given the organizational and financial difficulties, and the formation of the NAACP in 1910, his desire was to be unfulfilled. The NAACP had its origin in a reaction to a lynching in Springfield, Illinois, in 1908. The incident spurred a group of Northern white liberals to form a committee to discuss the status and problems of black Americans. Du Bois was invited to this initial meeting, which led to a second conference in 1909 for the purpose of forming a new civil-rights organization to work for the full equality of black Americans. Most of the members of the defunct Niagara Movement, including Du Bois, joined the new organization, which became incorporated as the National Association for the Advancement of Colored People. Du Bois was the only black man among the five incorporators, and he was the first black staff-executive as the founder and editor of their official publication, *The Crisis*. His primary role in the new organization was to edit and publish *The Crisis*. In retrospect, he wrote: "The span of my life from 1910 to 1934 is chiefly the story of *The Crisis* under my editorship, but it had also an astonishing variety of subsidiary interests and activities." [63]

As editor of *The Crisis*, Du Bois held that the opinion expressed therein was to be his personal opinion and not that of the NAACP. In short, it was to be almost exclusively his personal publication. He was so successful in his new role that the circulation skyrocketed, and as a consequence, the journal began to pay its own way. By 1915, following the death of Booker T. Washington, Du Bois became "the most prominent prophet in the Negro race." [54] However, Du Bois' success and prominence did little to alter the view of the NAACP that *The Crisis* should represent the organization and its viewpoints, not those of its editor. Thus a breach was established between the unyielding editor and the board of directors.

Each issue of the periodical contained numerous editorials, many of which were decidedly provocative. Du Bois denounced, among other things, whites, white Christian churches, particular denominations, black churches, the government, politicians, and various white institutions. Through his editorials, Du Bois, as perhaps the foremost spokesman for black Americans, told his readers, among other things, how to live, how to protest, what to read, and who to like and dislike.

Despite his editorial independence, Du Bois did support the efforts of the organization and dutifully reported their activities. However, in 1914 his editorial independence brought him criticism from the association's chairman of the board, and an organizational storm ensued which was not satisfactorily resolved. Again in 1934 the matter of editorial independence arose when Du Bois began to editorialize about his plan for black self-sufficiency, which ran counter to the assimilationist aims of the parent organization.

His plan was called nondiscriminatory segregation, which meant the development of black culture within white America. The plan included voluntary residential segregation, which Du Bois thought would serve effectively to unite blacks. The NAACP was opposed to any program of segregation, even if proposed and espoused by the eminent Dr. Du Bois. The long-standing feud over control of *The Crisis*, together with this new episode, led the board of directors to again rebuke Du Bois. The strong-willed editor replied only that *The Crisis* "never was and never was intended to be an organ of the Association in the sense of simply reflecting its official position."[55] Unable to comply with the demands of the board, Du Bois resigned from the NAACP in 1934.

The effect of Du Bois and *The Crisis* on black America during the twenty-four years that he served as editor was immense. *The Crisis* was the first general publication and, at that time, the only national publication written by a black for black consumption. Du Bois inspired over a generation of black Americans with his brilliant editorials, informed them of current events of interest to blacks, and regularly published the work of aspiring young black writers. *The Crisis* was the only publication repeatedly and strongly urging and clamoring for civil rights. Langston Hughes, for one, has written about the influence of Du Bois and *The Crisis* on his life:

> So many thousands of my generation were uplifted and inspired by the written and spoken words of . . . Du Bois that for me to say I was so inspired would hardly be unusual. My earliest memories of written words are those of Du Bois and the Bible. My maternal grandmother read to me as a child from both the Bible and *The Crisis*. And one of the first books I read on my own was *The Souls of Black Folk*. Years later, my earliest poems were accepted for publication by *The Crisis* under the editorship of Dr. Du Bois. It seems as if, one way or another, I knew Dr. Du Bois all my life. Through his work, he became a part of my life.[56]

During the period that Du Bois was with the NAACP, although most of his time and energy was devoted to *The Crisis*, he nevertheless continued his writing and speaking engagements. His theme by this time was settled—civil rights for blacks. In 1911 he read a paper before the Sociological Society in England.[57] This event is particularly noteworthy, since it was the only time in his long and illustrious career that he read a paper at a formal sociological meeting. The invitation coincided with the Universal Races Congress held in London in July 1911, where he had been named a cosecretary, representing the United States. The paper that he read before the congress, "The Negro Race in the United States of America," was judged by the

Manchester Guardian as the best presented there. Among others who participated were Franz Boas, Ferdinand Toennies, Felix Adler, and Israel Zangwill. Du Bois maintained that if it had not been for World War I, which so quickly followed, the congress would have established a new epoch in the cultural and racial history of the world.[58] It should be emphasized that Du Bois was the only American sociologist invited to present a paper at this first international scientific gathering on race.

He was the chief organizer of the First Modern Pan-African Conference in Paris in 1919, called to consider the interests of Africa following World War I. He attended and was deeply involved in the Second Pan-African Conference in 1921 and in a third conference two years later. The crusading scholar remained keenly interested and personally involved in African affairs throughout his life, fighting against the neocolonialist policies of the Western world and continuing to help gain black African unity.

Throughout the early 1920s Du Bois and Marcus Garvey waged editorial battles in their respective periodicals; Du Bois called his rival a "little fat, Black man; ugly but with intelligent eyes and a big head." Garvey countered with the claim that Du Bois was "the most dangerous enemy of the Negro Race in America," and he had his organization, the United Negro Improvement Association, exile Du Bois in 1924 from the Negro race.[59]

During the 1920s, Du Bois' influence among blacks seems to have diminished. There were more black newspapers and journals to compete with *The Crisis*; many blacks became more militant than the aging scholarly editor in defending their rights. He was never an active leader and manifested obvious shortcomings as a leader. Black society was moving away from his ideas of racial separation toward an integrationist mood. Although he was on the downgrade from his previous pinnacle of leadership, Du Bois was still very much in the forefront of the black civil-rights movement.

VII

In 1930 William Edward Burghardt Du Bois was sixty-two years old and was accomplished in four professions—sociologist, historian, educator, and journalist. He was nearing the age of retirement, when most American males begin to think of resting on their laurels. However, the indefatigable scholar never seemed to think of the quiet life of retirement when so much remained to be done in the matter of race relations. In 1933, at the age of sixty-five, Du Bois returned to Atlanta University as a visiting professor in the Department of Economics and Sociology to give a series of lectures. He thought that a return to Atlanta would have a certain poetic justice and would also relieve the NAACP from the financial burden of paying his salary during the depression.

The next year, after resigning from the NAACP, he was hired by Atlanta as head of the Department of Economics and Sociology. With Du Bois in the department were Walter Chivers, Ira De A. Reid (who also had joined Atlanta in 1934), and Hersey Strong. The department offered twelve courses at the time, including Sociology of the American Negro, 1850-1876; Karl Marx and the Negro; Seminar in Economic and Social Cooperation among American Negroes; and Seminar in Sociological Problems. By 1937-38, the department, under Du Bois' guidance, was offering seventeen courses. New course offerings were African Culture, Asiatic Culture, American Negro Culture, Race Problems, Urban Sociology, Social Conflict, and Social Institutions. By 1940, twenty-two courses were offered. Some of the new courses were: The Negro Family in The United States, Race Problems in the Modern World, Sociology of the South, and European Sociology.

Concerning his return to Atlanta University and academic life, Du Bois remarked: "I returned to my ivory tower, not so much for new research, as for interpretation and reflection; and for making a record of what I had seen and experienced."[60] Although he had returned to academic life and sociology, he retained enough of his propagandistic bent to impair his objectivity as a social scientist. More simply, he was no longer the objective, empirically oriented sociologist who had taught at Atlanta from 1897 to 1910; he was now more action-oriented, politicized, and "radical."

Still, one of his primary interests was reviving the old Atlanta University Conferences; he desired to model a new program after the old Atlanta program of collecting and disseminating empirically based information about blacks and black life. In 1940 he founded and became editor of a new scholarly journal, *Phylon*, an Atlanta University "Review of Race and Culture," which is still in existence. In 1941 he began to organize the first Phylon Conference in the hope of reviving the former Atlanta University Conferences.

The twenty-sixth Atlanta University Conference met in Atlanta in 1943 with thirty-four persons, representing thirty institutions, attending. The conferees included many prominent sociologists. Among those present were E. Franklin Frazier, Library of Congress; Charles S. Johnson, Fisk University; Howard W. Odum, University of North Carolina; E. B. Reuter, University of Iowa; T. Lynn Smith, Louisiana State University; Edgar T. Thompson, Duke University; Donald Young, Social Science Research Council; and William Earle Cole, University of Tennessee.[61] One of the results of the conference was an attempt to get black colleges to initiate a series of cooperative studies of black social conditions. Du Bois was singularly honored when he was selected as the official coordinator. Because the meeting was considered very important as an attempt to advance black studies, a second conference was planned for the following year.

Shortly after this moment of acclaim, without notice of any kind, Du Bois was suddenly retired as professor and head of the Atlanta Department of Sociology. He spoke of his feelings and frustrations about leaving the newly initiated Atlanta research program: "The result of this action was disastrous; not merely to me but to the American Negro. Up until this time the Negro himself had led in the study and interpretation of the conditions of his race in the United States. Beginning in 1944, with accelerated speed the study of the Negro passed into the hands of whites and increasingly Southern whites."[62]

Du Bois, at age 76, found himself unemployed—his career seemingly over, and his plans for the systematic study of blacks once more thwarted. At first he received several offers of part-time employment and lecturing from black colleges; Howard University, for example, extended him an invitation to join its faculty. In the midst of these opportunities, an unexpected offer came from the NAACP to rejoin them as director of special research, an offer he unhesitatingly accepted.

VIII

Du Bois was happy to return to the NAACP, the organization which he had helped to found, and wanted only the leisure time to write, assuring the association that he expected no role in the executive department. He offered to revive the Pan-African movement and pay special attention to international aspects of the race problem. Soon after he began work, he discovered that Walter White, then secretary of the association, expected him to serve as a ghost writer and general representative at White's discretion. The ambiguity of his status became a grave concern, and in general he was unhappy about his new working conditions.

Du Bois and White attended the initial United Nations organizational meetings in San Francisco in 1945, representing the NAACP. Du Bois remained active in the Pan-African congresses, attended various meetings and conferences (both Pan-African and other) and traveled 20,000 miles delivering lectures for the NAACP. In 1946, on behalf of the NAACP, he planned an appeal to the Human Rights Commission of the United Nations, which was eventually delivered to a member of the United Nations Secretariat.[63] This document was Du Bois' protest to the world's highest international body about the prejudice and discrimination practiced against a segment of the population by one of the founding members.

His second tenure with the NAACP lasted only four years. In 1948, on White's request, Du Bois was dismissed by the Board of Directors for issuing a provocative memorandum which criticized both White and the association.

Following his dismissal from the NAACP, Du Bois accepted an honorary position as vice-chairman of the Council on African Affairs, an organization which appeared on the attorney-general's list of subversive organizations. He also was appointed chairman of the Peace Information Center, another reputedly subversive organization, which he had helped to found. During the late 1940s, Du Bois altered his thinking in several ways. His writings became more emotional, ideological, bombastic, and replete with "communist" and "leftist" phraseology, and they were more often published in so-called leftist publications. His behavior clearly manifested a heightened interest in international affairs, a tendency which had been building up for years.

Beginning in the late 1940s his efforts toward achieving world peace in the shadow of the Cold War and a threatened confrontation between democracy and communism became more open. He was invited to join a small group which eventually planned the Cultural and Scientific Conference for World Peace. The conference, which met in New York in 1949, was sponsored by 550 "outstanding leaders of American cultural and liberal thought."[64] Leading intellectuals in the arts and sciences from over seventeen nations on both sides of the Iron Curtain were invited; Du Bois commented that the conference "marked an era in the cultural history of the United States."[65] The *New York Times* reported the meeting as one of the most controversial in recent city history.

Later in 1949 Du Bois attended a world peace meeting in Paris which he called "the greatest demonstration for peace in modern times" and the "greatest meeting of human beings that he had ever attended."[66] In August 1949, twenty-five prominent Americans were invited to attend a Soviet peace conference in Moscow; because of the violent and bitter reception given the New York conference, and for other obvious reasons, all but Du Bois declined the invitation. As was so often the case with Du Bois, he was again ahead of his time— he had urged civil rights upon a nation that was not ready, and now he was involved in efforts for world peace during an era when such ideas were considered heretical and un-American.

In late winter 1950, the aging scholar-activist received a telegram from an old friend urging him to attend a meeting to discuss new activities to promote world peace. The meeting resulted in the establishment of the Peace Information Center, an organization dedicated to tell the people of the United States what other nations were doing about war and peace. The group periodically sent out informative notices called peacegrams and, among other activities, collected signatures for the Stockholm Appeal, a petition demanding an absolute ban on the use of atomic weapons and a strict enforcement of that ban. Dean Acheson, then secretary of state, called the petition a propaganda trick of the Soviet Union by which the American people would not be fooled.[67] Du Bois replied, defending the organization and providing the press with a list of the renowned intellectuals who had signed the petition.

En route home after attending a peace conference in Prague, Du Bois received a cable from an officer of the Peace Information Center informing him that the government had demanded their registration as agents of a foreign principal. In their response to the Department of Justice, spokesmen for the center maintained that they were "American in conception and formation," were only interested in peace, and were agents of no government, American or foreign. Because of this stance, they did not comply with the government's request, and in early 1951 the organization and its officers were formally indicted as "an agent of a foreign principal." Du Bois' embittered words about the condemnation are poignant:

> I have faced during my life many unpleasant experiences; the growl of a mob; the personal threat of murder; the scowling distaste of an audience. But nothing has so cowed me as that day, November 8, 1951, when I took my seat in a Washington court-room as an indicted criminal. I was not a criminal. I had broken no law, consciously or unwittingly. Yet I sat with four other American citizens of unblemished character, never before accused even of misdemeanor, in the seats often occupied by murderers, forgers, and thieves; accused of a felony and liable to be sentenced before leaving this court to five years of imprisonment, a fine of $10,000 and loss of my civil and political rights as a citizen, representing five generations of Americans.[68]

The trial began in November 1951, and after five days of prosecution testimony, the judge acquitted the defendants, ruling that the government had failed to support the allegations in the indictment. Even so, Du Bois was now more than ever a marked and tainted figure—acquitted of the alleged crime, but nevertheless deeply and irrevocably stigmatized; innocent, yet guilty of being accused.

During this period, Du Bois returned briefly to academia. In 1948 he taught a course called "The Negro in American History" at the New School for Social Research in New York City. Here again Du Bois was ahead of his time, teaching black history at a white institution. In the early 1950s he taught courses in African and

Afro-American history at the Thomas Jefferson School in New York, until the government closed the school.

Despite his age, Du Bois continued to write. He completed *In Battle for Peace*, the account of his indictment and trial, and in 1957 the first novel in the *Black Flame* trilogy was published.[69] The trilogy is a fictional account of black history in the United States from Reconstruction to 1961.

During an extensive trip in 1959, primarily to China and the USSR, Du Bois attended, in Stockholm, the tenth anniversary of the World Council for Peace, of which he had at one time been vice-president. He also presented to Mr. Khrushchev a proposal for a Soviet based Institute of African Studies, and this was in fact opened in Moscow the following year.

IX

Dr. and Mrs. Du Bois were invited to attend the Independence Ceremony in Ghana in 1957, but difficulty in obtaining passports prevented their attendance. During this period Du Bois had to turn down many offers to travel abroad because of the State Department's refusal to issue him a passport. He finally wrote the passport office: "My beliefs are none of your business. I repeat my demand for a passport in accordance with the Constitution of the United States, the laws of the land, and the decision of the courts."[70]

In 1960 Du Bois again had trouble obtaining a passport to attend the celebration of the founding of the Republic of Ghana, but this time his passport was finally issued. While he was in Ghana, Kwame Nkrumah asked him to return to Africa to begin work on an encyclopedia Africana. Du Bois was delighted with such an opportunity but was reluctant because of his age and the amount of time necessary even to begin to outline the vast undertaking. The offer was left open. After returning home, he undertook some preliminary research seeking opinions about the project from other scholars and research bodies throughout the world. The response overall was favorable, and in 1961 Du Bois wrote Nkrumah informing him that he would come to Ghana to begin work on the project. Aged 93, he was aware that this would be his final move, and he looked forward to the encyclopedia Africana as the pinnacle of his career.

Du Bois took over the encyclopedia Africana project in Ghana in 1961 and, except for some brief bouts of illness and periods of recuperation, organized the preliminary groundwork. This lasted until he died in his sleep on August 27, 1963, the eve of the massive civil rights march on Washington, D.C., for which he had spent a lifetime laying the groundwork.

In 1961, shortly before the aging activist left for Ghana, he wrote a letter to Gus Hall, chairman of the American Communist party, seeking membership.[71] In the letter, Du Bois spoke of his political development and his evolution from socialism to communism, and he offered the American Communist party a ten-point program which he declared would restore democracy to the nation. Although there had been accusations and innuendos for decades about Du Bois' ideology, he had not, up until this time, been a member of the Communist party.

Du Bois' close friend, historian Herbert Aptheker, has written of a speech into which Du Bois put extraordinary effort and thought and which Du Bois presented many times in 1953. Part of the speech reads:

> This brings me to the crux of my message. We Negroes are not fighting tonight against slavery. That fight is won. We are now not fighting in vain for the ballot. We hold the balance of power in the North, and either we get the vote in the South or we come North and get it here. But we are fighting desperately the economic battle for the right to work and to get from our work food, housing, education, health, and a chance to live as human beings. But in this fight we are not alone. With us stand and must stand, whether they will or not, the white workers of America and the World.[72]

Aptheker claims that "It was this kind of emphasis and this insight that brought him . . . into the communist party."[73] St. Clair Drake commented that Du Bois' "defection" was related to his impatience "with what he considered an unforgivably slow rate of change in the status of Black men in America during a period when the winds of change were blowing with revolutionary velocity elsewhere."[74]

X

During the period 1896–1910, Du Bois was an unusually productive sociologist. His major sociological work, *The Philadelphia Negro*, based on social survey and participant observation, was published in 1899, two years after publication of Durkheim's *Le Suicide*. His Atlanta Studies initiated the technique of measuring social change through continuous resurveys of particular social phenomena; they remain classic statements about black conditions at the turn of the century. In addition, Du Bois authored some unpublished papers as well as over thirty published papers ranging from community studies to explanations of criminality among blacks. His sociological writings stand alone as the significant body of descriptive and empirically based information about black Americans in the early twentieth century.

Du Bois was generally critical of many of his sociological peers and their work, claiming that they were unnecessarily impeding the new discipline by providing an arm-chair, speculative orientation rather than an inductive, empirical approach. His primary concern was to make a science of sociology by emulating the orientation of the physical sciences. He had entered sociology with the hope that his work would alleviate the race problem; he felt that knowledge was the key, and that ignorance and misinformation were, in large part, the problem. He sought "the truth" by means of his empirical investigations, believing that the truth would alleviate the problem by bringing the facts to well-intentioned, but ignorant whites.

Early in his life he dedicated himself to this goal; however, as a practicing sociologist, he slowly began to realize that facts, valid as they might be, would not provide the solution. Because of this and lack of support for his work, he left the academy to become an activist and propagandist for his race. He wrote: "Two considerations . . . broke in upon my work and eventually disrupted it: First, one could not be a calm, cool, and detached scientist while Negroes were lynched, murdered, and starved; and secondly, there was no such definite demand for scientific work of the sort that I was doing as I had confidently assumed would be easily forthcoming."[75]

Du Bois' sociological writings offer a rich and sophisticated body of empirically grounded sociological information. He never set forth a formal statement of his conception of sociology, which is somewhat out of character because he was a prolific writer and sociology was very important to him. This is also puzzling in view of the fact that he was so outspoken about how sociologists should perceive and analyze social phenomena. One explanation of this omission, perhaps, is that he was too involved in studying blacks and "the Negro problems" to take time for such an academic effort; that is, his interest in collecting and analyzing socioeconomic data was more pressing than reflection upon the nature of sociology. Another factor may have been that his training in history and his lack of formal instruction in sociology left him unprepared to adequately discuss the nature of sociology. Also, Du Bois might have felt that his sociological studies were tantamount to a statement of his conception of sociology. It is possible, as a matter of fact, to construct his conception of the new discipline of sociology from his early writings, primarily those of this early, sociological period.

In one of his earliest comments about the discipline of sociology, Du Bois noted that it was concerned with current social conditions and methods of social regeneration. Although he clearly favored an empirical approach, he did not at that time consider sociology a science, because it had neither definitely stated laws nor any body of carefully systematized facts. Nevertheless, he thought that the sociological study of society had begun to provide some evidence of social laws, and he was optimistic about sociology's future. Sociology was a "vast and fruitful field of inquiry into the mysterious phenomena of human action."[76] In another early study, he noted that sociology had examined all phases of society and, even with its crude or imperfect methods, had collected a great body of data: "the phenomena of society are worth the most careful and systematic study, and whether or not this study may eventually lead to a systematic body of knowledge deserving the name of science, it cannot in any case fail to give the world a mass of truth worth the knowing."[77]

Defining sociology more explicitly in a speech around 1900, he said that it attempts to study "the mighty subject of human cooperation in modern society." But the study of society, he went on to say, is both slow and difficult, and sociologists cannot lay claim to laws and accurate measurements, as is common in the hard sciences. Another problem he saw was that the facts with which sociology must deal are extremely multitudinous and intricate. Although no startling laws had been discovered, he continued to remain positive regarding the future of sociology. He claimed, for example, that sociology was responsible for collecting "a mass of material of supreme interest and value and of such nature that no modern thinker who is interested in the condition and destiny of human beings can afford to ignore its methods and results."[78] Later he reaffirmed this point, stating that everyone feels the necessity of sociological study because of the widespread ignorance of social facts and processes in our times; he stated that, with regard to social facts, "we still linger in a Middle Age of credulity and superstition."[79]

He observed that the development of sociology was going through a "trying" period. "It is the period of observation, research and comparison—work always wearisome, often aimless, without well-settled principles and guiding lines, and subject ever to the pertinent criticism: What, after all, has been accomplished?"[80] Elaborating on his conception of sociology, he wrote, "We have sought to build upon a plan the breadth of which is not limited even by the ends of the world; and have taken all human action for our province."[81] But the appropriate unit of investigation, he claimed, was individual or real man. There had been, he continued, some attempts to replace this perplexing element with more tractable concepts, such as economic man, because he is guaranteed to act from a singular motive with little or nothing left to chance. "But common sense won and real men were studied—not metaphysical lay figures."[82]

Du Bois used census data in many of his sociological studies; however, he noted that such data are sensitive only to the broader and more simple aspects of human society. The national census was unsuited to measure "the more delicate and intricate questions of social life." He called for the use of more detailed studies, an approach which had become known by the term *social study*: "such investigations ... seek to go further and deeper than a national census and study definitely and, within limits, exhaustively, the conditions of life and action in certain localities." The use of this type of study is a difficult undertaking; nevertheless, the social study approaches "as nearly as anything the ideal of measuring and classifying human action."[83]

In an unpublished article written shortly after the turn of the century, Du Bois set forth perhaps his most formal statement about sociology.[84] He began by claiming that sociology was in difficulty, partly because of a confusion regarding the method of sociology. He chided Comte for "steering curiously by the deeds of men as objects of scientific study." Sociology, to Du Bois, was the study of human behavior. He was unimpressed with Herbert Spencer's "verbal jugglery," which he said would lead ultimately to such gross and troublesome abstractions as Gidding's "consciousness of kind." Such sociological forays, he stated, would lead to a descriptive sociology utilizing and revolving around imperfect and unscientific methods. The result would be that their shadowy outline would remain to be completed by precise scientific measurement and more intense analysis.

He was curious why Comte had hesitated to delimit the parts which constitute society.[85] Clearly, Du Bois reflected, sociology is the study of men, which includes the notion that their behavior is a function of rhythm (recurring regularities) and incalculable factors. Sociology is the analysis of the rhythms and the incalculable which underlay human action: "I saw the action of physical law in the actions of men; but I saw more than that: I saw rhythms and tendencies; coincidences and probabilities; and I saw that, which for want of any other word, I must in accord with the strict tenets of Science, call Chance."[86] In short, he was saying that sociology was the attempt to discover the laws that govern the conduct of men. Du Bois' sociology stands between that school of thought that considers all human behavior subject to laws and the proponents of free will, who refuse to conceive of man's behavior as governed by laws. He held an affinity to the unity of science orientation and discussed a "future path" where sociology and physics might work together, and in this he indicates a preference for the positivistic argument and reductionism.[87]

In a reaction against the "grand theoretical" approach common around the turn of the century, Du Bois wrote that sociology must concentrate more and more upon "the minute study of limited fields of human action, where observation and accurate measurement are possible and where real illuminating knowledge can be had." The ideal of the twentieth-century sociologist, he continued, is the careful and exhaustive study of the isolated group. [88] This observation served to reinforce his research of black Americans: "Social scientists were . . . still thinking in terms of theory and vast and eternal laws, but I had a concrete group of living beings . . . capable of almost laboratory experiment." [89]

Sociology, according to Du Bois, must be scientific and have "but one simple aim: the discovery of truth." Although the results of science are open for all men to use, the guiding, singular aim must be "simple truth." To give science a double aim by including social reform with truth would inevitably tend to defeat both goals: "the frequent alliance of sociological research with various panaceas and particular schemes of reform, has resulted in closely connecting social investigation with a good deal of groundless assumption and humbug in the popular mind." [90] More succinctly he stated, "We simply collect the facts. Others may use them as they will." But facts, he urged, were essential. [91]

Even though he saw truth unequivocally as the paramount goal of sociological research, he was not interested in studying social phenomena out of mere curiosity or intellectual interest. He felt that "the truth" discovered by sociologists could and should have some practical value so that it could be utilized to reform society. Du Bois saw social change as a normal, evolutionary process which man should attempt to control. There was little or no question whether or not to guide society; the paramount question was, do we have enough accurate information? He believed that his approach would provide the information.

Du Bois' statement that much sociological research was intertwined with various social panaceas and social reform and had, as a consequence, compromised the image of sociology seems to be a reaction against many of his contemporaries, whom he felt were more interested in reform than in "the truths." He strongly believed that the truths generated by empirical research would and should ultimately lead to social reform; he also believed, however, that the sociologist qua scientist must concentrate on the former. His viewpoint shows the influence of his German mentor, Gustav Schmoller, who urged his students to study what is and leave what should be to others.[92]

Although Du Bois considered sociology the study of present social conditions, he held that sociological descriptions and explanations should be grounded upon an accurate and adequate historical base. For example, in a paper about the study of the Negro problem, which was presented to the American Academy of Political and Social Science, he claimed that "Scientific work must be subdivided, but conclusions which affect the whole subject must be based on a study of the whole," and "that one cannot study the Negro in freedom and come to general conclusions about his destiny without knowing his history in slavery."[93] Many of his studies began with an historical sketch. *The Philadelphia Negro*, for example, a survey of the socioeconomic conditions of a segment of the Philadelphia black population, begins with a history of the Negro in Philadelphia. Similarly, a discussion of black criminality in Philadelphia begins with a history of black crime in the city.

Later he wrote:

> We can only understand the present by continually referring to and studying that past; when any one of the intricate phenomena of our daily life puzzles us; when there arises religious problems, political problems, race problems, we must always remember that while their solution lies in the present, their cause and their explanation lie in the past. Study the past then, if you would comprehend the present; read history if you would know how to vote intelligently, read history if you do not know what sound money is, read history if you cannot grasp the Negro problem.[94]

He reinforced his argument by writing that "in the cold, bare facts of history, so much was omitted from the complete picture that it could only be recovered as complete scientific knowledge if we could read back into the past enough to piece out the reality."[95]

Throughout his life, Du Bois remained adamant that the success of sociology would be related to its use of measurement and direct observation. In an article written late in life, he spoke of the use of measurement in sociology:

One of the causes of this change of attitude [in race relations] has been the increasing willingness and, indeed, compulsion among observers of social phenomena to depend upon some kind of social measurement for their judgments rather than upon individual observation. Consequently, today we have some increase in measurements for social phenomena; they are not many and scientists have not quite made up their minds that it is possible to measure the acts of men. It is undoubtedly difficult and calls for much more careful methods than we have put in practice; but the time is coming when we are going to measure human action and more and more depends upon such measurements for our social welfare.[96]

He was firm in his commitment to the use of sociological measurement to describe and delimit social phenomena. He felt that proper measurement of social conditions would provide a rational basis for sound social judgments. Implicit in this belief was a more general belief in the worth of a quantitative, empirically based sociology which, if properly practiced, would form the foundation of social policy.

Du Bois' empirical orientation led him toward a methodology based on direct and prolonged observation. In Philadelphia, for example, he used participant observation, living in the seventh ward for a year "in the midst of ... dirt, drunkenness, poverty, and crime."[97] He used the term *car-window sociologist* in reference to sociologists who, while attempting to understand the South or black Americans, spent a few leisurely hours on holiday, riding in a Pullman car through the South, generally not venturing into communities. He pointedly told Walter Willcox, a Cornell professor, that he was seeking to understand "the Negro problem" from his office.[98] He was adamant in his claim that to fully understand the Negro problems, which must include their history, one must study them first-hand.

His empirical orientation showed an impatience with the philosophical speculations and armchair theorizing of sociologists like Herbert Spencer and Franklin Giddings:

Social thinkers were engaged in vague statements and were seeking to lay down the method by which, in some not too distant future, social laws analogous to physical law would be discovered. Herbert Spencer finished his ten volumes of synthetic philosophy in 1896. The biological analogy, the vast generalizations, were striking, but actual scientific accomplishments lagged. For me an opportunity seemed to present itself. I could not lull my mind to hypnosis by regarding a phrase like 'consciousness of kind' as a scientific law. But turning my gaze from fruitless words, twisting and facing the facts of my own situation and racial world, I determined to put science into sociology through a study of the conditions and problems of my own group.[99]

This seems to demonstrate Du Bois' opinion of social philosophy and of much of the sociology of his era as compared with his empirical approach, geared toward generating social laws. It also appears to suggest a distaste for armchair social theory; yet he did realize the value of theory and claimed that theory and empirical research should be brought closer together. He stated that there were two kinds of sociological materials:

A number of thick books full of generalizations more or less true and more or less systematic, but all liable to the same criticism, namely that while they have said many things well, they have neither permanently increased the amount of our knowledge nor introduced in the maze of fact any illuminating system or satisfying interpretation. On the other hand we have a growing tangled mass of facts arising from social investigations, of all degrees of worth and reliability, bewildering in their quantity and baffling in their hidden meaning.[100]

In the same vein, Du Bois argued that some sociological instruction turns into prolonged discussions of society and social units; this, in turn, might easily degenerate into bad metaphysics or false psychology, or venture into so many statistics that students forget or neglect the "concrete facts" behind the statistics.[101] According to Du Bois, what was necessary to overcome this situation was to attempt to bring theory and empirical work closer together: "Now the work of the next fifty years is to bring theory and practice ... nearer together, to connect more logically the statement and the demonstration and to make in truth the science of human action a true and systematic statement of the verifiable facts as ascertained by observation and measurement." To gain this end, we must limit ourselves to "the minute study of limited fields of human action." Sociology is too vast and we cannot effectively study all human action in time and eternity: "much valuable time has already been wasted in trying to do the impossible under the brilliant but questionable leadership of Herbert Spencer."[102] Du Bois frequently emphasized the necessity of smaller, minute studies of limited fields of social action where observation and measurement were more readily applicable. The ideal study, he held, was the careful and exhaustive analysis of the isolated group from many points of view.

XI

Du Bois rightly deserves a place among the giants of sociology for his work during the years 1896-1910, when sociology was being established as an academic discipline. He established a department of sociology at Atlanta University, created a laboratory of sociology, instituted a program of systematic research, founded and conducted regular sociological conferences on research, founded two journals (*Crisis* and *Phylon: A Journal of Race Relations*), attempted to organize a sociological society in 1897, or eight years before the American Sociological Society developed out of the American Economic Association, and he established a record of valuable publications which has rarely been equaled by any sociologist. Atlanta University over the years became the site where such renowned sociologists as E. Franklin Frazier, Ira De Augustine Reid, Mozell Hill, and others could find employment in the early years of their sociological careers.

Important and valuable as his contributions may be, historically or currently, Du Bois has not been accorded by early or later white sociologists the respect and recognition that he deserves. His continuous neglect by the sociological fraternity (hereafter meaning white sociologists only) until 1971 constitutes an interesting and perhaps instructive datum for the "sociology of sociology." It is of interest, however, to note the recent establishment of two awards which carry Du Bois' name.[103]

Indicators of Du Bois' neglect by sociologists are the frequency and kind of citations of him and his sociological works which are found in published overviews of sociological subtopics.[104] Overviews of the history of sociology or sociological thought rarely mention Du Bois. Of twenty-seven books and three journal overviews published between 1916 and 1969, only four mention Du Bois even once, and each of these cite a somewhat different point. Of the four, it is only Howard Odum, in his chronicle of United States sociology from its beginning to 1950, who clearly treats Du Bois as an important "being" in the sociological enterprise.[105] In his chapter titled "Special Sociology: Race, Ethnic, Groups, Folk," Odum lists in chronological order the principal volumes by sociologists and includes the publications of Du Bois from 1896 (his doctoral dissertation, which was published as the first volume in Harvard's Historical series) to 1945 (his *Color and Democracy*). Of the eighty-five books Odum lists, all 12 books from the earliest years to 1908 are by Du Bois.

Odum fails, however, in the other chapters of his book to point out how Du Bois contributed to the specialities of research methods, social problems, the community, the family, and population/ecology. If, for example, Odum had classified Du Bois' *The Health and Physique of the Negro American* (1906) under "population/ecology" as well as under "race/ethnic/groups/folk", then he would have acknowledged that Du Bois' contribution to population greatly anteceded Thompson's *Population* (1915) and Woofter's *Negro Migration* (1920)—the first two books which Odum placed under population.

Overviews of research methods similarly ignore Du Bois' contributions. Of eleven publications between 1911 and 1952 which review the use of the social survey in sociology, only one mentions Du Bois.[106] Beyond the review of the social survey, the one general methodological overview which at least obliquely suggests Du Bois' uses of the survey, participant-observation, and the ecological method is a paper concerned with research in Europe, not the United States. In his survey of early social research in Europe, N. Glazer, commenting on the influence of Charles Booth in the United States, says: "W.E.B. Du Bois' *The Philadelphia Negro*, a particularly fine work of 1899, is specifically indebted to Booth, down to the color of the maps."[107] But, Glazer does not say how he learned of Du Bois' indebtedness.

Of all the specialities in sociology, it is only in the area of race relations that Du Bois fares somewhat well. In a nonrandom sample of sixty-one books published between 1908 and 1968, Du Bois' status is as follows: he is not mentioned in sixteen; he is mentioned but identified as other than sociologist in thirty-five; and he is mentioned and identified as a sociologist in ten of them. Of the forty-five books citing Du Bois, eight do so just once, fourteen do so from two to five times, and fourteen others do so from six to nine times. The median number of citations is five.[108] The most frequent citations are fifty-eight times in Frazier and eighty times in Myrdal, and in these books Du Bois is mentioned more often than any other writer.[109]

The pattern of citations is indeed an interesting one. The tendency of those who cite Du Bois often (above the median) is to fail to define him as a sociologist or to mention only his nonsociological publications, or both. The tendency of those who cite Du Bois less often is to ignore his status as a sociologist and the existence of his sociological publications. A few examples are in order. Arnold Rose almost deviates from both tendencies: he cites Du Bois fifteen times, referring to him as a scholar and a social scientist, and says that Du Bois organized many facts about blacks from a new viewpoint, their meaning for a sense of group membership; but he omits to cite Du Bois' sociological writings. Park presents Du Bois only as a "Negro leader" and an "editor of *Crisis*" and cites only his nonsociological writings. Reuter labels him as an agitator who heightened the racial problem, an educator, an author, and a prominent mulatto, while Miller limits the labels to editor and agitator.[110]

Du Bois' neglect meant that generations of sociologists, graduate students, and undergraduates in sociology would obtain no knowledge of him, or at best only a faint, blurred image of him as a black intellectual, but not ås a sociologist. To understand the neglect of Du Bois during the period 1896–1910, at least three kinds of data are needed: an understanding of the system of race relations in the United States during that period; evidence that this system was incorporated into the sociological enterprise; and evidence that such an incorporation would result either in neglect or in a faint, blurred image of Du Bois and his sociological expertise.

Two general sociocultural themes present in United States society and in sociology at that time made it socially "proper" for sociologists to overlook Du Bois' sociology. These two themes are structural and sociopsychological and interrelated: one is a racial caste-like system of social organization, and the other is an ideology which combines the doctrines of manifest destiny, social Darwinism, and racism. A caste system, as an ideal type in the Weberian sense, is a social arrangement whereby groups are permanently placed in positions of superordination and subordination to one another in all relationships, because of a difference between them in racial identity or some other ascriptive trait. In referring to Du Bois' era, Broderick, the historian, speaks of it as the "most oppressive era in the history of Black Americans since the Civil War; historian Rayford Logan has appropriately called it the 'Nadir.' "[111] The great political and educational gains (for example, the creation of a public school system in the South) which the black Reconstruction (1865–76) and the following era had brought to blacks, as well as to lower-class whites, were largely aborted through the caste-like system which segregated blacks "by occupation and privileges and to some extent by dwelling place, to the end that they (a) submit permanently to an inferior position, or (b) die out, or (c) migrate."[112]

The new economics of the South reduced the political power of black laborers in the region and promoted a series of labor laws which sanctioned their raw exploitation. Irrespective of ability, the black man was to be denied all positions of authority, employment in certain lines of industry, promotion to higher grades, competition on equal terms with white laborers, the purchase of land, and membership in labor unions.[113]

Political acts coincided with economic ones to intensify the evolving caste-like system for black oppression. The financing of public education for blacks was arbitrarily and drastically reduced, and many private schools were forced to retrench severely or to close.[114] Admission to college often involved special consideration or blunt refusal. Judicial decisions and administration declared the legality of black subjugation. Distinctions among legal, extralegal, and illegal acts were blurred; thus, while 1,183 blacks are known to have been lynched, without legal trial, during 1900–1916, white lynchers were rarely brought before the courts for their acts.[115] "Race riots" was the euphemism for unconscionable white mob attacks on groups of blacks. Social relations were governed by a "social etiquette" which unequivocally communicated the white's superiority and the black's inferiority.[116] Irrespective of achieved status, blacks were subject to peculiar and galling sorts of injustice in daily life."[117]

This caste-like organization of United States society was manifest in all major institutions, separating blacks and whites rather completely from each other. Such organization was evident in the university, giving rise to schools for whites and schools for blacks, an aspect of what the late sociologist Louis Wirth of Chicago termed a system of "cultural parallelism."

Ideological currents during this era both created and sustained the caste-like system for black oppression in the United States. They constituted a complex of the simpler ideologies of social Darwinism, manifest destiny, and racism. The belief systems of both social Darwinism and manifest destiny operated to support and rationalize the social system of race relations. Noting that social Darwinism and manifest destiny projected a dual system of rights and privileges based on a hierarchy of social position and were used to justify the colonization of areas of Africa, China, Cuba, and the Philippine Republic, Du Bois commented sharply:

> Making all due allowances for different ways of interpreting facts, it must be confessed by all honest men that a theory of human civilization which stands sponsor for the enormities committed by European civilization on native races is an outrage and a lie.
>
> But do the theories of Darwin and Spencer, properly interpreted, support any crude views of justice and right and the spread of civilization as those current to-day? It may be safely answered they do not. Ignorant and selfish interpretation of great sociological laws must not any longer be allowed to obscure and degrade those laws.[118]

During the Du Bois era, the sociological fraternity was beginning to develop an element of intellectual autonomy but was nevertheless still strongly influenced and conditioned by the greater American culture. It was caste-like in having an entirely white membership, and the writings of some of its most prominent figures reflected the ideology of manifest destiny, social Darwinism, and racism. It should not be overlooked, however, that during the decade of the 1890s, sociologists were engaged in a frontal criticism of biological determinism which was destined to undermine both "racist" and "sexist" theories of society.

Before the turn of the century, sociology departments were established at Chicago, Columbia, Pennsylvania, and Atlanta, and then at Brown, Yale, Wisconsin, Michigan, and Illinois Wesleyan. Professional positions, except at Atlanta, were restricted to whites, although in the 1870s a few blacks had held such positions in, for example, the University of South Carolina. While Pennsylvania sociologists claim that Du Bois was a member of their department in 1896-97, it should be noted that Du Bois was brought to Pennsylvania on the initiative of the Quaker Susan P. Wharton, a member of the executive committee of the Philadelphia College Settlement; the official correspondence of the then provost, C. C. Harrison, clearly shows that Du Bois' appointment was to the settlement—not the sociology department—for one year only and specifically to study the blacks of the seventh ward (Pennsylvania territory); and that Du Bois, while identifying his position as "assistant in sociology," said that the only students whom he handled were a group of ruffians whom he took on a one-day tour of the seventh ward.[119]

During his lengthy career, Du Bois was never offered a position at a white university.[120] In retrospect, Du Bois felt that his career had suffered because of the lack of affiliation with a major university. Commenting on this regarding his research in Philadelphia, he noted:

> It would have been a fine thing if after this difficult piece of work, the University of Pennsylvania had at least offered me a temporary instructorship in the college or in the Wharton School. Harvard had never dreamed of such a thing; a half century later one of Harvard's professors said of a gifted Negro student: 'We'd give

him a position if he were not a Negro!' White classmates of lower academic rank than I became full professors at Pennsylvania and Chicago. Here in my case an academic accolade from a great American University would have given impetus to my life work.[121]

The "glass wall" of casteism was not, of course, a personal but a group phenomenon. Augmenting Du Bois' difficulty in this regard was the weak institutionalization of the discipline of sociology at this time, and more specifically, the fact that his alma mater, Harvard, did not have a sociology department to assist him in obtaining a position befitting his stature and ability. Exclusion from the competitive scholarly game was also the fate of other blacks receiving the Ph.D. in sociology from United States universities at this early time: James R. Diggs from Illinois Wesleyan in 1906, Richard R. Wright from Pennsylvania in 1911, and George Edward Haynes from Columbia in 1912.[122] This pattern of exclusion continued through decades, with the result that E. Franklin Frazier, a graduate of Chicago, whose book *The Negro Family in the United States* (1939) Ernest Burgess defined as the most important contribution to the literature on the family since *The Polish Peasant*,[123] and who in 1948 became the first (and only) black president of ASA, never held more than part-time or visiting positions in white universities and colleges.[124] What particularly bothered Du Bois and Frazier was their being cut off from needed research facilities for sociological work, and the general irrationality of a caste-like system based on racism.[125] Frazier expressed his disdain for this system in a brilliant paper which had as its theme "the Negro-in-America ... is a form of insanity that overtakes white men."[126]

The societal ideology comprising social Darwinism, manifest destiny, and racism was one of the dominant themes of United States sociology during Du Bois' early era, even though, at the same time, one could find in the same discipline some of the earliest critiques of biological racism. After noting that the word *sociology* was first used in the United States in a polemical defense of slavery by Henry Hughes (*Treatise on Sociology*, 1854) and by George Fitzhugh (*Sociology for the South*, 1854), Maus says that a "biologically based development ... dominated American sociology from the seventies on, when the work of Spencer and Darwin became known."[127] Odum, after reviewing the race/ethnic relations literature, says that the earlier literature assumed that "race was a relatively fixed and stable biological heritage, with sub-assumptions of superior and inferior capabilities." Odum goes on to note how changing societal ideology generated sociological revisionism:

> Our main point here . . . is that in the total story of American sociology this changed viewpoint and accelerated moral motivation make this particular area [race/ethnic relations] rate a continuous review, for, if we seek to analyze the whole field into its parts, it seems likely that in no aspect of society has the sociological approach changed more than in that of race, region, folk, and intercultural relations. In the writings of the earlier sociologists each of these represented a sort of fixed value in the total evolutionary structure of society. . . . Intercultural relations were bottomed in class, caste, nations, international levels, empire, on the one hand; or in academic appraisal of status and philanthropic intervention, on the other hand. These assumptions no longer predominate, not primarily because of what sociologists have done, but because of the sweep of social change. Here again, sociology, even as education and economics, follows the trend, seeking to effect adjustment more than it creates movements or directs evolution.[128]

Examination of the writings of presidents of ASA from 1905, when the association was founded, to 1914, reveals the presence of this general ideology, varying from one president to another in its degree of subtlety. The differences in these men's attitudes regarding Darwin and biological determinism, however, must not be minimized nor neglected. In particular, the critical outlook of Small, as well as his colleague W. I. Thomas, revealed emerging trends. Key's analysis of the writings of Sumner, Giddings, Small, Ward, and Ross leads him to conclude:

> The racism of the pioneer sociologists and the incidents of racism found in their works seem to range from unashamed bigotry to tacit acceptance. Their racism can be understood in the same manner by which their theories and prophecies can be understood; with reference to the socio-culture in which they took meaning and shape; their opportunity structures, "styles of life," and world views.[129]

Of the Big Five, each of whom spent two years in the presidency of ASA, this general ideology is most explicit in the writings of Giddings and Sumner. Speaking of Giddings, Odum says:

> First, he stressed ethnic and kinship groups as basic to societal evolution. Next, as a sort of corollary of his concept of the 'consciousness of kind', he explained political groupings, classes, racial exclusiveness by pointing out, on page 18 of his *Principles*, that "within racial lines, the ethnical and political groupings, it is the basis of class distinctions, of innumerable forms of alliance, of rules of intercourse, and of peculiarities of policies. Our conduct toward those whom we feel to be most like ourselves is instinctively and rationally different from our conduct toward others." And again on page 191 of his *Civilization and Society*, he held that race prejudice develops out of the racial struggle for existence.[130]

The behavioral, psychological, and emotional commitment of society and the white sociological fraternity to a caste-like system premised on white superiority-black inferiority, and to an ideology comprising social Darwinism, manifest destiny, and racism during the era 1896–1910 probably accounts for the ignoring of Du Bois as sociologist. By the white "definition of the situation," social and intellectual creativity and talent were prerogatives of the white caste exclusively. The credibility of these claims in the minds of white sociologists and the public was established by the dual processes of categorically neglecting all black sociologists and glorifying the achievements of white sociologists. Claims are cumulative, today's histories being composed out of the themes of yesterday's histories. Over time, with the expansion of the academy and its clientele— both white and black—the claims echo loudly, then more loudly.

The early white sociological fraternity was aware of Du Bois through his publications in the *Annals of the American Academy of Political and Social Sciences* and the leading United States intellectual magazines, his invitation to and participation in a race relations seminar at the University of Chicago, and in sundry other significant ways. Du Bois' exclusion from the chronicles of the history of sociology was, in part, the result of the institutional structure of sociology before World War I, which was local and fragmented and therefore did not enforce norms and practices that were oriented toward universalistic intellectual goals. Du Bois' life and contributions to the sociological enterprise, if disinterestedly assessed in their time, would have stood as contradictions to the caste-like system of the white sociological subcaste. It is particularly noteworthy that Max Weber knew of Du Bois and his work. When Weber visited the United States in 1904, Du Bois was among those whom he met. Weber had Du Bois write an article for the journal which he edited; the article, "Die Negerfrage in den Vereington Staaten," published in 1906, was the only article to appear in the journal by an American sociologist.[131]

Our book seeks to bring Du Bois' sociological contributions to the attention of contemporary and future sociologists. It may serve to provide this profession with a true statement of its history in the United States. It may also serve to suggest to some the advantages to a profession and a discipline of a universalistic rather than particularistic orientation.

DAN S. GREEN and EDWIN D. DRIVER

THE TASKS OF SOCIOLOGY

This section presents Du Bois' conception of sociology and why he believed that the study of the Afro-American was especially valuable to the development of a science of sociology. To Du Bois, sociology was "the science that seeks to measure the limits of chance in human action." While recognizing that sociologists seek laws which are historically and universally true for the human group, Du Bois felt that sociology's best possibility of generating laws was through the exhaustive study of the small, isolated group. For this purpose, the Afro-American was ideally suited. Here, by virtue of historical social forces, was a group diverse enough in cultural forms to mirror the stages of evolution experienced at one time or another by most other social groups.

The purpose of the program outlined in "The Atlanta Conferences" (1904) was the systematic and scientific study of the Afro-American. The aspects of his condition were to be divided into ten large subjects, and each year one subject was to be studied until the cycle was completed. Then the cycle would begin again. The plan was that in a course of a century "we shall have a continuous record on the condition and development of a group of 10 to 20 millions of men—a body of sociological material unsurpassed in human annals."

As the second paper, "The Laboratory in Sociology at Atlanta University" (1903), makes clear, Atlanta University was important to the implementation of this plan. It was located near the geographical center of the black population of the nation and was therefore near the center of the congeries of human problems which cluster around the black Americans. Upper classmen at Atlanta University were therefore trained to systematically study conditions of living around the university and, when possible, to compare these with conditions elsewhere. At the graduate level, students were to collect and analyze primary source data obtained through interviews and schedules, discuss the findings, and prepare written reports. While the "social study," or intensive study of a local community proved successful and had its unique advantages, Du Bois recognized that it was geographically limited and could not provide the kind of national statistics needed for discussions about the status of the Afro-American.

In the third paper, "The Twelfth Census and the Negro Problems" (1900), he proposed that the United States Census schedules be extended to incorporate questions specifically addressed to the status of the Afro-American and that these parts of the schedules later be turned over to an unpaid committee of twenty-five distinguished persons, from the North and South and both black and white, for an unbiased analysis and reporting of the findings.

The fourth paper, "The Study of the Negro Problems" (1898), presents Du Bois' conception of a social problem. It is "the failure of an organized social group to realize its group ideals through the inability to adapt a certain desired line of action to given conditions of life." He offered four considerations for the study of the social problems of black Americans: the historical development of the problems; the necessity for their diligent, systematic study; the results of scientific analyses of the Negro; and the scope and method to be used by future analysis. He deplored the fact that so much of the work done on the Negro question had been "uncritical from lack of discrimination in the selection and weighing of evidence; uncritical in choosing the proper point of view from which to study these problems; and, finally, uncritical from the distinct bias in the minds of so many writers." In the future, the proper scientific study of the Negro would have to make explicit the premises from which it began and would, for the sake of logical clarity, have to separately investigate the Negro as a social group, and his peculiar social environment. The study of the Negro as a social group would have to combine the approaches of history, statistics, anthropology, and sociology.

The final paper, "The Negro Race in the United States of America" (1911), demonstrates Du Bois' careful, early use of these various disciplines in providing us with a general portrait.

1

THE ATLANTA CONFERENCES

The present condition of sociological study is peculiar and in many respects critical. Amid a multitude of interesting facts and conditions we are groping after a science—after reliable methods of observation and measurement, and after some enlightening way of systematizing and arranging the mass of accumulated material. Moreover the very immensity of the task gives us pause. What after all are we trying to do but to make a science of human action? And yet such a task seems so preposterous that there is scarce a sociologist the world over that would acknowledge such a plan. Rather, turning from so startling a task, they have assured the world that their object is to study a certain metaphysical entity called society—and when they have been asked earnestly and rather insistently just what society is, they have replied in language at once curious, mystical and at times contradictory. Has not the time come however when we should face our problem? In reality we seek to know how much of natural law there is in human conduct. Sociology is the science that seeks to measure the limits of chance in human action, or if you will excuse the paradox, it is the science of free will. Leaving then the definition of the science in this rather stupendous form we must turn to the fact that in reality we have sought to build upon a plan the breadth of which is not limited even by the ends of the world; and have taken all human action for our province and made the endeavor to collate and systematize the facts of human progress and organization; and the result is two sorts of sociological material—a number of thick books full of generalization

Reprinted from *Voice of the Negro* 1 (March 1904): 85–89.

more or less true and more or less systematic, but all liable to the same criticism, namely that while they have said many things well, they have neither permanently increased the amount of our own knowledge nor introduced in the maze of fact any illuminating system or satisfying interpretation. On the other hand we have a growing tangled mass of facts arising from social investigations, of all degrees of worth and reliability, bewildering in their quantity and baffling in their hidden meaning.

Now the work of the next fifty years is to bring theory and practice in sociology nearer together, to connect more logically the statement and the demonstration and to make in truth the science of human action a true and systematic statement of the verifiable facts as ascertained by observation and measurement.

Now to bring about this result it is certain that we cannot at once compass all human action in time and eternity—the field is too vast and much valuable time has already been wasted in trying to do the impossible under the brilliant but questionable leadership of Herbert Spencer. We must more and more school ourselves to the minute study of limited fields of human action, where observation and accurate measurement are possible and where real illuminating knowledge can be had. The careful exhaustive study of the isolated group then is the ideal of the sociologist of the 20th century—from that may come a real knowledge of natural law as locally manifest—a glimpse and revelation of rhythm beyond this little center and at last careful, cautious generalization and formulation.

For such work there lies before the sociologist of the United States a peculiar opportunity. We have here going on before our eyes the evolution of a vast group of men from simpler primitive conditions to higher more complex civilization. I think it may safely be asserted that never in the history of the modern world has there been presented to men of a great nation so rare an opportunity to observe and measure and study the evolution of a great branch of the human race as is given to Americans in the study of the American Negro. Here is a crucial test on a scale that is astounding and under circumstances peculiarly fortunate. By reason of color and color prejudice the group is isolated—by reason of incentive to change, the changes are rapid and kaleidoscopic; by reason of the peculiar environment, the action and reaction of social forces are seen and can be measured with more than usual ease. What is human progress and how is it emphasized? How do nations rise and fall? What is the meaning and value of certain human actions? Is there rhythm and law in the mass of the deeds of men—and if so how can it best be measured and stated—all such questions can be studied and answered in the case of the American Negro, if he shall be studied closely enough in a way to enlighten science and inspire philanthropy. Instead of vainly attacking the whole race mass of the world—instead of vainly seeking to attack the problems of social relations among all men and all peoples at all times, why in the name of common sense, does it not occur to American sociologists that their time and labor would be infinitely more effective for real scientific advance if applied to the study of the one rapidly developing group of people?

Instead of this nothing can exceed our remarkable and reprehensible ignorance of the Negro people. Even for the purposes of practical philanthropy, for the aid of education theories, for the knowledge of rare characteristics our ignorance is astounding. If the Negroes were still lost in the forests of central Africa we could have a government commission to go and measure their heads, but with 10 millions of them here under your noses I have in the past besought the Universities almost in vain to spend a single cent in a rational study of their characteristics and conditions. We can go to the South Sea Islands half way around the world and beat and shoot a weak people longing for freedom into the slavery of American color prejudice at the cost of hundreds of millions, and yet at Atlanta University we beg annually and beg in vain for the paltry sum of $500 simply to aid us in replacing gross and vindictive ignorance of race conditions with enlightening knowledge and systematic observation. There is no question before the scientific world in regard to which there is more guess work and wild theorizing than in regard to causes and characteristics of the diverse human species. And yet here in America we have not only the opportunity to observe and measure nearly all the world's great races in juxta-position, but more than that to watch a long and intricate process of amalgamation carried on hundreds of years and resulting in millions of men of mixed blood. And yet because the subject of amalgamation with black races is a sore point with us, we have hitherto utterly neglected and thrown away every opportunity to study and know this vast mulatto population and have deliberately and doggedly based our statements and conclusions concerning this class upon pure fiction or unvarnished lies. We do not even know the number of mixed bloods, the extent of the mixture, the characteristics, stature, or ability of the mixed; and yet there is scarcely a man or woman who would not be able or willing at a moment's notice to express a full and definite opinion concerning American Mulattoes, both here and everywhere, in time and eternity.

Such an attitude is allowable to the ignorant—it is expected among horses and among the uncultivated masses of men, but it is not expected of the scientific leaders of a great nation. On the contrary, it is fair to ask of them, first, to approach the question of the scientific study of a great race with open-mindedness and simple-hearted desire for truth, and in the second place that they let slip no such opportunity as this of widening the narrow boundaries of scientific truth.

It is of course perfectly clear as to why scientific men have long fought shy of this field. The presence of the Negro in America has long been the subject of bitter and repeated controversy—of war and hate, of strife and turmoil. It has been said that so dangerous a field, where feelings were deep-seated and turbulent, was not the place for scientific calm of clear headed investigation. The nation will come to see—I trust is already beginning to realize—that this is a mistake; that no subject is so intricate and dangerous, as not to be infinitely more approachable in the clear light of knowledge than in the fog of prejudice and bitter feeling, and that the first business of any nation distracted by a great social problem is thoroughly to study and understand this problem.

The study of men however, is peculiar in being especially liable to the influences of prejudice which makes the inevitable scientific assumption with which all investigators must start difficult to agree upon. For instance, if the Negroes are not ordinary human beings, if their development is simply the retrogression of an inferior people, and the only possible future for the Negro, a future of inferiority, decline and death, then it is manifest that a study of such a group, while still of interest and scientific value is of less pressing and immediate necessity than the study of a group which is distinctly recognized as belonging to the great human family, whose advancement is possible, and whose future depends on its own efforts and the fairness and reasonableness of the dominant and surrounding group.

Now some assumptions of this kind are necessary. They must be held tentatively ever subject to change and revision; and yet the scientific investigation must start with them. Now we at Atlanta University in making some small beginning toward the scientific study of the American Negro have made certain tentative assumptions. We have assumed that the Negro is a constituent member of the great human family, that he is capable of advancement and development, that mulattoes are not necessarily degenerates and that it is perfectly possible for the Negro people to become a great and civilized group. In making these assumptions we have kept before us the facts that every student knows, namely: That there is no adequate historical warrant for pronouncing the Negro race inferior to the other races of the world in a sense of unalterable destiny. To be sure we do not dogmatically assert what place the Negro really occupies in the human scale. We merely assume that clear evidence to the contrary being absolutely wanting, it is fair to place a great race of men who have for centuries come in contact with the world's greatest civilizations as a part and parcel of that world of men. We assume further the Negro's capability of advancement, not so much because of the progress he has already made, as because of the repeated failure of those theories that have placed metes and bounds to his development. We assume the essential manhood and capabilities of mulattoes because in the history of the race no differences between the blacks and half-bloods have been clearly enough established to warrant other assumptions. And above all we assume that given such effort as the Negroes are capable of and such response as the environment may give, the black people of the land will become as civilized as their fellows. We assume this because all the evidence which is reliable, points this way and the evidence on the other side is rather wish and prejudice than fact and observation.

Now, as I have said before, we take none of these positions dogmatically. We never consciously conceal an unpleasant truth that militates against our assumptions, nor do we allow ourselves to be swept by the prevailing dislike of the race into conclusions unwarranted by the facts or beyond the evidence. We are seeking the truth and seeking it despite the urging of friends and clamor of enemies; and in this seeking we demand and think we deserve the sympathy and aid of scientific men.

The object of the Atlanta Conference is to study the American Negro. The method employed is to divide the various aspects of his social condition into ten great subjects. To treat one of these subjects each year as carefully and exhaustively as means will allow until the cycle is completed. To begin then again on the same cycle for a second ten years. So that in the course of a century, if the work is well done we shall have a continuous record on the condition and development of a group of 10 to 20 millions of men—a body of sociological material unsurpassed in human annals. Such an ambitious program is of course difficult to realize. We have, however, reached already the eighth year of the first cycle and have published seven reports and have the eighth in preparation; the sequence of subjects studied has not been altogether logical but will in the end be exhaustive.

In 1896 we studied the subject of health among the Negroes; in 1897, the subject of homes; in 1898, the question of organization; in 1899, the economic development in business lines; in 1900 the higher education of Negroes; in 1901, the common schools and in 1902, another phase of the economic developments—the Negro artisans. In 1903 we investigated the Negro church, and have still to take up the subjects of crime and the suffrage. We shall then begin the cycle again, studying in succession for the second decade, health, homes, occupations, organizations, religion, crime and suffrage.

We have been greatly hampered in this work as I have intimated. First we have been unable as yet to convince any considerable number of the American people of the burning necessity of work of this sort and its deep scientific significance. We do not pretend that Atlanta University is the only fit centre for this work or that we are doing it in the best way. We do contend that the work ought to be done and that we are doing it better than any one else is trying. We receive some encouragement: the libraries are buying our reports; newspapers and periodicals are at times willing to assist in spreading our results and scientific workers give us aid and sympathy. The mass of thinking people, however, fail to realize the true significance of an attempt to study systematically the greatest social problem that has ever faced a great modern nation. We raise with difficulty $250 to $350 annually to carry on the work and we are not sure how long even that meagre sum will be forthcoming. Nevertheless, by the voluntary co-operation of Negro college bred men throughout the land and the goodness of other persons black and white we have succeeded in doing some reliable work.

The work on death rates was our first effort and necessarily limited. The study of homes and social conditions, however, was better done and its results were published by the United States Bureau of Labor, besides the papers in our report. The study of efforts at organization and social betterment entered a unique field and showed with interesting detail the progress of civilizing a group of men in the simple matters of every day life. In the economic field we sought to study the efforts by which the driven slave when emancipated had been made to become himself a master of men in the modern economic world. It was a story of struggle, failure and success and threw no little light on economic development in general. Then came a study of education; how far the higher training of Negroes fitting of unfitting men for real work—was an undue number studying Latin and Greek and was an appalling number of colleges opening their doors to black men. The result of this report corrected many misapprehensions. It showed only 2,500 college graduates among nine million of people, which does not look particularly alarming. It showed that fully 90 per cent. of them were in useful regular occupations and were property holders and respected citizens. It showed that there were too many Negro colleges of poor ranks and too few of high rank and adequate equipment. We showed the history of the public school for both races in the rural districts of the South and we insisted upon the novel, but as we think perfectly clear, proposition that Negro taxes, direct and indirect have since the war, entirely paid for Negro schools and that they have in no sense been a burden on the white tax payer. In 1902 we took up the subject of the Negro Artisan. We investigated the work of industrial schools, received returns from every National Trades Union in America and, three-fourths of the city central labor councils; in conjunction with the greatest Southern Industrial paper, the Chattanooga Tradesman, we made an investigation among employees of skilled Negro labor and finally corresponded with thousands of Negro artisans. The report on the Negro church is in press.

2

THE LABORATORY IN SOCIOLOGY
AT ATLANTA UNIVERSITY

There is some ground for suspicion when a small institution of learning offers courses in sociology. Very often such work means simply prolonged discussions of society and social units, which degenerate into bad metaphysics and false psychology, or it may take a statistical turn and the student become so immersed in mere figures as to forget, or be entirely unacquainted with, the concrete facts standing back of the counting.

On the other hand every one feels how necessary social study is,—how widespread in modern times is our ignorance of social facts and processes. In such matters we still linger in a Middle Age of credulity and superstition. We print in the opening chapters of our children's histories theories of the origin and destiny of races over which the gravest of us must smile; we assume, for instance, elaborate theories of an "Aryan" type of political institution, and then discover in the pitso of the South African Basutos as perfect an agora or tungemot as ever existed among Greeks or Germans. At the same time all of us feel the rhythm in human action; we are sure that the element of chance is at least not supreme, and no generation has taken to the study of social phenomena more energetically or successfully than ours. Have we, however, accomplished enough or settled the matter of scope and method sufficiently to introduce the subject of sociology successfully into the small college or the high school?

I am not sure that our experience at Atlanta University contributes much toward answering this question, for our position is

2

Reprinted from *The Annals of the American Academy of Political and Social Science* 21 (May 1903), 503–5.

somewhat exceptional, and yet I think it throws light on it. Atlanta University is situated within a few miles of the geographical centre of the negro population of the nation, and is, therefore, near the centre of that congeries of human problems which cluster round the black American. This institution, which forms in itself a "negro problem," and which prepares students whose lives must of necessity be further factors in this same problem, cannot logically escape the study and teaching of some things connected with that mass of social questions. Nor can these things all be reduced to history and ethics—the mass of them fall logically under sociology.

We have arranged, therefore, what amounts to about two years of sociological work for the junior and senior college students, and we carry on in our conferences postgraduate work in original research. The undergraduate courses in sociology are simply an attempt to study systematically conditions of living right around the university and to compare these conditions with conditions elsewhere about which we are able to learn. For this purpose one of the two years is taken up principally with a course in economics. Here the methods of study are largely inductive, going from field work and personal knowledge to the establishment of the main principles. There is no text-book, but a class-room reference library with from five to ten duplicate copies of well-known works.

In the next year the study comes nearer what is understood by sociology. Here again, after much experiment, we have discarded the text-book, not because a book of a certain sort would not be valuable in the hands of students, but rather because available text-books are distinctly and glaringly unsuitable. The book most constantly referred to is Mayo-Smith's "Statistics and Sociology," and after that the United States censuses. Our main object in this year of work is to find out what characteristics of human life can be known, classified and compared. Students are expected to know what the average death-rate of American negroes is, how it varies, and what it means when compared with the death-rates of other peoples and classes. When they learn by search in the census and their own mathematical calculations that 30 per cent of the negroes of New York City are twenty to thirty years of age, they immediately set to work to explain this anomaly, and so on. A large part of their work consists of special reports, in which the results of first-hand study of some locality or some characteristic of negro life are compared with general conditions in the United States and Europe. Thus in a way we measure the negro problem.

Sometimes these studies are of real scientific value: the class of '99 furnished local studies, which, after some rearrangement, were published in No. 22 of the Bulletin of the United States Department of Labor; the work of another class was used in a series of articles on the housing of the negro in the *Southern Workman*, and a great deal of the work of other classes has been used in the reports of the Atlanta Conferences. Our main object in the undergraduate work, however, is human training and not the collection of material, and in this we have been fairly successful. The classes are enthusiastic and of average intelligence, and the knowledge of life and of the meaning of life in the modern world is certainly much greater among these students than it would be without such a course of study.

Our postgraduate work in sociology was inaugurated with the thought that a university is primarily a seat of learning, and that Atlanta University, being in the midst of the negro problems, ought to become a centre of such a systematic and thoroughgoing study of those problems as would gradually raise many of the questions above the realm of opinion and guess into that of scientific knowledge. It goes without saying that our ideals in this respect are far from being realized. Although our researches have cost less than $500 a year, yet we find it difficult and sometimes impossible to raise that meagre sum. We lack proper appliances for statistical work and proper clerical aid; notwithstanding this, something has been done. The plan of work is this: a subject is chosen; it is always a definite, limited subject covering some phase of the general negro problem; schedules are then prepared, and these with letters are sent to the voluntary correspondents, mostly graduates of this and other negro institutions of higher training. They, by means of local inquiry, fill out and return the schedules; then other sources of information, depending on the question under discussion, are tried, until after six or eight months' work a body of material is gathered. Then a local meeting is held, at which speakers, who are specially acquainted with the subject studied, discuss it. Finally, about a year after the beginning of the study, a printed report is issued, with full results of the study, digested and tabulated and enlarged by the addition of historical and other material. In this way the following reports have been issued:

No. 1. Mortality among Negroes in Cities. 51 pp. 1896.

No. 2. Social and Physical Conditions of Negroes in Cities. 86 pp. 1897.

No. 3. Some Efforts of Negroes for Social Betterment. 66 pp. 1898.

No. 4. The Negro in Business. 78 pp. 1899.

No. 5. The College-Bred Negro. 115 pp. 1900. The College-Bred Negro. Second edition, abridged. 32 pp.

No. 6. The Negro Common School. 118 pp. 1901.

No. 7. The Negro Artisan. 200 pp. 1902.

No. 8. The Negro Church. (1903.)

Of the effect of this sociological work it is difficult for us who are largely responsible for it to judge. Certain it is that there is a call for scientific study of the American negro, and it is also clear that no agency is doing anything in this line except Atlanta University, the United States Census Bureau and the United States Department of Labor. In general our reports have been well received, both in this country and in England, and their material has been widely used. In fact they have not received as much criticism as they deserved, which is perhaps one discouraging feature.

Upon the school, the community and the negro race, the emphasis put on this sort of study has undoubtedly exerted a wholesome influence. It has directed thought and discussion into definite and many times unnoticed channels; it has led to various efforts at social betterment, such as the formation of the National Negro Business League, and it has stimulated healthy self-criticism based on accurate knowledge.

3

THE TWELFTH CENSUS
AND THE NEGRO PROBLEMS

The Spanish war and its various sequels have gravely increased some of our difficulties in dealing with the Negro problems. There has come a significant change in public opinion—a growing indifference to human suffering, a practical surrender of the doctrine of equality, of citizenship, and a new impetus to the cold commercial aspect of racial intercourse; all this means increased difficulty in stirring the heart of the nation to such great reformatory movements as the proper solution of the Negro problems demands. Under such circumstances any significant disagreement among the friends of reform, and especially any wide-spread and acknowledged ignorance of the real facts and conditions, is bound to multiply the impediments in the path of humantarian effort. In the last ten years we have had the spectacle of the friends of the Negro bickering among themselves as to the aim and method of their work. And especially have we for full fifty years felt the hopelessness of many set arguments on the Negro question because of the absence of any common authoritative basis of fact. Just the other day two speakers in the University Extension Series of Philadelphia made substantially the following statements:

> The freedman bought land in Georgia, but his sons have not, and are even losing what he had owned. The later generation make such poor workmen that corporations often offer higher wages for convict than for free labor.

Abridged from *The Southern Workman* 29 (May 1900): 305–9.

The ownership of land by Georgia Negroes has increased by leaps and bounds, save at a few temporary periods of financial depression or political unrest, and the material advance of the great mass of the black people of that state cannot be denied.

This is but a single instance of the almost daily contradiction as to elementary facts which greets the layman who seeks lights on the present condition of the Negro: Is the Negro buying land or is he not? Is he losing or gaining in the skilled trades? How does his physical health compare with that of the past? Does he receive living wages? Can he vote? What does the graduate of the schools find to do?—all these are specimens of the important questions which to-day can be given no comprehensive or authoritative answer covering large and typical areas. And yet most of them are vitally necessary to a preliminary understanding of the Negro problems, not to say to intelligent plans for reform.

If we look about for agencies which can reasonably be expected to give us at least a partial collection of authoritative data, the most conspicuous is undoubtedly the United States census. So far the census reports are almost our sole source of information as to the condition of the Negro population in general, and for this reason peculiar interest attaches to the Twelfth Census as marking in a peculiar sense the end of an era in the solution of the Negro Question as well as in other matters. Some circumstances connected with the preliminary organization of this census lead us to expect from it a somewhat higher degree of accuracy than in the past or at least an avoidance of the faults of the discredited ninth and eleventh censuses. As an instrument for social investigation there are certain obvious limitations to the national census. It can successfully measure only the broader and simpler aspects of human society— the number, distribution, age, sex, conjugal condition, and occupations of men. Such matters are easily counted, there is, comparatively speaking, small room for error, and no other agency but the government could command the requisite funds and authority for covering so vast a field. Other data such as those relating to illiteracy, deaths, industries, etc. are less obviously suited to census methods and yet we have just now no better agency. When, however, it comes to matters of land and property, education, crime, and the more delicate and intricate questions of social life, the ordinary machinery of the census is obviously unsuited to the work.

The rather indefinite term "Social Study" has come to be applied to such investigations as seek to go further and deeper than a national census and study definitely and, within limits, exhaustively, the conditions of life and action in certain localities. Such difficult undertakings have very obvious limitations: they must necessarily be confined to small geographical areas; they can after all measure only the more powerful economic and social forces and must largely omit the deeper spiritual and moral impulses; and above all they require for their successful pursuit a high order of ability, insight, and tact, They are also very costly when the paucity of definite or immediately usable results is considered. Nevertheless the Social Study manifestly approaches as nearly as anything the ideal of measuring and classifying human activity.

Here we have then the two agencies upon which we must depend for our knowledge of social conditions and development—the broad general measurements of the Census, the limited specific investigations of the Social Study. It is clear that these two agencies may to a large extent supplement each other. For a given city or town the census furnishes the mass data as to number, age, sex, etc. With this broad outline in hand the sociologist seeks to fill in the details of the picture so as to classify and weigh the life and action of that community. So with any particular social problem or series of problems, the careful investigation based upon the census is our best method of acquiring reliable and definite knowledge of social conditions. It is the object of this paper, therefore, to suggest a method of careful co-operation between the authorities in charge of the Twelfth Census and a Special Committee for the Study of the Negro Problems, of such a nature as to give to social reformers the most authoritative and reliable light possible on this grave question.

For the best success of this plan it is necessary that, first, the Twelfth Census be taken with some special reference to gathering material on the Negro in such shape as to be most available for further investigation: for instance, pains should be taken to count the Negro population thoroughly; to class those of African descent together and not confound with them groups socially so diverse as the Japanese and Indians, to have especial care taken with the age classifications and the statistics of conjugal condition where large errors creep in among the Negro statistics for obvious reasons; above all, the Negro statistics should be so collected as to be easily segregated and counted by themselves. Special pains should be taken to count and classify returns as to Negroes somewhat minutely and elaborately in a special census volume.

As soon as practical, duplicate copies of the original returns as to Negroes should be put in the hands of a Special Committee for the Study of the Negro Problems covering such cities and other areas as they may elect. Upon the appointment of this committee the whole plan, of course, stands or falls. I only insist upon the necessity of some steps to make plain the truth: with all our simple optimism the race problem is assuming grave aspects that demand study. An ordinary congressional committee would be unsuitable for this work for political reasons. The best agency would be a voluntary committee of men something like the Committee of Fifty who studied the liquor problem—chosen, as it were, by common consent, but carrying with it the confidence of the better half of the nation.

Some such committee as this should have general oversight of a series of social studies into the condition of the American Negro. The object of this investigation should not be philanthropic but scientific—it should aim to collect a reliable and authoritative body of facts and not to point out methods of reform; and it should be the province of the supervising committee simply to guarantee the honest, unbiased, and thorough character of the research. The members of this committee should serve without salary and they should appoint for the actual work of investigation a body of five—possibly ten—trained specialists of recognized ability who should be salaried men, and should conduct in a number of typical districts and other localities throughout the United States a series of social studies into the condition of the Negro, based primarily on the original returns of the Twelfth Census. From ten to twenty-five such studies should be made covering a space of five years and involving a total expenditure of not less than $250,000 or more than $500,000. The returns from these studies should be duly classified and various sub-committees of the Committee of Twenty-five should review the evidence collected and determine the final form of its presentation.

The scope of the inquiry should be well defined. It could without difficulty take up the following three subjects:

1. Occupations and Wages.
2. Land, Property, and Taxation.
3. Education.

And with more difficulty it could throw some light on two other subjects:

4. Crime and Punishment.
5. The Right of Suffrage.

This plan is of course capable of any amount of modification: it might be reduced to the carrying out of two or three local studies by means of private benevolence or it might be expanded to a thorough and exhaustive study of the American Negro. In all cases, however, the fundamental propositions which seem to me vital are:

a. A census taken with especial care as regards the Negro.

b. A supervising committee of national reputation.

c. The placing of the original returns of the census in the hands of experts under the guidance of the committee.

d. A series of social studies based primarily on this data.

Finally, I cannot too strongly insist that the present condition of the Race Question in the United States is critical, and that the Policy of Drift is not the policy that should appeal to a sensible, righteous people. For half the cost of an ironclad to sail about the world and get us into trouble we might *know* instead of *think* about the Negro problems.

4

THE STUDY OF THE NEGRO PROBLEMS

The present period in the development of sociological study is a
trying one; it is the period of observation, research and comparison
—work always wearisome, often aimless, without well-settled principles and guiding lines, and subject ever to the pertinent criticism:
What, after all, has been accomplished? To this the one positive
answer which years of research and speculation have been able to
return is that the phenomena of society are worth the most careful
and systematic study, and whether or not this study may eventually
lead to a systematic body of knowledge deserving the name of
science, it cannot in any case fail to give the world a mass of truth
worth the knowing.

Being then in a period of observation and comparison, we must
confess to ourselves that the sociologists of few nations have so good
an opportunity for observing the growth and evolution of society as
those of the United States. The rapid rise of a young country, the
vast social changes, the wonderful economic development, the bold
political experiments, and the contact of varying moral standards—
all these make for American students crucial tests of social action,
microcosmic reproductions of long centuries of world history, and
rapid—even violent—repetitions of great social problems. Here is a
field for the sociologist—a field rich, but little worked, and full of
great possibilities. European scholars envy our opportunities and it
must be said to our credit that great interest in the observation of
social phenomena has been aroused in the last decade—an interest

Abridged from *The Annals of the American Academy of Political and Social
Science*, 11 (January 1898): 1–23.

of which much is ephemeral and superficial, but which opens the way for broad scholarship and scientific effort.

In one field, however,—and a field perhaps larger than any other single domain of social phenomena, there does not seem to have been awakened as yet a fitting realization of the opportunities for scientific inquiry. This is the group of social phenomena arising from the presence in this land of eight million persons of African descent.

It is my purpose in this paper to discuss certain considerations concerning the study of the social problems affecting American Negroes; first, as to the historical development of these problems; then as to the necessity for their careful systematic study at the present time; thirdly, as to the results of scientific study of the Negro up to this time; fourthly, as to the scope and method which future scientific inquiry should take, and, lastly, regarding the agencies by which this work can best be carried out.

1. DEVELOPMENT OF THE NEGRO PROBLEMS

A social problem is the failure of an organized social group to realize its group ideals, through the inability to adapt a certain desired line of action to given conditions of life. If, for instance, a government founded on universal manhood suffrage has a portion of its population so ignorant as to be unable to vote intelligently, such ignorance becomes a menacing social problem. The impossibility of economic and social development in a community where a large per cent of the population refuse to abide by the social rules of order, makes a problem of crime and lawlessness. Prostitution becomes a social problem when the demands of luxurious home life conflict with marriage customs.

Thus a social problem is ever a relation between conditions and action, and as conditions and actions vary and change from group to group from time to time and from place to place, so social problems change, develop and grow. Consequently, though we ordinarily speak of the Negro problem as though it were one unchanged question, students must recognize the obvious facts that this problem, like others, has had a long historical development, has changed with the growth and evolution of the nation; moreover, that it is not *one* problem, but rather a plexus of social problems, some new, some old, some simple, some complex; and these problems have their one bond of unity in the act that they group themselves about those Africans whom two centuries of slave-trading brought into the land.

2. THE PRESENT NEGRO PROBLEMS

Such are some of the changes of condition and social movement which have, since 1619, altered and broadened the social problems grouped about the American Negro. In this development of successive questions about one centre, there is nothing peculiar to American history. Given any fixed condition or fact—a river Nile, a range of Alps, an alien race, or a national idea—and problems of society will at every stage of advance group themselves about it. All social growth means a succession of social problems—they constitute growth, they denote that laborious and often baffling adjustment of action and condition which is the essence of progress, and while a particular fact or circumstance may serve in one country as a rallying point of many intricate questions of adjustment, the absence of that particular fact would not mean the absence of all social problems. Questions of labor, caste, ignorance and race were bound to arise in America; they were simply complicated here and intensified there by the presence of the Negro.

Turning now from this brief summary of the varied phases of these questions, let us inquire somewhat more carefully into the form under which the Negro problems present themselves to-day after 275 years of evolution. Their existence is plainly manifested by the fact that a definitely segregated mass of eight millions of Americans do not wholly share the national life of the people; are not an integral part of the social body. The points at which they fail to be incorporated into this group life constitute the particular Negro problems, which can be divided into two distinct but correlated parts, depending on two facts:

First—Negroes do not share the full national life because as a mass they have not reached a sufficiently high grade of culture.

Secondly—They do not share the full national life because there has always existed in America a conviction—varying in intensity, but always widespread—that people of Negro blood should not be admitted into the group life of the nation no matter what their condition might be.

Considering the problems arising from the backward development of Negroes, we may say that the mass of this race does not reach the social standards of the nation with respect to

a. Economic condition.
b. Mental training.
c. Social efficiency.

Even if special legislation and organized relief intervene, freedmen always start life under an economic disadvantage which generations, perhaps centuries, cannot overcome. Again, of all the important constituent parts of our nation, the Negro is by far the most ignorant; nearly half of the race are absolutely illiterate, only a minority of the other half have thorough common school training, and but a remnant are liberally educated. The great deficiency of the Negro, however, is his small knowledge of the art of organized social life—that last expression of human culture. His development in group life was abruptly broken off by the slave ship, directed into abnormal channels and dwarfed by the Black Codes, and suddenly wrenched anew by the Emancipation Proclamation. He finds himself, therefore, peculiarly weak in that nice adaptation of individual life to the life of the group which is the essence of civilization. This is shown in the grosser forms of sexual immorality, disease and crime, and also in the difficulty of race organization for common ends in economic or in intellectual lines.

For these reasons the Negro would fall behind any average modern nation, and he is unusually handicapped in the midst of a nation which excels in its extraordinary economic development, its average of popular intelligence and in the boldness of its experiments in organized social life.

These problems of poverty, ignorance and social degradation differ from similar problems the world over in one important particular, and that is the fact that they are complicated by a peculiar environment. This constitutes the second class of Negro problems, and they rest, as has been said, on the widespread conviction among Americans that no persons of Negro descent should become constituent members of the social body. This feeling gives rise to economic problems, to educational problems, and nice questions of social morality; it makes it more difficult for black men to earn a living or spend their earnings as they will; it gives them poorer school facilities and restricted contact with cultured classes; and it becomes, throughout the land, a cause and excuse for discontent, lawlessness, laziness and injustice.

3. THE NECESSITY OF CAREFULLY STUDYING THESE PROBLEMS

Such, barely stated, are the elements of the present Negro problems. It is to little purpose, however, to name the elements of a problem unless we can also say accurately to what extent each element enters into the final result: whether, for instance, the present difficulties arise more largely from ignorance than from prejudice, or *vice versa*. This we do not know, and here it is that every intelligent discussion of the American Negro comes to a standstill. Nearly a hundred years ago Thomas Jefferson complained that the nation had never studied the real condition of the slaves and that, therefore, all general conclusions about them were extremely hazardous. We of another age can scarcely say that we have made material progress in this study. Yet these problems, so vast and intricate, demanding trained research and expert analysis, touching questions that affect the very foundation of the republic and of human progress, increasing and multiplying year by year, would seem to urge the nation with increasing force to measure and trace and understand thoroughly the underlying elements of this example of human evolution.

Now first we should study the Negro problems in order to distinguish between the different and distinct problems affecting this race. Nothing makes intelligent discussion of the Negro's position so fruitless as the repeated failure to discriminate between the different questions that concern him. If a Negro discusses the question, he is apt to discuss simply the problem of race prejudice; if a Southern white man writes on the subject he is apt to discuss problems of ignorance, crime and social degradation; and yet each calls the problem he discusses *the* Negro problem, leaving in the dark background the really crucial question as to the relative importance of the many problems involved. Before we can begin to study the Negro intelligently, we must realize definitely that not only is he affected by all the varying social forces that act on any nation at his stage of advancement, but that in addition to these there is reacting upon him the mighty power of a peculiar and unusual social environment which affects to some extent every other social force.

In the second place we should seek to know and measure carefully all the forces and conditions that go to make up these different problems, to trace the historical development of these conditions, and discover as far as possible the probable trend of further development. Without doubt this would be difficult work, and it can with much truth be objected that we cannot ascertain, by the methods of sociological research known to us, all such facts thoroughly and accurately. To this objection it is only necessary to answer that however difficult it may be to know all about the Negro, it is certain that we can know vastly more than we do, and that we can have our knowledge in more systematic and intelligible form. As things are, our opinions upon the Negro are more matters of faith than of knowledge. Every schoolboy is ready to discuss the matter, and there are few men that have not settled convictions. Such a situation is dangerous. Whenever any nation allows impulse, whim or hasty conjecture to usurp the place of conscious, normative, intelligent action, it is in grave danger. The sole aim of any society is to settle its problems in accordance with its highest ideals, and the only rational method of accomplishing this is to study those problems in the light of the best scientific research.

Finally, the American Negro deserves study for the great end of advancing the cause of science in general. No such opportunity to watch and measure the history and development of a great race of men ever presented itself to the scholars of a modern nation. If they miss this opportunity—if they do the work in a slip-shod, unsystematic manner—if they dally with the truth to humor the whims of the day, they do far more than hurt the good name of the American people; they hurt the cause of scientific truth the world over, they voluntarily decrease human knowledge of a universe of which we are ignorant enough, and they degrade the high end of truth-seeking in a day when they need more and more to dwell upon its sanctity.

4. THE WORK ALREADY ACCOMPLISHED

It may be said that it is not altogether correct to assert that few attempts have been made to study these problems or to put the nation in possession of a body of truth in accordance with which it might act intelligently. It is far from my purpose to disparage in any way the work already done by students of these questions; much valuable effort has without doubt been put upon the field, and yet a careful survey of the field seems but to emphasize the fact that the work done bears but small proportion to the work still to be done.

Moreover the studies made hitherto can as a whole be justly criticised in three particulars: (1) They have not been based on a thorough knowledge of details; (2) they have been unsystematical; (3) they have been uncritical.

In few subjects have historians been more content to go on indefinitely repeating current traditions and uninvestigated facts. We are still gravely told that the slave trade ceased in 1808, that the docility of Africans made slave insurrections almost unknown, and that the Negro never developed in this country a self-conscious group life before 1860. In the hasty endeavor to cover a broad subject when the details were unknown, much superficial work has been current, like that, for instance, of a newspaper reporter who spent "the odd intervals of leisure in active newspaper work" for "nearly eighteen months," in the District of Columbia, and forthwith published a study of 80,000 Negroes, with observations on their institutions and development.

Again, the work done has been lamentably unsystematic and fragmentary. Scientific work must be subdivided, but conclusions which affect the whole subject must be based on a study of the whole. One cannot study the Negro in freedom and come to general conclusions about his destiny without knowing his history in slavery. A vast set of problems having a common centre must, too, be studied according to some general plan, if the work of different students is to be compared or to go toward building a unified body of knowledge. A plan once begun must be carried out, and not like that of our erratic census reports, after allowing us to follow the size of farms in the South for three decades, suddenly leave us wondering as to the relation of farms and farm families. Students of black codes should not stop suddenly with 1863, and travelers and observers whose testimony would be of great value if arranged with some system and reasonably limited in time and space, must not ramble on without definite plan or purpose and render their whole work of doubtful value.

Most unfortunate of all, however, is the fact that so much of the work done on the Negro question is notoriously uncritical; uncritical from lack of discrimination in the selection and weighing of evidence; uncritical in choosing the proper point of view from which to study these problems, and, finally, uncritical from the distinct bias in the minds of so many writers. To illustrate, the layman who does not pretend to first hand knowledge of the subject and who would learn of students is to-day woefully puzzled by absolutely contradictory evidence. One student declares that Negroes are advancing in knowledge and ability; that they are working, establishing homes, and going into business, and that the problem will soon be one of the past. Another student of equal learning declares that the Negro is degenerating—sinking into crime and social immorality, receiving little help from education, still in the main a menial servant, and destined in a short time to settle the problem by dying entirely out. Such and many other contradictory conclusions arise from the uncritical use of material. A visitor to a great Negro school in the South catches the inspiration of youth, studies the work of graduates, and imbibes the hopes of teachers and immediately infers from the situation of a few hundred the general condition of a population numbering twice that of Holland. A college graduate sees the slums of a Southern city, looks at the plantation field hands, and has some experience with Negro servants, and from the laziness, crime and disease which he finds, draws conclusions as to eight millions of people, stretched from Maine to Texas and from Florida to Washington. We continually judge the whole from the part we are familiar with; we continually assume the material we have at hand to be typical; we reverently receive a column of figures without asking who collected them, how they were arranged, how far they are valid and what chances of error they contain; we receive the testimony of men without asking whether they were trained or ignorant, careful or careless, truthful or given to exaggeration, and, above all, whether they are giving facts or opinions. It is so easy for a man who has already formed his conclusions to receive any and all testimony in their favor without carefully weighing and testing it, that we sometimes find in serious scientific studies very curious proof of broad conclusions. To cite an extreme case, in a recently published study of the Negro, a part of the argument as to the physical condition of all these millions, is made to rest on the measurement of fifteen black boys in a New York reformatory.

The widespread habit of studying the Negro from one point of view only, that of his influence on the white inhabitants, is also responsible for much uncritical work. The slaves are generally treated as one inert changeless mass, and most studies of slavery apparently have no conception of a social evolution and development among them. The slave code of a state is given, the progress of anti-slavery sentiment, the economic results of the system and the general influence of man on master are studied, but of the slave himself, of his group life and social institutions, of remaining traces of his African tribal life, of his amusements, his conversion to Christianity, his acquiring of the English tongue—in fine, of his whole reaction against his environment, of all this we hear little or nothing, and would apparently be expected to believe that the Negro arose from the dead in 1863. Yet all the testimony of law and custom, of tradition and present social condition, shows us that the Negro at the time of emancipation had passed through a social evolution which far separated him from his savage ancestors.

The most baneful cause of uncritical study of the Negro is the manifest and far-reaching bias of writers. Americans are born in many cases with deep, fierce convictions on the Negro question, and in other cases imbibe them from their environment. When such men come to write on the subject, without technical training, without breadth of view, and in some cases without a deep sense of the sanctity of scientific truth, their testimony, however interesting as opinion, must of necessity be worthless as science. Thus too often the testimony of Negroes and their friends has to be thrown out of court on account of the manifest prejudice of the writers; on the other hand, the testimony of many other writers in the North and especially in the South has to be received with reserve on account of too evident bias.

Such facts make the path of students and foreign observers peculiarly thorny. The foreigner's views, if he be not exceptionally astute, will depend largely on his letters of introduction; the home student's views, on his birthplace and parentage. All students are apt to fail to recognize the magnitude and importance of these problems, and to succumb to the vulgar temptation of basing on any little contribution they make to the study of these problems, general conclusions as to the origin and destiny of the Negro people in time and eternity. Thus we possess endless final judgments as to the American Negro emanating from men of influence and learning, in the very face of the fact known to every accurate student, that there exists to-day no sufficient material of proven reliability, upon which any scientist can base definite and final conclusions as to the present condition and tendencies of the eight million American Negroes; and that any person or publication purporting to give such conclusions simply makes statements which go beyond the reasonably proven evidence.

5. A PROGRAM OF FUTURE STUDY

If we admit the deep importance of the Negro problems, the necessity of studying them, and certain shortcomings in work done up to this time, it would seem to be the clear duty of the American people, in the interests of scientific knowledge and social reform, to begin a broad and systematic study of the history and condition of the American Negroes. The scope and method of this study, however, needs to be generally agreed upon beforehand in its main outlines, not to hinder the freedom of individual students, but to systematize and unify effort so as to cover the wide field of investigation.

The scope of any social study is first of all limited by the general attitude of public opinion toward truth and truth-seeking. If in regard to any social problem there is for any reason a persistent refusal on the part of the people to allow the truth to be known, then manifestly that problem cannot be studied. Undoubtedly much of the unsatisfactory work already done with regard to the Negro is due to this cause; the intense feeling that preceded and followed the war made a calm balanced research next to impossible. Even to-day there are certain phases of this question which we cannot hope to be allowed to study dispassionately and thoroughly, and these phases, too, are naturally those uppermost in the public mind. For instance, it is extremely doubtful if any satisfactory study of Negro crime and lynching can be made for a generation or more, in the present condition of the public mind, which renders it almost impossible to get at the facts and real conditions. On the other hand, public opinion has in the last decade become sufficiently liberal to open a broad field of investigation to students, and here lies the chance for effective work.

The right to enter this field undisturbed and untrammeled will depend largely on the attitude of science itself. Students must be careful to insist that science as such—be it physics, chemistry, psychology, or sociology—has but one simple aim: the discovery of truth. Its results lie open for the use of all men—merchants, physicians, men of letters, and philanthropists, but the aim of science itself is simple truth. Any attempt to give it a double aim, to make social reform the immediate instead of the mediate object of a search for truth, will inevitably tend to defeat both objects. The frequent alliance of sociological research with various panaceas and particular schemes of reform, has resulted in closely connecting social investigation with a good deal of groundless assumption and humbug in the popular mind. There will be at first some difficulty in bringing the Southern people, both black and white, to conceive of an earnest, careful study of the Negro problem which has not back of it some scheme of race amalgamation, political jobbery, or deportation to Africa. The new study of the American Negro must avoid such misapprehensions from the outset, by insisting that historical and statistical research has but one object, the ascertainment of the facts as to the social forces and conditions of one-eighth of the inhabitants of the land. Only by such rigid adherence to the true object of the scholar, can statesmen and philanthropists of all shades of belief be put into possession of a reliable body of truth which may guide their efforts to the best and largest success.

In the next place, a study of the Negro, like the study of any subject, must start out with certain generally admitted postulates. We must admit, for instance, that the field of study is large and varying, and that what is true of the Negro in Massachusetts is not necessarily true of the Negro in Louisiana; that what was true of the Negro in 1850 was not necessarily true in 1750; and that there are many distinct social problems affecting the Negro. Finally, if we would rally to this common ground of scientific inquiry all partisans and advocates, we must explicitly admit what all implicitly postulate —namely, that the Negro is a member of the human race, and as one who, in the light of history and experience, is capable to a degree of improvement and culture, is entitled to have his interests considered according to his numbers in all conclusions as to the common weal.

With these preliminary considerations we may say that the study of the Negro falls naturally into two categories, which though difficult to separate in practice, must for the sake of logical clearness, be kept distinct. They are (*a*) the study of the Negro as a social group, (*b*) the study of his peculiar social environment.

The study of the Negro as a social group may be, for convenience, divided into four not exactly logical but seemingly most practicable divisions, viz:

1. Historical study.
2. Statistical investigation.
3. Anthropological measurement.
4. Sociological interpretation.

The material at hand for historical research is rich and abundant; there are the colonial statutes and records, the partially accessible archives of Great Britain, France and Spain, the collections of historical societies, the vast number of executive and congressional reports and documents, the state statutes, reports and publications, the reports of institutions and societies, the personal narratives and opinions of various observers and the periodical press covering nearly three centuries. From these sources can be gathered much new information upon the economic and social development of the Negro, upon the rise and decline of the slave-trade, the character, distribution and state of culture of the Africans, the evolution of the slave codes as expressing the life of the South, the rise of such peculiar expressions of Negro social history, as the Negro church, the economics of plantation life, the possession of private property by slaves, and the history of the oft-forgotten class of free Negroes. Such historical research must be sub-divided in space and limited in time by the nature of the subject, the history of the different colonies and groups being followed and compared, the different periods of development receiving special study, and the whole subject being reviewed from different aspects.

The collection of statistics should be carried on with increased care and thoroughness. It is no credit to a great modern nation that so much well-grounded doubt can be thrown on our present knowledge of the simple matters of number, age, sex and conjugal condition in regard to our Negro population. General statistical investigations should avoid seeking to tabulate more intricate social conditions than the ones indicated. The concrete social status of the Negro can only be ascertained by intensive studies carried on in definitely limited localities, by competent investigators, in accordance with one general plan. Statistical study by groups is apt to be more accurately done and more easily accomplished, and able to secure more competent and responsible agents than any general census. General averages in so complicated a subject are apt to be dangerously misleading. This study should seek to ascertain by the most approved methods of social measurement the size and condition of families, the occupations and wages, the illiteracy of adults and education of children, the standard of living, the character of the dwellings, the property owned and rents paid, and the character of the organized group life. Such investigations should be extended until they cover the typical group life of Negroes in all sections of the land and should be so repeated from time to time in the same localities and with the same methods, as to be a measure of social development.

The third division of study is anthropological measurement, and it includes a scientific study of the Negro body. The most obvious peculiarity of the Negro—a peculiarity which is a large element in many of the problems affecting him—is his physical unlikeness to the people with whom he has been brought into contact. This difference is so striking that it has become the basis of a mass of theory, assumption and suggestion which is deep-rooted and yet rests on the flimsiest basis of scientific fact. That there are differences between the white and black races is certain, but just what those differences are is known to none with an approach to accuracy. Yet here in America is the most remarkable opportunity ever offered of studying these differences, of noting influences of climate and physical environment, and particularly of studying the effect of amalgamating two of the most diverse races in the world—another subject which rests under a cloud of ignorance.

The fourth division of this investigation is sociological interpretation; it should include the arrangement and interpretation of historical and statistical matter in the light of the experience of other nations and other ages; it should aim to study those finer manifestations of social life which history can but mention and which statistics can not count, such as the expression of Negro life as found in their hundred newspapers, their considerable literature, their music and folklore and their germ of esthetic life—in fine, in all the movements and customs among them that manifest the existence of a distinct social mind.

The second category of studies of the Negro has to do with his peculiar social environment. It will be difficult, as has been intimated, to separate a study of the group from a study of the environment, and yet the group action and the reaction of the surroundings must be kept clearly distinct if we expect to comprehend the Negro problems. The study of the environment may be carried on at the same time with a study of the group, only the two sets of forces must receive distinct measurement.

In such a field of inquiry it will be found difficult to do more than subdivide inquiry in time and space. The attempt should be made to isolate and study the tangible phenomena of Negro prejudice in all possible cases; its effect on the Negro's physical development, on his mental acquisitiveness, on his moral and social condition, as manifested in economic life, in legal sanctions and in crime and lawlessness. So, too, the influence of that same prejudice on American life and character would explain the otherwise inexplicable changes through which Negro prejudice has passed.

The plan of study thus sketched is, without doubt, long, difficult and costly, and yet is not more than commensurable with the size and importance of the subject with which it is to deal. It will take years and decades to carry out such a plan, with the barest measure of success, and yet there can be no doubt that this plan or something similar to it, points to the quickest path toward the ultimate solution of the present difficulties.

5

THE NEGRO RACE
IN THE UNITED STATES OF AMERICA

There were in 1900 in the United States and its dependencies 8,840,789 persons of acknowledged Negro descent. To-day the number is probably ten millions. These persons are almost entirely descendants of the African slaves brought to America in the sixteenth, seventeenth, eighteenth, and nineteenth centuries.

I. The Slave Trade

The African slave trade to America arose from the desire of the Spanish and other nations to exploit rapidly the resources of the New World. The attempt to use the native races for this purpose failed because of the weakness and comparative scarcity of the Indians. Conditions in Africa, on the other hand, favoured the organisation of the slave traffic. A strong Negro-Arabian civilisation in the Soudan had forced back the barbarians to the fever-cursed Centre and West, and there the stronger and fiercer Bantu and other nations dominated and enslaved the weaker tribes. The coming of the Portuguese in the middle of the fifteenth century was the occasion of transporting some of these slaves to Portugal, and from this, in time, came the slave trade to the West Indies.

The African slave trade soon became a profitable venture, for which the Portuguese, Dutch, and English competed. Finally, in 1714, the English secured a virtual monopoly of the North American

Reprinted from *Papers on Inter-racial Problems Communicated to the First Universal Races Congress Held at University of London, July 26–29, 1911*, G. Spiller, ed. (London: P.S. King & Son, 1911).

trade and poured large numbers of slaves into the West. The exact number of slaves imported is not known. Dunbar estimates that nearly 900,000 came to America in the sixteenth century, 2,750,000 in the seventeenth, 7,000,000 in the eighteenth, and over 4,000,000 in the nineteenth, perhaps 15,000,000 in all. It goes without saying that the cruelty incident in this forced migration of men was very great. For a long time the policy of the slave owners was to kill off the Negroes by over-work and buy more. Family life was impossible, there being few women imported, and sexual promiscuity and concubinage ensued. When finally, for physical and moral reasons, the supply of slaves began to fall off a new development began.

II. GROWTH AND PHYSIQUE OF THE NEGRO-AMERICAN POPULATION

The growth of the Negro population in the English colonies in America may be estimated as follows:—

1710	50,000
1725	75,000
1750	220,000
1754	260,000
1760	310,000
1770	462,000
1780	462,000

The United States censuses give the following figures:

Date	Total Negroes	Per Cent. of Increase	Per Cent. of Increase of Whites	Per Cent. of Negroes in Total Population
1790	757,208	—	—	19.27
1800	1,002,037	32.33	35.76	18.88
1810	1,377,808	37.50	36.12	19.03
1820	1,771,656	28.59	34.12	18.39
1830	2,328,642	31.44	34.03	18.10
1840	2,873,648	23.40	34.72	16.84
1850	3,638,808	26.63	37.74	15.69
1860	4,441,830	22.07	37.69	14.13
1870	4,880,009	9.86	24.76	12.66

cont. Date	Total Negroes	Per Cent. of Increase	Per Cent. of Increase of Whites	Per Cent. of Negroes in Total Population
1880	6,580,793	34.85	29.22	13.12
1890	7,488,789	13.79	26.68	11.93
1900	8,840,789	18.1	21.4	11.6
1910	10,000,000 (estimated)	—	—	—

The census of 1870 was defective, and probably that of 1890 also, which would explain the chief irregularities in the rate of increase of Negroes. The higher rate of increase of the whites is due mainly to the large immigration.

The present so-called "Negro" population of the United States is:

1. A mixture of the various African populations—Bantu, Soudanese, West Coast Negroes, some dwarfs, &c. There are traces of Arab and Semitic blood.

2. A mixture of these strains with the blood of white Americans through a long system of concubinage of coloured women in slavery days together with some legal intermarriage. The official figures for mulattoes are as follows:

1850, mulattoes formed 11.2 per cent. of the total Negro population.
1860, mulattoes formed 13.2 per cent. of the total Negro population.
1870, mulattoes formed 12 per cent. of the total Negro population.
1890, mulattoes formed 15.2 per cent. of the total Negro population.

Or in actual numbers:

> 1850, 405,751 mulattoes.
> 1860, 588,352 mulattoes
> 1870, 585,601 mulattoes.
> 1890, 1,132,060 mulattoes.

These figures are of doubtful validity and officially acknowledged to be misleading. From observation and local studies in all parts of the United States I am inclined to believe that at least one-third of the Negroes of the United States have distinct traces of white blood, and there is also a large amount of Negro blood in the white population. This blending of the races has led to new and interesting human types, but race prejudice has hitherto prevented any scientific study of the matter.

Scientific physical measurements of Negro-Americans have not been made on any sufficiently large scale for valuable conclusions to be formed.

The Negro population shows, so far as known, a greater death-rate than the white. Throughout the registration area of the United States the figures are:

DEATH-RATE PER 1,000 LIVING, UNITED STATES
REGISTRATION AREA

	1890	1900
Coloured	29.9	29.6
White	19.1	17.3

These figures apply to only 1¼ million of the Negro population, and those mainly in cities. Of the death-rate of the mass of the population living in the country we know nothing. The chief causes of death among Negroes are: Consumption, pneumonia, nervous disorders, malaria, and infant mortality. The figures are:

DEATHS PER 100,000 LIVING NEGROES

	1890	1900
Consumption	546	485
Pneumonia	279	355
Nervous disorders	333	308
Malaria	72	63

To every 1,000 living coloured children, there were each year the following number who died:

CHILDREN UNDER 1 YEAR OF AGE

	1890	1900
Registration States	458	344
Cities	580	397
Country	204	219

The birth-rate is conjectural:

NUMBER OF CHILDREN UNDER 5 YEARS OF AGE TO 1,000 FEMALES 15 TO
44 YEARS OF AGE FOR THE CONTINENTAL UNITED STATES

	Total	White	Coloured	Excess of Coloured
1900	474	465	543	78
1890	485	473	574	101
1880	559	537	706	169
1870	572	562	641	79
1860	634	627	675	48
1850	626	613	694	81
1840 *	—	744	—	—
1830 *	—	781	—	—

* Women 15 to 49 years of age.

From this we may conclude:

1. The Negro birth-rate exceeds and has always exceeded the white birth-rate.

2. The Negro birth-rate probably decreased largely until 1870; then it possibly increased somewhat, and afterwards rapidly decreased.

3. The Negro birth-rate in the country districts is high. In the city it is low because of the immigrant character of the population.

In general the Negro population of the United States is brown in colour, darkening to almost black and shading off in the other directions to yellow and white, indistinguishable in many cases from the white population. The race is strong and virile, and, although hard pressed by economic and mental strain, is more than holding its own.

III. SOCIAL HISTORY

Negroes came to America with the early explorers, and they took some part in exploration. Stephen Dorantes, a Negro of the Fray Marcos Expedition, was the discoverer of the South-Western part of

North America; and there were many Negroes with Balboa, Pizarro, D'Ayllon, and Cortez. As the Dutch and English slave trade of the seventeenth century poured in larger numbers of Negroes, the question of their control and organisation became serious. They were carefully mixed by race and language so as to prevent conspiracy, and worked in gangs by severe taskmasters. This led to repeated revolts throughout the islands and on the Continent. Only two of these were large and successful—that of the Maroons in Jamaica in the seventeenth century, and of Touissant L'Ouverture in Hayti in the eighteenth century.

The moral theory of early Negro slavery was that the heathen were by this means brought to Christianity, and efforts were gradually made to convert them. The result was that after slow and hesitating advance the slaves were by the middle of the nineteenth century nominal Christians, and spoke the English tongue. The work of conversion and uplift was, however, greatly retarded by the rapid importation of Negroes after the Assiento treaty between England and Spain in 1714. England forced slaves on the colonies, and found them at first complacent; but at last they were frightened, and a distinct moral revolt against the system arose.

Finally a sort of new American feudalism was evolved out of which free Negroes from time to time escaped into the full privileges of freemen.

This was the situation at the time of the War for Independence with England. Probably ten thousand Negro soldiers fought for the independence of the American colonies, and they were recognised as citizens. The undoubted thought of the founders of the Republic was that slavery would gradually die out, and the Negroes either become American citizens or migrate to Africa. This assumption received encouragement by the economic failure of slavery in the North and the emancipation of slaves.

Among the Negroes there were signs of awakening. The freedmen began to demand the ballot in Massachusetts and to organise churches and associations in Rhode Island, New York, and Pennsylvania, and some black persons of distinction arose like Benjamin Banneker, the almanac maker, and Phillis Wheatley, the poet. Negroes fought in the war of 1812—there being black sailors with

Perry and McDonough, and four hundred coloured soldiers with Jackson at New Orleans. About this time, too, definite steps were taken to suppress the slave trade from Africa.

Gradually, however, the strength of this liberal movement waned as the importance of the cotton crop increased. Signs of increased severity against slaves were manifest, and several slave revolts were attempted, that of Nat Turner, in 1831, being the most bloody.

From 1830 on the South took a new tone and began to defend slavery as an economic system against the growing attacks of the abolitionists, while the systematic running away of slaves gave rise to bitterness and recrimination. The free Negroes began to meet in conventions, the anti-slavery crusade was organised, and gradually slavery became the burning political issue. Negro leaders like Frederick Douglass now came forward, Harriet Beecher Stowe's *Uncle Tom's Cabin* was published, fugitive slaves increased in number, and the nation was in a ferment.

When the civil war broke out because of the slavery issue, Negro soldiers were at first refused, but eventually two hundred thousand were enlisted, and even the South tried to arm the slaves.

From the first these slaves were a source of weakness and apprehension to the South. During most of the war the blacks remained quiet, and protected the white women and children while the masters were in the field fighting for their enslavement. Gradually, however, the meaning of the war dawned on them and they began to run away and join the Northern armies. Finally, as a war measure, the mass of them were emancipated, and this was later confirmed by a constitutional amendment.

When after the declaration of peace the question of the protection of the new freedmen arose, the nation paused in puzzled hesitation. Three courses were open:

a. To leave the Negroes to the mercy of the whites, on condition that the whites accepted the constitutional amendment abolishing slavery.

b. To put the Negroes under special guardianship designed to help them as labourers, educate them, and secure justice for them in the courts.

c. To give the Negroes the power of self-protection by insisting on full manhood suffrage in the States with any restrictions the State wished to impose except restrictions based on "race, colour, or previous condition of servitude."

The first method was tried by Johnson. The result was a series of "black codes" which practically restored Negro slavery in almost every essential except name. As Carl Schurz reported:

> Some planters held back their former slaves on their plantations by brute force. Armed bands of white men patrolled the country roads to drive back the Negroes wandering about. Dead bodies of murdered Negroes were found on and near the highways and by-paths. Gruesome reports came from the hospitals— reports of coloured men and women whose ears had been cut off, whose skulls had been broken by blows, whose bodies had been slashed by knives or lacerated with scourges. A number of such cases I had occasion to examine myself. A veritable reign of terror prevailed in many parts of the South. The Negro found scant justice in the local courts against the white man. He could look for protection only to the military forces of the United States still garrisoning the "States lately in rebellion," and to the Freedmen's Bureau.

The second method was tried in the establishment of the Freedmen's Bureau, but the North demurred at the cost, the South complained at the principle, and the Bureau itself was not well managed. The Government was, therefore, as a last resort, literally forced to the third method which involved Negro voters. The argument for this was thus stated by Carl Schurz:

> The emancipation of the slaves is submitted to only in so far as chattel slavery in the old form could not be kept up. But although the freedman is no longer considered the property of the individual master, he is considered the slave of society, and all independent State legislation will share the tendency to make him such.
>
> The solution of the problem would be very much facilitated by enabling all the loyal and free-labour elements in the South to exercise a healthy influence upon legislation. It will hardly be possible to secure the freedman against oppressive class legislation and private persecution, unless he be endowed with a certain measure of political power.

To the argument of ignorance Schurz replied:

The effect of the extension of the franchise to the coloured people upon the development of free labour and upon the security of human rights in the South being the principle object in view, the objections raised on the ground of the ignorance of the freedmen become unimportant. Practical liberty is a good school.... It is idle to say that it will be time to speak of Negro suffrage when the whole coloured race will be educated, for the ballot may be necessary to him to secure his education.

The Negroes themselves said to President Johnson through their spokesman, Frederick Douglass:

Your noble and humane predecessor placed in our hands the sword to assist in saving the nation, and we do hope that you, his able successor, will favourably regard the placing in our hands the ballot with which to save ourselves.

The result of the new basis of suffrage was at first demoralisation. The better class of Southern whites refused to take part in government even when they could, and the new and ignorant Negro voters were delivered into the hands of Northern and Southern demagogues, who looted the State treasuries. Finally, however, the Negroes secured a better class of white and Negro leaders, revolted from the carnival of stealing, and began honest advance and reform. They succeeded in giving to the new South:

1. A more democratic form of government.
2. Free public schools.
3. The beginnings of a new social legislation.

Before this work was finished they were intimidated and put out of power by force and fraud, but as a prominent white leader said:

During their ascendency they obeyed the Constitution of the United States.... They instituted a public school system in a realm where public schools had been unknown. They opened the ballot box and jury box to thousands of white men who had been debarred from them by a lack of earthly possessions. They introduced home rule into the South. They abolished the whipping post, the branding iron, the stocks, and other barbarous forms of punishment which had up to that time prevailed. They reduced capital felonies from about twenty to two or three. In an age of extravagance they were extravagant in the sums appropriated for public works. In all of that time no man's rights of person were invaded under the forms of law. Every Democrat's life, home, fireside, and business were safe. No man obstructed any white man's way to the ballot box, interfered with his freedom of speech, or boycotted him on account of his political faith.

Despite this, the South was determined to deprive the Negroes of political power and force them to occupy the position of a labouring caste.

This was done first by open intimidation, murder, and fraud, through secret societies like the Ku Klux Klan. Finally, beginning in 1890, a new set of disfranchising laws were passed. These laws ostensibly disfranchised the ignorant and poor, but they allowed poor and ignorant whites to vote by a provision known as the "grandfather clause," which admitted to the polls any person whose father or grandfather had the right to vote before the coloured men were enfranchised. At the same time, these laws excluded from the polls not only the ignorant, but nearly all the intelligent Negroes, by making the local registrars judicial officers from whose decision as to fitness there was practically no appeal. These registrars were, of course, invariably white.

With this legislation have gone various restrictive laws to curtail the social, civil, and economic freedom of all persons of Negro descent. The question as to the validity and advisability of these laws, and as to the development of the freedom under them, and speculation as to the future of the race in America constitutes the Negro problem.

IV. SOCIAL CONDITION OF THE NEGRO-AMERICAN

After such a social history, what is the present social condition of the ten millions of persons of Negro descent in the United States, fully one-third of whom have more or less white blood? We may best consider this under certain subheads:

    a. Distribution. The distribution of the Negro American population is very uneven, the coloured people being largely concentrated in the former slave States of the South-East.

In the last decade—1900-1910—there has been a considerable migration from country to city and from North to South, which will change these maps to some extent. The relation of the Negro to cities in 1900 is shown by this table from the census:

POPULATION CLASSIFIED BY RACE AND CLASS OF PLACE OF RESIDENCE AND PER CENT. OF DISTRIBUTION, 1900

Class of Place of Residence	Number of Cities, 1900	White	Negro
Continental United States	—	66,809,196	8,833,994
Cities having at least 2,500 inhabitants	1,861	28,506,146	2,004,121
Cities having a Population of—			
100,000 and over	38	13,507,327	668,254
25,000 to 100,000	122	5,021,827	468,209
8,000 to 25,000	385	4,866,928	399,295
4,000 to 8,000	612	3,098,048	274,492
2,500 to 4,000	704	2,012,016	193,871
Country districts	—	38,303,050	6,829,873

PER CENT. DISTRIBUTION BY CLASS OF PLACE OF RESIDENCE, 1900

Class of Place of Residence	White	Negro
Continental United States	100.0	100.0
Cities having at least 2,500 inhabitants	42.7	22.7
Cities having a Population of—		
100,000 and over	20.2	7.6
25,000 to 100,000.	7.5	5.3
8,000 to 25,000	7.3	4.5
4,000 to 8,000	4.7	3.1
2,500 to 4,000	3.0	2.2
Country districts	57.3	77.3

NUMBER AND PER CENT. DISTRIBUTION OF NEGRO POPULATION OF CONTINENTAL
UNITED STATES BY DIVISION OF RESIDENCE, 1900

	Negro Population, 1900	Per Cent. of Negro Population of Continental United States Living in Specified Division, 1900
Continental United States	8,833,994	100.0
North Atlantic Division—	385,020	4.4
New England	59,099	0.7
Southern North Atlantic	325,921	3.7
South Atlantic Division—	3,729,017	42.2
Northern South Atlantic	1,056,684	12.0
Southern South Atlantic	2,672,333	30.2
North Central Division—	495,751	5.6
Eastern North Central	257,842	2.9
Western North Central	237,909	2.7
South Central Division—	4,193,952	47.5
Eastern South Central	2,499,886	28.3
Western South Central	1,694,066	19.2
Western Division—	30,254	0.3
Rocky Mountain	12,936	0.1
Basin and Plateau	2,654	(*)
Pacific	14,664	0.2

* Less than one-tenth of 1 per cent.

b. Sex, Age, and Conjugal Condition.—In the sex statistics of Negro-Americans one can see easily their social history—the disproportionate number of male slaves imported, the killing of the men during the Civil War and later, &c.

PROPORTION OF MALES AND FEMALES IN EVERY 10,000

DATE	NEGROES		WHITES	
	Male	Female	Male	Female
1820	5,082	4,918	5,080	4,920
1830	5,074	4,926	5,077	4,923
1840	5,014	4,986	5,090	4,910
1850	4,978	5,022	5,104	4,896
1860	4,990	5,010	5,116	4,844
1870	4,905	5,095	5,056	4,944
1880	4,942	5,057	5,088	4,912
1890	4,986	5,014	5,121	4,879
1900	4,969	5,030	5,108	4,892

The median age of Negroes has increased as follows:

MEDIAN AGE OF THE COLOURED POPULATION, CLASSIFIED,
CONTINENTAL UNITED STATES: 1820 TO 1900

1900	19.70	1850	17.33
1890	17.83	1840	17.27
1880	18.01	1830	16.90
1870	18.49	1820	17.75
1860	17.65		

The general age composition is as follows by percentage:

NATIVE WHITES

	Under 15	15-59	60 and Over
1880	42.6	52.9	4.9
1890	40.0	54.8	5.2
1900	39.0	55.8	5.2

COLOURED

	Under 15	15-59	60 and Over
1880	44.2	51.2	4.6
1890	42.1	53.3	4.6
1900	39.5	55.6	4.9

The conjugal condition by sex and age is as follows:

PER CENT. DISTRIBUTION BY CONJUGAL CONDITION FOR THE NEGRO
POPULATION BY SEX AND AGE PERIODS: 1900

AGE PERIOD	PER CENT. OF NEGRO MALE POPULATION, 1900		
	SINGLE AND UNKNOWN	MARRIED	WIDOWED AND DIVORCED
Continental United States—			
15 years and over	39.8	54.0	6.2
15 to 19 years	98.2	1.7	0.1
20 to 24 years	64.9	33.8	1.3
25 to 29 years	33.4	63.3	3.3
30 to 34 years	21.4	73.7	4.9
35 to 44 years	13.5	79.1	7.4
45 to 54 years	7.4	81.4	11.2
55 to 64 years	5.5	78.6	15.9
65 years and over	5.0	69.6	25.4
Age unknown	46.7	47.4	5.9

These statistics can be appreciated only when we remember that there could be no legal family relations among slaves, and that the family therefore is an institution only a generation old for the mass of the coloured people. There are consequently still an abnormally large number of "widowed and separated," while economic pressure and sexual irregularity is setting the age of marriage very late. The improvement in family life in twenty-five years has, however, been enormous.

The average size of the Negro family is about five persons to-day. The percentage of illegitimacy is not accurately known, but is apparently about 20 per cent. in a city like Washington, D.C., which has 100,000 Negroes. It is, without doubt, rapidly decreasing.

c. Education. According to the United States census, the illiteracy of Negro-Americans has been as follows for persons ten years of age and over:

1870	79.9 per cent.
1880	70.0 per cent.
1890	57.1 per cent.
1900	44.5 per cent.

Probably to-day about two-thirds of the Negro population can at least write their names and read to some extent.

In the Northern States, with few exceptions, the coloured children attend the general public schools. In the former slave States, where the Negro population is massed, there are two separate systems of schools, one for the Negroes and one for the whites. Both systems are supported by public taxation and are supposed to offer equal facilities. As a matter of fact, while the Negroes form one-third of the school population they receive less than one-fifth of the school funds, except in the District of Columbia and in a few cities.

The result is a very inferior and inadequate set of Negro public schools with poor teachers, and poor superintendence. The attitude of the mass of southern whites is still inimical to schools for Negroes, and since the new disfranchisement laws the Negro schools have been more than usually neglected.

As a partial compensation for this neglect on the part of the States there are 132 private institutions for educating Negroes; a few of these receive State and national aid, but most of them are supported by private philanthropy, endowments, and tuition fees. They ante-date the public schools for Negroes and represent the original educational foundations which were established by the various church and philanthropic agencies directly after the Civil War.

They are of all degrees of efficiency. Some, like Atlanta, Fisk, Howard Universities, rank as small colleges and high schools doing work of a high grade. Other are high and normal schools. Some, like Hampton and Tuskegee, are trade and agricultural schools, and are rather more favoured by the South than the other schools.

These private institutions have over 40,000 pupils and 2,400 teachers, and represent an investment of $14,000,000, and an expenditure of $2,100,000 a year, of which the Negroes themselves pay about 30 per cent. In these schools most of the teachers and professional men and many of the artisans among Negroes have been trained. Their chief hindrance to-day is lack of sufficient funds for their growing work.

There are beside these some 200 small private elementary schools supported entirely by Negroes mostly through their Churches. They are designed to supplement poor public schools.

d. Occupations. Of the Negroes in the United States in 1900 there were 3,992,337 ten years of age and over who were in gainful occupations, or 45.2 per cent. of the total Negro population. The chief occupations were:

OCCUPATION

Continental United States—all occupations	3,992,337
Occupations giving employment to at least 10,000 Negroes in 1900	3,807,008
Agricultural labourers	1,344,125
Farmers, planters, and overseers	757,822
Labourers (not specified)	545,935
Servants and waiters	465,734
Launderers and laundresses	220,104
Draymen, hackmen, teamsters, &c.	67,585
Steam railroad employees	55,327
Miners and quarrymen	36,561
Saw and planing mill employees	33,266
Porters and helpers (in stores, &c.)	28,977
Teachers and professors in colleges, &c.	21,267
Carpenters and joiners	21,113
Turpentine farmers and labourers	20,744
Barbers and hairdressers	19,942
Nurses and midwives	19,431
Clergymen	15,528
Tobacco and cigar factory operatives	15,349
Hostlers	14,496
Masons (brick and stone)	14,386
Dressmakers	12,569
Iron and steel workers	12,327
Seamstresses	11,537
Janitors and sextons	11,536
Housekeepers and stewards	10,596
Fishermen and oystermen	10,427
Engineers and firemen (not locomotive)	10,224
Blacksmiths	10,100
Other occupations	185,329

To understand Negro occupations, one must remember that the slaves were emancipated and started as free labourers without land or capital. The result was that the mass of them became serfs and a system of peonage through alleged crime and debt was fastened on them; crime peonage consisted of leasing or parolling prisoners to a landlord who paid their fines or paid a stipulated sum to the State. Debt peonage consisted of keeping the labourer in debt and arresting him for breaking contract if he attempted to stop work. From this peonage larger and larger numbers are escaping; many are going to cities and becoming casual and day labourers; others of the better trained house-servant class are becoming land-owners and artisans, and others through education are entering the professional class. Roughly speaking, we may say that the Negro population consists of:

$$2,000,000 \text{ labourers} \begin{cases} 1,250,000 & \text{farm labourers.} \\ 500,000 & \text{day labourers.} \\ 250,000 & \text{washerwomen.} \end{cases}$$

These are a semi-submerged class, some held in debt peonage, all paid small wages, and kept largely in ignorance.

$$1,200,000 \text{ working-men} \begin{cases} 125,000 & \text{skilled artisans.} \\ 575,000 & \text{semi-skilled workers.} \\ 500,000 & \text{servants.} \end{cases}$$

This is the emerging group. They are handicapped by poor training and race prejudice, but they are pushing forward, saving something, and educating their children as far as possible.

$$250,000 \text{ independents} \begin{cases} 200,000 & \text{farmers.} \\ 40,000 & \text{professional men.} \\ 10,000 & \text{merchants.} \end{cases}$$

This is the leading group of Negro-Americans. The mass of them have common school training, and there are some 5,000 college-trained men. They are accumulating property and educating their children. Their advance is opposed by a bitter and growing race prejudice.

The exact amount of property accumulated by Negroes is not known.

A committee of the American Economic Association reported:

"The evidence in hand leads your Committee to the conclusion that the accumulated wealth of the Negro race in the United States in 1900 was approximately $300,000,000, and probably neither less than $250,000,000 nor more than $350,000,000."

Since 1900 the increase of Negro property holdings has been very rapid, as the records in three States show:

ASSESSED VALUE OF PROPERTY

	1900	1908
Georgia	$14,118,720	$27,042,672
Virginia	15,856,570	25,628,336
North Carolina	9,478,399	21,253,581
Total	$39,453,689	$73,924,589

Judging from these figures, and the report of the American Economic Association quoted above, it would seem fair to infer that the total property of Negro-Americans aggregated $560,000,000 in 1908.

In 1900 the census said:

"We find that the total owned land of coloured farmers in continental United States in 1900 amounted to 14,964,214 acres, or 23,382 square miles—an area nearly as large as Holland and Belgium—and constituted 35.8 per cent. of all the land operated by coloured farmers."

Of the proportion of farm ownership the census says that between 1890 and 1900, while the number of Negro farmers probably increased by about 36 or 38 per cent., the number of Negro owners increased over 57 per cent., and the percentage of ownership increased by 3.5 per cent. So that 187,799 Negro farms, or 25.2 per cent. of all Negro farms were owned.

V. RELIGION

The Christian Church did but little to convert the slaves from their Obeah worship and primitive religion until the establishment of the Society for the Propagation of the Gospel in Foreign Parts in 1701; this Society, and the rising Methodists and Baptists, rapidly brought the body of slaves into nominal communion with the Christian Church. No sooner, however, did they appear in the Church than discrimination began to be practised, which the free Negroes of the North refused to accept. They therefore withdrew into the African Methodist and Zion Methodist Churches. The Baptists, even among the slaves, early had their separate Churches, and these Churches in the North began to federate about 1836. In 1871 the Methodist Church, South, set aside their coloured members into the Coloured Methodist Episcopal Church, and the other Southern Churches drove their members into the other coloured Churches. The remaining Northern denominations retained their Negro members, but organised them for the most part into separate congregations.

Practically, then, the seven-eighths of the whole Negro population is included in its own self-sustaining, self-governing Church bodies.

The statistics for Negro churches in 1906, according to the United States census, was as follows:

"The total number of communicants or members, as reported by 36,563 organisations, is 3,685,097; of these, as shown by the returns for 34,648 organisations, 37.5 per cent. are males and 62.5 per cent. females."

According to the statistics, these organisations have 35,160 church edifices; a seating capacity for church edifices of 10,481,738, as reported by 33,091 organisations; church property valued at $56,636,159, against which there appears an indebtedness of $5,005,905; halls, &c., used for worship by 1,261 organisations; and parsonages valued at $3,727,884. The number of Sunday Schools, as reported by 33,538 organisations, is 34,681, with 210,148 officers and teachers and 1,740,099 scholars.

As compared with the report of 1890, these figures show increases of 13,300 in the number of coloured organisations, 1,011,120 in the number of communicants or members, 11,390 in the number of church edifices, and $30,009,711 in the value of church property.

It was estimated in 1907 that these churches raised seven and a half million dollars a year. Most of the half million goes probably to pay high interest on a debt of five millions. The remaining seven millions goes chiefly to the support of the pastor, the maintenance of the plant, and general church purposes. A large and growing share, however, goes to "mission" work; part of this is proselytising, but the larger part of it is distinctly benevolence and work for social betterment. No complete record of this work can be obtained. Outside of these money contributions by far the larger part of the benevolent work of Negroes is the unorganised personal work of church members among the congregations. This consists of donations, visits, care of the sick, adoption of children, &c.

The leading denominations are as follows, according to membership:

Denomination	Total Number of Organisations, White and Coloured	Number of Coloured Organisations	Total Number of Members
Total	142,476	36,770	3,685,097
Baptist bodies	32,122	19,891	2,354,789
Churches of the Living God ..	68	68	4,276
Congregationalists	5,713	156	11,960
Disciples of Christians	10,942	170	11,233
Methodist bodies	44,861	15,317	1,182,131
Presbyterian bodies	14,226	659	47,116
Protestant Episcopal bodies ..	6,845	198	19,098
Roman Catholic Church	12,482	36	38,235
All others	15,317	275	66,259

VI. CRIME

Of 125,093 prisoners committed in 1904 in the United States 15.8 per cent. were Negroes, who form 11.5 per cent. of the population. This is not, however, a fair measure of Negro crime, since, on account of race prejudice, Negroes are more easily convicted in court and receive longer sentences—*e.g.*, there were 125,093 white prisoners committed to jail during 1904. On June 30, 1904, there were 55,111 white prisoners in jail, showing a large number of short sentences. On the other hand, there were 23,698 Negro prisoners committed during 1904, and on June 30th there were 26,087 Negroes in jail, showing a large number of long sentences. Over half the prisoners in the United States sentenced to prison for life are Negroes. This might be explained by the greater gravity of Negro crimes, but this does not seem true. The Negro is naturally good-tempered, and the current newspaper reports of the rape of white women are greatly exaggerated. On the other hand, accusation of crime and long sentences for petty offences have long been used as methods of securing cheap Negro labour both for private and public purposes in the South, and of the 2,500 Negroes known to have been lynched for alleged crime in the last 25 years, not 25 per cent. have been even accused of assaulting women.

Most Negro crime arises from the natural weakness of slaves—petty stealing and quarrelling. To this have been added in later years more serious crimes of revenge against whites, altercations arising between employers and labourers, and fights and murders arising from contact of the races.

VII. THE NEGRO PROBLEM

The American Negro problem is the question of the future status of the ten million Americans of Negro descent. It must be remembered that these persons are Americans by birth and descent. They represent, for the most part, four or five American born generations, being in that respect one of the most American groups in the land. Moreover, the Negroes are not barbarians. They are, as a mass, poor and ignorant; but they are growing rapidly in both wealth and intelligence, and larger and larger numbers of them demand the rights and privileges of American citizens as a matter of undoubted desert.

To-day these rights are largely denied. In order to realise the disabilities under which Negroes suffer regardless of education, wealth, or degree of white blood, we may divide the United States into three districts:

a. The Southern South, containing 75 per cent. of the Negroes.

b. The border States, containing 15 per cent. of the Negroes.

c. The North and West, containing 10 per cent. of the Negroes.

In the Southern South by law or custom Negroes—

1. Cannot vote, or their votes are neutralised by fraud.

2. Must usually live in the least desirable districts.

3. Receive very low wages.

4. Are, in the main, restricted to menial occupations or the lower grades of skilled labour and cannot expect preferment or promotion.

5. Cannot by law intermarry with whites.

6. Cannot join white churches or attend white colleges or join white cultural organisations.

7. Cannot be accommodated at hotels and restaurants or in any place of public entertainment.

8. Receive a distinct standard of justice in the courts and are especially liable to mob violence.

9. Are segregated so far as possible in every walk of life—in railway stations, railway trains, street-cars, lifts, &c., and usually made to pay equal prices for inferior accommodations.

10. Are often unable to protect their homes from invasion, their women from insult, and their savings from exploitation.

11. Are taxed for public facilities like parks and libraries, which they may not enter.

12. Are given meagre educational facilities and sometimes none at all.

13. Are liable to personal insult unless they appear as servants or menials or show deference to white folks by yielding the road, &c.

To many of these disabilities there are personal and local exceptions. In cities, for instance, the chance to defend the home, get an education, and somewhat better wages is greater, and mob violence less frequent. Then there are always some personal exceptions—cases of help and courtesy, of justice in the courts, and of good schools. These are, however, exceptions, and, as a rule, all Negroes, no matter what their training, possessions, or desert, are subjected to the above disabilities. Within the limits of these caste restrictions there is much goodwill and kindliness between the races, and especially much personal charity and help.

The 15 per cent. of the Negro population living on the border States suffer a little less restriction. They have some right of voting, are better able to defend their homes, and are less discriminated against in the expenditure of public funds. In the cities their schools are much better and public insult is less noticeable.

In the North the remaining 10 per cent. of the Negro population is legally undiscriminated against and may attend schools and churches and vote without restriction. As a matter of fact, however, they are made in most communities to feel that they are undesirable. They are either refused accommodation at hotels, restaurants, and theatres, or received reluctantly. Their treatment in churches and general cultural organisations is such that few join. Intermarriage with whites brings ostracism and public disfavour, and in courts Negroes often suffer undeservedly. Common labour and menial work is open to them, but avenues above this in skilled labour or the professions (save as they serve their own race), are extremely difficult to enter, and there is much discrimination in wages. Mob violence has become not infrequent in later years.

There are here also many exceptional cases; instances of preferment in the industrial and political world; and there is always some little social intercourse. On the whole, however, the Negro in the north is an ostracised person who finds it difficult to make a good living or spend his earnings with pleasure.

Under these circumstances there has grown up a Negro world in America which has its own economic and social life, its churches, schools, and newspapers; its literature, public opinion, and ideals. This life is largely unnoticed and unknown even in America, and travellers miss it almost entirely.

The average American in the past made at least pretence of excusing the discrimination against Negroes, on the ground of their ignorance and poverty and their tendencies to crime and disease. While the mass is still poor and unlettered, it is admitted by all to-day that the Negro is rapidly developing a larger and larger class of intelligent property-holding men of Negro descent; notwithstanding this more and more race lines are being drawn which involve the treatment of civilised men in an uncivilised manner. Moreover, the crux of the question to-day is not merely a matter of social eligibility. For many generations the American Negro will lack the breeding and culture which the most satisfactory human intercourse requires. But in America the discrimination against Negroes goes beyond this, to the point of public discourtesy, civic disability, injustice in the courts, and economic restriction.

The argument of those who uphold this discrimination is based primarily on race. They claim that the inherent characteristics of the Negro race show its essential inferiority and the impossibility of incorporating its descendants into the American nation. They admit that there are exceptions to the rule of inferiority, but claim that these but prove the rule. They say that amalgamation of the races would be fatal to civilisation and they advocate therefore a strict caste system for Negroes, segregating them by occupations and privileges, and to some extent by dwelling-place, to the end that they (*a*) submit permanently to an inferior position, or (*b*) die out, or (*c*) migrate.

This philosophy the thinking Negroes and a large number of white friends vigorously combat. They claim that the racial differences between white and black in the United States offer no essential barrier to the races living together on terms of mutual respect and helpfulness. They deny, on the one hand, that the large amalgamation of the races already accomplished has produced degenerates, in spite of the unhappy character of these unions; on the other hand, they deny any desire to lose the identity of either race through intermarriage. They claim that it should be possible for a civilised black man to be treated as an American citizen without harm to the republic, and that the modern world must learn to treat coloured races as equals if it expects to advance.

They claim that the Negro race in America has more than vindicated its ability to assimilate modern culture. Negro blood has furnished thousands of soldiers to defend the flag in every war in which the United States has been engaged. They are a most important part of the economic strength of the nation, and they have furnished a number of men of ability in politics, literature, and art, as, for instance, Banneker, the mathematician; Phillis Wheatley, the poet; Lemuel Haynes, the theologian; Ira Aldridge, the actor; Frederick Douglass, the orator; H. O. Tanner, the artist; B. T.

Washington, the educator; Granville Woods, the inventor; Kelly Miller, the writer; Rosamond Johnson and Will Cook, the musical composers; Dunbar, the poet; and Chestnut, the novelist. Many other Americans, whose Negro blood has not been openly acknowledged, have reached high distinction. The Negroes claim, therefore, that a discrimination which was originally based on certain social conditions is rapidly becoming a persecution based simply on race prejudice, and that no republic built on caste can survive.

At the meeting of two such diametrically opposed arguments it was natural that councils of compromise should appear, and it was also natural that a nation, whose economic triumphs have been so noticeable as those of the United States, should seek an economic solution to the race question. More and more in the last twenty years the business men's solution of the race problem has been the development of the resources of the South. Coincident with the rise of this policy came the prominence of Mr. B. T. Washington. Mr. Washington was convinced that race prejudice in America was so strong and the economic position of the freedmen's sons so weak that the Negro must give up or postpone his ambitions for full citizenship and bend all his energies to industrial efficiency and the accumulation of wealth. Mr. Washington's idea was that eventually when the dark man was thoroughly established in the industries and had accumulated wealth, he could demand further rights and privileges. This philosophy has become very popular in the United States, both among whites and blacks.

The white South hastened to welcome this philosophy. They thought it would take the Negro out of politics, tend to stop agitation, make the Negro a satisfied labourer, and eventually convince him that he could never be recognised as the equal of the white man. The North began to give large sums for industrial training, and hoped in this way to get rid of a serious social problem.

From the beginning of this campaign, however, a large class of Negroes and many whites feared this programme. They not only regarded it as a programme which was a dangerous compromise, but they insisted that to stop fighting the essential wrong of race prejudice just at the time, was to encourage it.

This was precisely what happened. Mr. Washington's programme was announced at the Atlanta Exposition in 1896. Since that time four States have disfranchised Negroes, dozens of cities and towns have separated the races on street cars, 1,250 Negroes have been publicly lynched without trial, and serious race riots have taken place in nearly every Southern State and several Northern States, Negro public school education has suffered a set back, and many private schools have been forced to retrench severely or to close. On the whole, race prejudice has, during the last fifteen years, enormously increased.

This has been coincident with the rapid and substantial advance of Negroes in wealth, education, and morality, and the two movements of race prejudice and Negro advance have led to an anomalous and unfortunate situation. Some, white and black, seek to minimise and ignore the flaming prejudice in the land, and emphasise many acts of friendliness on the part of the white South, and the advance of the Negro. Others, on the other hand, point out that silence and sweet temper are not going to settle this dangerous social problem, and that manly protest and the publication of the whole truth is alone adequate to arouse the nation to its great danger.

Moreover, many careful thinkers insist that, under the circumstances, the "business men's" solution of the race problem is bound to make trouble: if the Negroes become good cheap labourers, warranted not to strike or complain, they will arouse all the latent prejudice of the white working men whose wages they bring down. If, on the other hand, they are to be really educated as men, and not as "hands," then they need, as a race, not only industrial training, but also a supply of well-educated, intellectual leaders and professional men for a group so largely deprived of contact with the cultural leaders of the whites. Moreover, the best thought of the nation is slowly recognising the fact that to try to educate a working man, and not to educate the man, is impossible. If the United States wants intelligent Negro labourers, it must be prepared to treat them as intelligent men.

This counter movement of intelligent men, white and black, against the purely economic solution of the race problem, has been opposed by powerful influences both North and South. The South represents it as malicious sectionalism, and the North misunderstands it as personal dislike and envy of Mr. Washington. Political pressure has been brought to bear, and this insured a body of coloured political leaders who do not agitate for Negro rights. At the same time, a chain of Negro newspapers were established to advocate the dominant philosophy.

Despite this well-intentioned effort to keep down the agitation of the Negro question and mollify the coloured people, the problem has increased in gravity. The result is the present widespread unrest and dissatisfaction. Honest Americans know that present conditions are wrong and cannot last; but they face, on the one hand, the seemingly implacable prejudice of the South, and, on the other hand, the undoubted rise of the Negro challenging that prejudice. The attempt to reconcile these two forces is becoming increasingly futile, and the nation simply faces the question: Are we willing to do justice to a dark race despite our prejudices? Radical suggestions of wholesale segregation or deportation of the race have now and then been suggested; but the cost in time, effort, money, and economic disturbance is too staggering to allow serious consideration. The South, with all its race prejudice, would rather fight than lose its great black labouring force, and in every walk of life throughout the nation the Negro is slowly forcing his way. There are some signs that the prejudice in the South is not immovable, and now and then voices of protest and signs of liberal thought appear there. Whether at last the Negro will gain full recognition as a man, or be utterly crushed by prejudice and superior numbers, is the present Negro problem of America.

II

COMMUNITY STUDIES

The Philadelphia Negro: A Social Study (1899) is Du Bois' major sociological work and it certainly ranks high among his many publications. It is the earliest large-scale empirical study in the history of American sociology. Gunnar Myrdal, in *An American Dilemma*, referred to *The Philadelphia Negro* as the best model of "what a study of a Negro community should be." More recently, in his Introduction to a new edition of *The Philadelphia Negro* (New York: Schocken Books, 1967), E. Digby Baltzell noted the sociological significance of this book when he said that "there has not been a scholarly study of the American Negro in the twentieth century which has not referred to and utilized the empirical findings, the research methods, and the theoretical point of view of this seminal book." In the excerpts from *The Philadelphia Negro* which follow, there is an overview of the scope of the study, its general aim, methodology; comments on the credibility of the findings; and a statement on the plan for presenting the findings. Then the seventh ward—the main area of black settlement—is described in terms of population, the ecology of social classes, housing conditions, and patterns of in-out migration. The fact that many findings for Philadelphia are generalizable to blacks living in other Northern cities is evident in the second selection from Du Bois, "The Black North in 1901: New York City" (1901).

The other two selections are studies of small Southern communities. "The Negroes of Farmville, Virginia: A Social Study" (1898) was envisioned by Du Bois as "the first of a series of investigations of small, well-defined groups of Negroes in various parts of the country." Farmville, a market town of about 2500 inhabitants, was the trading center for six counties in the main tobacco-growing area of Virginia. Through participant observation and a detailed schedule which he administered to each family and individual, Du Bois was able to describe the people of Farmville in terms of population, conjugal condition, birthplace, farm tenure, acreage owned, principal products, assessed value of real estate, school attendance, and occupation. Of particular sociological significance is Du Bois' analysis and description of the occupational structure and social stratification system of Farmville. In the "Negroes of Dougherty County, Georgia" (1901), Du Bois describes the community structure and economic activities or rural inhabitants in the Black Belt. He emphasizes the very high proportions of men and women in gainful employment, the high ratio of agriculturalists to other occupations, and the presence of economic classes. One of the notable social changes, having several positive and negative aspects, is the rise of the "metayer system" in the rural South—a system of sharing crops and costs which brings a new merchant into relationships with the landless laborers.

6

THE PHILADELPHIA NEGRO

The Scope of this Study

General Aim. This study seeks to present the results of an inquiry undertaken by the University of Pennsylvania into the condition of the forty thousand or more people of Negro blood now living in the city of Philadelphia. This inquiry extended over a period of fifteen months and sought to ascertain something of the geographical distribution of this race, their occupations and daily life, their homes, their organizations, and, above all, their relation to their million white fellow-citizens. The final design of the work is to lay before the public such a body of information as may be a safe guide for all efforts toward the solution of the many Negro problems of a great American city.

The Methods of Inquiry. The investigation began August the first, 1896, and, saving two months, continued until December the thirty-first, 1897. The work commenced with a house-to-house canvass of the Seventh Ward. This long narrow ward, extending from South Seventh street to the Schuylkill River and from Spruce street to South street, is an historic centre of Negro population, and contains to-day a fifth of all the Negroes in this city.[1] It was therefore thought best to make an intensive study of conditions in this district, and afterward to supplement and correct this information by general observation and inquiry in other parts of the city.

Six schedules were used among the nine thousand Negroes of this

Abridged from W.E.B. Du Bois, *The Philadelphia Negro: A Social Study* (1899; New York: Benjamin Blom, distributed by Arno Press, Inc., 1967), pp. 1-9, 58-65, 73-82, 287-99, 305-9.

ward; a family schedule with the usual questions as to the number of members, their age and sex, their conjugal condition and birthplace, their ability to read and write, their occupation and earnings, etc.; an individual schedule with similar inquiries; a home schedule with questions as to the number of rooms, the rent, the lodgers, the conveniences, etc.; a street schedule to collect data as to the various small streets and alleys, and an institution schedule for organizations and institutions; finally a slight variation of the individual schedule was used for house-servants living at their places of employment.

This study of the central district of Negro settlement furnished a key to the situation in the city; in the other wards therefore a general survey was taken to note any striking differences of condition, to ascertain the general distribution of these people, and to collect information and statistics as to organizations, property, crime and pauperism, political activity, and the like. This general inquiry, while it lacked precise methods of measurement in most cases, served nevertheless to correct the errors and illustrate the meaning of the statistical material obtained in the house-to-house canvass.

Throughout the study such official statistics and historical matter as seemed reliable were used, and experienced persons, both white and colored, were freely consulted.

The Credibility of the Results. The best available methods of sociological research are at present so liable to inaccuracies that the careful student discloses the results of individual research with diffidence; he knows that they are liable to error from the seemingly ineradicable faults of the statistical method, to even greater error from the methods of general observation, and, above all, he must ever tremble lest some personal bias, some moral conviction or some unconscious trend of thought due to previous training, has to a degree distorted the picture in his view. Convictions on all great matters of human interest one must have to a greater or less degree, and they will enter to some extent into the most cold-blooded scientific research as a disturbing factor.

Nevertheless here are social problems before us demanding careful study, questions awaiting satisfactory answers. We must study, we must investigate, we must attempt to solve; and the utmost that the world can demand is, not lack of human interest and moral conviction, but rather the heart-quality of fairness, and an earnest desire for the truth despite its possible unpleasantness.

In a house-to-house investigation there are, outside the attitude of the investigator, many sources of error: misapprehension, vagueness and forgetfulness, and deliberate deception on the part of the persons questioned, greatly vitiate the value of the answers; on the other hand, conclusions formed by the best trained and most conscientious students on the basis of general observation and inquiry are really inductions from but a few of the multitudinous facts of social life, and these may easily fall far short of being essential or typical.

The use of both of these methods which has been attempted in this study may perhaps have corrected to some extent the errors of each. Again, whatever personal equation is to be allowed for in the whole study is one unvarying quantity, since the work was done by one investigator, and the varying judgments of a score of census-takers was thus avoided.

Despite all drawbacks and difficulties, however, the main results of the inquiry seem credible. They agree, to a large extent, with general public opinion, and in other respects they seem either logically explicable or in accord with historical precedents. They are therefore presented to the public, not as complete and without error, but as possessing on the whole enough reliable matter to serve as the scientific basis of further study, and of practical reform.

THE PROBLEM

The Negro Problems of Philadelphia. In Philadelphia, as else-where in the United States, the existence of certain peculiar social problems affecting the Negro people are plainly manifest. Here is a large group of people—perhaps forty-five thousand, a city within a city—who do not form an integral part of the larger social group. This in itself is not altogether unusual; there are other unassimilated groups: Jews, Italians, even Americans; and yet in the case of the Negroes the segregation is more conspicuous, more patent to the eye, and so intertwined with a long historic evolution, with peculiarly pressing social problems of poverty, ignorance, crime and labor, that the Negro problem far surpasses in scientific interest and social gravity most of the other race or class questions.

The student of these questions must first ask, What is the real condition of this group of human beings? Of whom is it composed, what sub-groups and classes exist, what sort of individuals are being considered? Further, the student must clearly recognize that a complete study must not confine itself to the group, but must specially notice the environment; the physical environment of the city, sections and houses, the far mightier social environment—the surrounding world of custom, wish, whim, and thought which envelops this group and powerfully influences its social development.

Nor does the clear recognition of the field of investigation simplify the work of actual study; it rather increases it, by revealing lines of inquiry far broader in scope than first thought suggests. To the average Philadelphian the whole Negro question reduces itself to a study of certain slum districts. His mind reverts to Seventh and Lombard streets and to Twelfth and Kater streets of to-day, or to St. Mary's in the past. Continued and widely known charitable work in these sections makes the problem of poverty familiar to him; bold and daring crime too often traced to these centres has called his attention to a problem of crime, while the scores of loafers, idlers and prostitutes who crowd the sidewalks here night and day remind him of a problem of work.

All this is true—all these problems are there and of threatening intricacy; unfortunately, however, the interest of the ordinary man of affairs is apt to stop here. Crime, poverty and idleness affect his interests unfavorably and he would have them stopped; he looks upon these slums and slum characters as unpleasant things which should in some way be removed for the best interests of all. The social student agrees with him so far, but must point out that the removal of unpleasant features from our complicated modern life is a delicate operation requiring knowledge and skill; that a slum is not a simple fact, it is a symptom and that to know the removable causes of the Negro slums of Philadelphia requires a study that takes one far beyond the slum districts. For few Philadelphians realize how the Negro population has grown and spread. There was a time in the memory of living men when a small district near Sixth and Lombard streets comprehended the great mass of the Negro population of the city. This is no longer so. Very early the stream of the black population started northward, but the increased foreign immigration of 1830 and later turned it back. It started south also but was checked by poor houses and worse police protection. Finally with gathered momentum the emigration from the slums started west, rolling on slowly and surely, taking Lombard street as its main thoroughfare, gaining early foothold in West Philadelphia, and turning at the Schuylkill River north and south to the newer portions of the city.

Thus to-day the Negroes are scattered in every ward of the city, and the great mass of them live far from the whilom centre of colored settlement. What, then, of this great mass of the population? Manifestly they form a class with social problems of their own—the problems of the Thirtieth Ward differ from the problems of the Fifth, as the black inhabitants differ. In the former ward we have represented the rank and file of Negro working-people; laborers and servants, porters and waiters. This is at present the great middle class of Negroes feeding the slums on the one hand and the upper class on the other. Here are social questions and conditions which must receive the most careful attention and patient interpretation.

Not even here, however, can the social investigator stop. He knows that every group has its upper class; it may be numerically small and socially of little weight, and yet its study is necessary to the comprehension of the whole—it forms the realized ideal of the group, and as it is true that a nation must to some extent be measured by its slums, it is also true that it can only be understood and finally judged by its upper class.

The best class of Philadelphia Negroes, though sometimes forgotten or ignored in discussing the Negro problems, is nevertheless known to many Philadelphians. Scattered throughout the better parts of the Seventh Ward, and on Twelfth, lower Seventeenth and Nineteenth streets, and here and there in the residence wards of the northern, southern, and western sections of the city is a class of caterers, clerks, teachers, professional men, small merchants, etc., who constitute the aristocracy of the Negroes. Many are well-to-do, some are wealthy, all are fairly educated, and some liberally trained. Here too are social problems—differing from those of the other classes, and differing too from those of the whites of a corresponding grade, because of the peculiar social environment in which the whole race finds itself, which the whole race feels, but which touches this highest class at most points and tells upon them most decisively.

Many are the misapprehensions and misstatements as to the social environment of Negroes in a great Northern city. Sometimes it is said, here they are free; they have the same chance as the Irishman, the Italian, or the Swede; at other times it is said, the environment is such that it is really more oppressive than the situation in Southern cities. The student must ignore both of these extreme statements and seek to extract from a complicated mass of facts the tangible evidence of a social atmosphere surrounding Negroes, which differs from that surrounding most whites; of a different mental attitude, moral standard, and economic judgment shown toward Negroes than toward most other folk. That such a difference exists and can now and then plainly be seen, few deny; but just how far it goes and how large a factor it is in the Negro problems, nothing but careful study and measurement can reveal.

Such then are the phenomena of social condition and environment which this study proposes to describe, analyze, and, so far as possible, interpret.

Plan of Presentment. The study as taken up here divides itself roughly into four parts: the history of the Negro people in the city, their present condition considered as individuals, their condition as an organized social group, and their physical and social environment. To the history of the Negro but two chapters are devoted—a brief sketch—although the subject is worthy of more extended study than the character of this essay permitted.

Six chapters consider the general condition of the Negroes: their number, age and sex, conjugal condition, and birthplace; what degree of education they have obtained, and how they earn a living. All these subjects are treated usually for the Seventh Ward somewhat minutely, then more generally for the city, and finally such historical material is adduced as is available for comparison.

Three chapters are devoted to the group life of the Negro; this includes a study of the family, of property, and of organizations of all sorts. It also takes up such phenomena of social maladjustment and individual depravity as crime, pauperism and alcoholism.

One chapter is devoted to the difficult question of environment, both physical and social, one to certain results of the contact of the white and black races, one to Negro suffrage, and a word of general advice in the line of social reform is added.

SIZE, AGE AND SEX

We shall now make a more intensive study of the Negro population, confining ourselves to one typical ward for the year 1896. Of the nearly forty thousand Negroes in Philadelphia in 1890, a little less than a fourth lived in the Seventh Ward, and over half in this and the adjoining Fourth, Fifth and Eighth Wards.

The Seventh Ward starts from the historic centre of Negro settlement in the city, South Seventh street and Lombard, and includes the long narrow strip, beginning at South Seventh and extending west, with South and Spruce streets as boundaries, as far as the Schuylkill River. The colored population of this ward numbered 3621 in 1860, 4616 in 1870, and 8861 in 1890. It is a thickly populated district of varying character; north of it is the residence and business section of the city; south of it a middle class and workingmen's residence section; at the east end it joins Negro, Italian and Jewish slums; at the west end, the wharves of the river and an industrial section separating it from the grounds of the University of Pennsylvania and the residence section of West Philadelphia.

Starting at Seventh street and walking along Lombard, let us glance at the general character of the ward. Pausing a moment at the corner of Seventh and Lombard, we can at a glance view the worst Negro slums of the city. The houses are mostly brick, some wood, not very old, and in general uncared for rather than dilapidated. The blocks between Eighth, Pine, Sixth and South have for many decades been the centre of Negro population. Here the riots of the thirties took place, and here once was a depth of poverty and degradation almost unbelievable. Even to-day there are many evidences of degradation, although the signs of idleness, shiftlessness, dissoluteness and crime are more conspicuous than those of poverty. The alleys[2] near, as Ratcliffe street, Middle alley, Brown's court, Barclay street, etc., are haunts of noted criminals, male and female, of gamblers and prostitutes, and at the same time of many poverty-stricken people, decent but not energetic. There is an abundance of political clubs, and nearly all the houses are practically lodging houses, with a miscellaneous shifting population. The corners, night and day, are filled with Negro loafers—able-bodied young men and women, all cheerful, some with good-natured, open faces, some with traces of crime and excess, a few pinched with poverty. They are mostly gamblers, thieves and prostitutes, and few have fixed and steady occupation of any kind. Some are stevedores, porters, laborers and laundresses. On its face this slum is noisy and dissipated, but not brutal, although now and then highway robberies and murderous assaults in other parts of the city are traced to its denizens. Nevertheless the stranger can usually walk about here day and night with little fear of being molested, if he be not too inquisitive.[3]

Passing up Lombard, beyond Eighth, the atmosphere suddenly changes, because these next two blocks have few alleys and the residences are good-sized and pleasant. Here some of the best Negro families of the ward live. Some are wealthy in a small way, nearly all are Philadelphia born, and they represent an early wave of emigration from the old slum section.[4] To the south, on Rodman street, are families of the same character. North of Pine and below Eleventh there are practically no Negro residences. Beyond Tenth street, and as far as Broad street, the Negro population is large and varied in character. On small streets like Barclay and its extension below Tenth—Souder, on Ivy, Rodman, Salem, Heins, Iseminger, Ralston, etc., is a curious mingling of respectable working people and some of a better class, with recent immigrations of the semi-criminal class from the slums. On the larger streets, like Lombard and Juniper, there live many respectable colored families—native Philadelphians, Virginians and other Southerners, with a fringe of more questionable families. Beyond Broad, as far as Sixteenth, the good character of the Negro population is maintained except in one or two back streets.[5] From Sixteenth to Eighteenth, intermingled with some estimable families, is a dangerous criminal class. They are not the low, open idlers of Seventh and Lombard, but rather the graduates of that school: shrewd and sleek politicians, gamblers and confidence men, with a class of well-dressed and partially undetected prostitutes. This class is not easily differentiated and located, but it seems to centre at Seventeenth and Lombard. Several large gambling houses are near here, although more recently one has moved below Broad, indicating a reshifting of the criminal centre. The whole community was an earlier immigration from Seventh and Lombard. North of Lombard, above Seventeenth, including Lombard street itself, above Eighteenth, is one of the best Negro residence sections of the city, centering about Addison street. Some undesirable elements have crept in even here, especially since the Christian League attempted to clear out the Fifth Ward slums,[6] but still it remains a centre of quiet, respectable families, who own their own homes and live well. The Negro population practically stops at Twenty-second street, although a few Negroes live beyond.

We can thus see that the Seventh Ward presents an epitome of nearly all the Negro problems; that every class is represented, and varying conditions of life. Nevertheless one must naturally be careful not to draw too broad conclusions from a single ward in one city. There is no proof that the proportion between the good and the bad here is normal, even for the race in Philadelphia; that the social problems affecting Negroes in large Northern cities are presented here in most of their aspects seems credible, but that certain of those aspects are distorted and exaggerated by local peculiarities is also not to be doubted.

In the fall of 1896 a house-to-house visitation was made to all the Negro families of this ward. The visitor went in person to each residence and called for the head of the family. The housewife usually responded, the husband now and then, and sometimes an older daughter or other member of the family. The fact that the University was making an investigation of this character was known and discussed in the ward, but its exact scope and character was not known. The mere announcement of the purpose secured, in all but about twelve cases,[7] immediate admission. Seated then in the parlor, kitchen, or living room, the visitor began the questioning, using his discretion as to the order in which they were put, and omitting or adding questions as the circumstances suggested. Now and then the purpose of a particular query was explained, and usually the object of the whole inquiry indicated. General discussions often arose as to the condition of the Negroes, which were instructive. From ten minutes to an hour was spent in each home, the average time being fifteen to twenty-five minutes.

Usually the answers were prompt and candid, and gave no suspicion of previous preparation. In some cases there was evident falsification or evasion. In such cases the visitor made free use of his best judgment and either inserted no answer at all, or one which seemed approximately true. In some cases the families visited were not at home, and a second or third visit was paid. In other cases, and especially in the case of the large class of lodgers, the testimony of landlords and neighbors often had to be taken.

No one can make an inquiry of this sort and not be painfully conscious of a large margin of error from omissions, errors of judgment and deliberate deception. Of such errors this study has, without doubt, its full share. Only one fact was peculiarly favorable and that is the proverbial good nature and candor of the Negro. With a more cautious and suspicious people much less success could have been obtained. Naturally some questions were answered better than others; the chief difficulty arising in regard to the questions of age and income. The ages given for people forty and over have a large margin of error, owing to ignorance of the real birthday. The question of income was naturally a delicate one, and often had to be gotten at indirectly. The yearly income, as a round sum, was seldom asked for; rather the daily or weekly wages taken and the time employed during the year.

On December 1, 1896, there were in the Seventh Ward of Philadelphia 9675 Negroes; 4501 males and 5174 females. This total includes all persons of Negro descent, and thirty-three intermarried whites.[8] It does not include residents of the ward then in prisons or in almshouses. There were a considerable number of omissions among the loafers and criminals without homes, the class of lodgers

NEGRO POPULATION OF SEVENTH WARD

Age	Male	Female
Under 10	570	641
10 to 19	483	675
20 to 29	1,276	1,444
30 to 39	1,046	1,084
40 to 49	553	632
50 to 59	298	331
60 to 69	114	155
70 and over	41	96
Age unknown	120	116
Total	4,501	5,174

Grand total	9,675

and the club-house habitués. These were mostly males, and their inclusion would somewhat affect the division by sexes, although probably not to a great extent.[9] The increase of the Negro population in this ward for six and a half years is 814, or at the rate of 14.13 per cent per decade. This is perhaps somewhat smaller than that for the population of the city at large, for the Seventh Ward is crowded and overflowing into other wards. Possibly the present Negro population of the city is between 43,000 and 45,000. At all events it is probable that the crest of the tide of immigration is passed, and that the increase for the decade 1890-1900 will not be nearly as large as the 24 per cent of the decade 1880-1890.

The division by sex indicates still a very large and, it would seem, growing excess of women. The return shows 1150 females to every 1000 males. Possibly through the omission of men and the unavoidable duplication of some servants lodging away from their place of service, the disproportion of the sexes is exaggerated. At any rate it is great, and if growing, may be an indication of increased restriction in the employments open to Negro men since 1880 or even since 1890.

The age structure also presents abnormal features.[10] Comparing the age structure with that of the large cities of Germany, we have:

Age	Negroes of Philadelphia	Large Cities of Germany
Under 20	25.1	39.3
20 to 40	51.3	37.2
Over 40	23.6	23.5

Comparing it with the Whites and Negroes in the city in 1890, we have:

Age	Negroes of Philadelphia, 1896, Seventh Ward	Negroes* of Philadelphia, 1890	Native Whites of Philadelphia, 1890
Under 10	12.8%	15.31%	24.6%
10 to 20	12.3	16.37	19.5
20 to 30	28.7	27.08	18.5
30 and over	46.2	41.24	37.4

*Includes 1003 Chinese, Japanese and Indians.

As was noticed in the whole city in 1890, so here is even more striking evidence of the preponderance of young people at an age when sudden introduction to city life is apt to be dangerous, and of an abnormal excess of females.

Sources of the Negro Population

The Seventh Ward. We have seen that there is in Philadelphia a large population of Negroes, largely young unmarried folks with a disproportionate number of women. The question now arises, whence came these people? How far are they native Philadelphians, and how far immigrants, and if the latter, how long have they been here? Much depends on the answer to these questions; no conclusions as to the effects of Northern city conditions on Negroes, as to the effects of long, close contact with modern culture, as to the general question of social and economic survival on the part of this race, can be intelligently answered until we know how long these people have been under the influence of given conditions, and how they were trained before they came.[11]

It is often tacitly assumed that the Negroes of Philadelphia are one homogeneous mass, and that the slums of the Fifth Ward, for instance, are one of the results of long contact with Philadelphia city life on the part of this mass. There is just enough truth and falsehood in such an assumption to make it dangerously misleading. The slums of Seventh and Lombard streets are largely results of the contact of the Negro with city life, but the Negro in question is a changing variable quantity and has felt city influences for periods varying in different persons from one day to seventy years. A generalization then that includes a North Carolina boy who has migrated to the city for work and has been here for a couple of months, in the same class with a descendant of several generations of Philadelphia Negroes, is apt to make serious mistakes. The first lad may deserve to be pitied if he falls into dissipation and crime, the second ought perhaps to be condemned severely. In other words our judgment of the thousands of Negroes of this city must be in all cases considerably modified by a knowledge of their previous history and antecedents.

Of the 9675 Negroes in the Seventh Ward, 9138 gave returns as to their birthplace. Of these, there were born:

In Philadelphia	2939 or 32.1 per cent
In Pennsylvania, outside of Philadelphia	526 or 6.0 per cent
In the New England and Middle States	485 or 5.3 per cent
In the South	4980 or 54.3 per cent
In the West and in foreign lands	208 or 2.3 per cent

That is to say, less than one-third of the Negroes living in this ward were born here, and over one-half were born in the South. Separating them by sex and giving their birthplaces more in detail, we have:

Birthplace of Negroes, Seventh Ward

Born in	Males	Females	Total
Philadelphia	1,307	1,632	2,939
Pennsylvania, outside of Philadelphia	231	295	526
Virginia	939	1,012	1,951
Maryland	550	794	1,344
Delaware	168	296	464
New Jersey	141	190	331
District of Columbia	146	165	311
Other parts, and undesignated parts of the South	528	382	910
Other New England and Middle States	62	92	154
Western States	28	27	55
Foreign countries	110	43	153
Unknown	291	245	537
Total	4,501	5,174	9,675

This means that a study of the Philadelphia Negroes would properly begin in Virginia or Maryland and that only a portion have had the opportunity of being reared amid the advantages of a great city.

That the Negro immigration to the city is not an influx of whole families is shown by the fact that 83 per cent of the children under ten were born in Philadelphia. Of the youth from ten to twenty, about one-half were born in the city. The great influx comes in the years from twenty-one to thirty, for of these but 17 per cent were born in the city; of the men and women born between 1856 and 1865, that is, in war time, about one-seventh were born in the city; of the freedmen, that is those born before 1856, a larger portion, one-fifth, were born in Philadelphia.

Much of the immigration to Philadelphia is indirect; Negroes come from country districts to small towns; then go to larger towns; eventually they drift to Norfolk, Va., or to Richmond. Next they come to Washington, and finally settle in Baltimore or Philadelphia.[12]

Much light will be thrown on the question of migration if we take the Negro immigrants as a class and inquire how long they have lived in the city; we can separate the immigrants into four classes, corresponding to the waves of immigration: first, the ante-bellum immigrants, resident thirty-five years or more; second, the refugees of war time and the period following, resident twenty-one to thirty-four years; third, the laborers and sightseers of the time of the Centennial, resident ten to twenty years; fourth, the recent immigration, which may be divided into those resident from five to nine years, from one to four years, and those who have been in the city less than a year. Of 5337 immigrants,[13] the following classes may be made:

Arrived since December 1	Resident	Number	Per cent	Per cent	Per cent
	Years				
1895	Under 1	293	5.5 }	28.7 }	53.2
1892	1 to 4	1,242	23.2 }		
1887	5 to 9	1,308	24.5 }	45.9	
1875	10 to 20	1,143	21.4 }		
1862	21 to 34	1,040	19.4 }	25.4 }	46.8
Before 1860	35 and over	311	6.0 }		
Before 1896		5,337	100	100	100

Thus we see that the majority of the present immigrants arrived since 1887, and nearly 30 per cent since 1892.

The City. The available figures for the past are not many nor altogether reliable, yet it seems probable that the per cent of immigrants to-day is as large as at any previous time and perhaps larger. In 1848, 57.3 per cent of 15,532 Negroes were natives of the State, and the remaining 42.7 per cent immigrants. In 1890 we have only figures for the whole State, which show that 45 per cent of the Negroes were immigrants mainly from Virginia, Maryland, Delaware, New Jersey, North Carolina, etc. For Philadelphia the percentage would probably be higher.

The new immigrants usually settle in pretty well-defined localities in or near the slums, and thus get the worst possible introduction to city life. In 1848, five thousand of the 6600 immigrants lived in the narrow and filthy alleys of the city and Moyamensing. To-day they are to be found partly in the slums and partly in those small streets with old houses, where there is a dangerous intermingling of good and bad elements fatal to growing children and unwholesome for adults. Such streets may be found in the Seventh Ward, between Tenth and Juniper streets, in parts of the Third and Fourth wards and in the Fourteenth and Fifteenth wards. This mingling swells the apparent size of many slum districts, and at the same time screens the real criminals. Investigators are often surprised in the worst districts to see red-handed criminals and good-hearted, hard-working, honest people living side by side in apparent harmony. Even when the new immigrants seek better districts, their low standard of living and careless appearance make them unwelcome to the better class of blacks and to the great mass of whites. Thus they find themselves hemmed in between the slums and the decent sections, and they easily drift into the happy-go-lucky life of the lowest classes and rear young criminals for our jails. On the whole, then, the sociological effect of the immigration of Negroes is the same as that of illiterate foreigners to this country, save that in this case the brunt of the burden of illiteracy, laziness and inefficiency has been, by reason of peculiar social conditions, put largely upon the shoulders of a group which is least prepared to bear it.

THE ENVIRONMENT OF THE NEGRO

Houses and Rent. The inquiry of 1848 returned quite full statistics of rents paid by the Negroes.[14] In the whole city at that date 4019 Negro families paid $199,665.46 in rent, or an average of $49.68 per family each year. Ten years earlier the average was $44 per family. Nothing better indicates the growth of the Negro population in numbers and power when we compare with this the figures for 1896 for one ward; in that year the Negroes of the Seventh Ward paid $25,699.50 each month in rent, or $308,034 a year, an average of $126.19 per annum for each family. This ward may have a somewhat higher proportion of renters than most other wards. At the lowest estimate, however, the Negroes of Philadelphia pay at least $1,250,000 in rent each year.[15]

In 1848 the average Negro family rented by the month or quarter, and paid between four and five dollars per month rent. The highest average rent for any section was less than fifteen dollars a month. For such rents the poorest accommodations were afforded, and we know from descriptions that the mass of Negroes had small and unhealthful homes, usually on the back streets and alleys. The rents paid to-day in the Seventh Ward [can be summarized] as follows:

Under $5 per month	490 families, or 21.9 per cent
$ 5 and under $10	643 families, or 28.7 per cent
$10 and under $15	380 families, or 17.0 per cent
$15 and under $20	252 families, or 11.3 per cent
$20 and under $30	375 families, or 17.0 per cent
$30 and over	95 families, or 4.1 per cent

The lodging system so prevalent in the Seventh Ward makes some rents appear higher than the real facts warrant. This ward is in the centre of the city, near the places of employment for the mass of the people and near the centre of their social life; consequently people crowd here in great numbers. Young couples just married engage lodging in one or two rooms; families join together and hire one house; and numbers of families take in single lodgers; thus the population of the ward is made up of

Families owning or renting their homes and living alone	738, or	31 per cent
Families owning or renting their homes, who take lodgers or sub-renters	937, or	38 per cent
Families sub-renting under other families	766, or	31 per cent
Total individuals	7751	100 per cent
Total families		2441
Individuals lodging with families	1924	
Total individuals	9675	

The practice of sub-renting is found of course in all degrees: from the business of boarding-house keeper to the case of a family which rents out its spare bed-chamber. In the first case the rent is practically all repaid, and must in some cases be regarded as income; in the other cases a small fraction of the rent is repaid and the real rent and the size of the home reduced. Let us endeavor to determine what proportion of the rents of the Seventh Ward are repaid in sub-rents, omitting some boarding and lodging-houses where the sub-rent is really the income of the house-wife. In most cases the room-rent of lodgers covers some return for the care of the room.

Nearly $9000 is paid by the sub-renting families and lodgers to the renting families. A part of this ought to be subtracted from the total rent paid if we would get at the net rent; just how much, however, should be called wages for care of room, or other conveniences furnished sub-renters, it is difficult to say. Possibly the net rent of the ward is $20,000, and of the city about $1,000,000.[16]

The accommodations furnished for the rent paid must now be considered. The number of rooms occupied is the simplest measurement, but is not very satisfactory in this case owing to the lodging system which makes it difficult to say how many rooms a family really occupies. A very large number of families of two and three rent a single bedroom and these must be regarded as one-room tenants, and yet this renting of a room often includes a limited use of a common kitchen; on the other hand this sub-renting family cannot in justice·be counted as belonging to the renting family. The figures are:

829 families live in 1 room, including families lodging,	or 35.2 per cent
104 families live in 2 rooms	or 4.4 per cent
371 families live in 3 rooms	or 15.7 per cent
170 families live in 4 rooms	
127 families live in 5 rooms	or 12.7 per cent
754 families live in 6 rooms or more	or 32.0 per cent

The number of families occupying one room is here exaggerated as before shown by the lodging system; on the other hand the number occupying six rooms and more is also somewhat exaggerated by the fact that not all sub-rented rooms have been subtracted, although this has been done as far as possible.

Of the 2441 families only 334 had access to bathrooms and

water-closets, or 13.7 per cent. Even these 334 families have poor accommodations in most instances. Many share the use of one bathroom with one or more other families. The bath-tubs usually are not supplied with hot water and very often have no water-connection at all. This condition is largely owing to the fact that the Seventh Ward belongs to the older part of Philadelphia, built when vaults in the yards were used exclusively and bathrooms could not be given space in the small houses. This was not so unhealthful before the houses were thick and when there were large back yards. To-day, however, the back yards have been filled by tenement houses and the bad sanitary results are shown in the death rate of the ward.

Even the remaining yards are disappearing. Of the 1751 families making returns, 932 had a private yard 12 x 12 feet, or larger; 312 had a private yard smaller than 12 x 12 feet; 507 had either no yard at all or a yard and outhouse in common with the other denizens of the tenement or alley.

Of the latter only sixteen families had water-closets. So that over 20 per cent and possibly 30 per cent of the Negro families of this ward lack some of the very elementary accommodations necessary to health and decency. And this too in spite of the fact that they are paying comparatively high rents. Here too there comes another consideration, and that is the lack of public urinals and water-closets in this ward and, in fact, throughout Philadelphia. The result is that the closets of tenements are used by the public.

When, however, certain districts like the Seventh Ward became crowded and given over to tenants, the thirst for money-getting led landlords in large numbers of cases to build up their back yards.

This is the origin of numbers of the blind alleys and dark holes which make some parts of the Fifth, Seventh and Eighth Wards notorious. The closets in such cases are sometimes divided into compartments for different tenants, but in many cases not even this is done; and in all cases the alley closet becomes a public resort for pedestrians and loafers. The back tenements thus formed rent usually for from $7 to $9 a month, and sometimes for more. They consist of three rooms one above the other, small, poorly lighted and poorly ventilated. The inhabitants of the alley are at the mercy of its worst tenants; here policy shops abound, prostitutes ply their trade, and criminals hide. Most of these houses have to get their water at a hydrant in the alley, and must store their fuel in the house. These tenement abominations of Philadelphia are perhaps better than the vast tenement houses of New York, but they are bad enough, and cry for reform in housing.

The fairly comfortable working class live in houses of 3-6 rooms, with water in the house, but seldom with a bath. A three room house on a small street rents from $10 up; on Lombard street a 5-8 room house can be rented for from $18 to $30 according to location. The great mass of comfortably situated working people live in houses of 6-10 rooms, and sub-rent a part or take lodgers. A 5-7 room house on South Eighteenth street can be had for $20; on Florida street for $18; such houses have usually a parlor, dining room and kitchen on the first floor and two to four bedrooms, of which one or two are apt to be rented to a waiter or coachman for $4 a month, or to a married couple at $6-$10 a month. The more elaborate houses are on Lombard street and its cross streets.

The rents paid by the Negroes are without doubt far above their means and often from one-fourth to three-fourths of the total income of a family goes in rent. This leads to much non-payment of rent both intentional and unintentional, to frequent shifting of homes, and above all to stinting the families in many necessities of life in order to live in respectable dwellings. Many a Negro family eats less than it ought for the sake of living in a decent house.

Some of this waste of money in rent is sheer ignorance and carelessness. The Negroes have an inherited distrust of banks and companies, and have long neglected to take part in Building and Loan Associations. Others are simply careless in the spending of their money and lack the shrewdness and business sense of differently trained peoples. Ignorance and carelessness however will not explain all or even the greater part of the problem of rent among Negroes. There are three causes of even greater importance: these are the limited localities where Negroes may rent, the peculiar connection of dwelling and occupation among Negroes and the social organization of the Negro. The undeniable fact that most Philadelphia white people prefer not to live near Negroes[17] limits the Negro very seriously in the choice of a cheap home. Moreover, real estate agents knowing the limited supply usually raise the rent a dollar or two for Negro tenants, if they do not refuse them altogether. Again, the occupations which the Negro follows, and which at present he is compelled to follow, are of a sort that makes it necessary for him to live near the best portions of the city; the mass of Negroes are in the economic world purveyors to the rich— working in private houses, in hotels, large stores, etc.[18] In order to keep this work they must live near by; the laundress cannot bring her Spruce street family's clothes from the Thirtieth Ward, nor can the waiter at the Continental Hotel lodge in Germantown. With the mass of white workmen this same necessity of living near work, does not hinder them from getting cheap dwellings; the factory is surrounded by cheap cottages, the foundry by long rows of houses, and even the white clerk and shop girl can, on account of their hours of labor, afford to live further out in the suburbs than the black porter who opens the store. Thus it is clear that the nature of the Negro's work compels him to crowd into the centre of the city much more than is the case with the mass of white working people. At the same time this necessity is apt in some cases to be overestimated, and a few hours of sleep or convenience serve to persuade a good many families to endure poverty in the Seventh Ward when they might be comfortable in the Twenty-fourth Ward. Nevertheless much of the Negro problem in this city finds adequate explanation when we reflect that here is a people receiving a little lower wages than usual for less desirable work, and compelled, in order to do that work, to live in a little less pleasant quarters than most people, and pay for them somewhat higher rents.

The final reason of the concentration of Negroes in certain localities is a social one and one peculiarly strong: the life of the Negroes of the city has for years centred in the Seventh Ward; here are the old churches, St. Thomas', Bethel, Central, Shiloh and Wesley; here are the halls of the secret societies; here are the homesteads of old families. To a race socially ostracised it means far more to move to remote parts of a city, than to those who will in any part of the city easily form congenial acquaintances and new ties. The Negro who ventures away from the mass of his people and their organized life, finds himself alone, shunned and taunted, stared at and made uncomfortable; he can make few new friends, for his neighbors however well-disposed would shrink to add a Negro to their list of acquaintances. Thus he remains far from friends and the concentrated social life of the church, and feels in all its bitterness what it means to be a social outcast. Consequently emigration from the ward has gone in groups and centred itself about some church, and individual initiative is thus checked. At the same time color prejudice makes it difficult for groups to find suitable places to move to—one Negro family would be tolerated where six would be objected to; thus we have here a very decisive hindrance to emigration to the suburbs.

It is not surprising that his situation leads to considerable crowding in the homes, *i. e.,* to the endeavor to get as many people into the space hired as possible. It is this crowding that gives the casual observer many false notions as to the size of Negro families, since he often forgets that every other house has its sub-renters and lodgers. It is however difficult to measure this crowding on account of this very lodging system which makes it very often uncertain as to just the number of rooms a given group of people occupy. In the following table therefore it is likely that the number of rooms given is somewhat greater than is really the case and that consequently there is more crowding than is indicated. This error however could not be wholly eliminated under the circumstances; in the Seventh Ward there are 9302 rooms occupied by 2401 families, an average of 3.8 rooms to a family, and 1.04 individuals to a room. A division by rooms will better show where the crowding comes in.

Families occupying five rooms and less: 1648, total rooms per family, 2.17; total individuals per room, 1.53.

Families occupying three rooms and less: 1350, total rooms per family, 1.63; total individuals per room, 1.85.

The worst cases of crowding are as follows:

> Two cases of 10 persons in 1 room
> One case of   9 persons in 1 room
> Five cases of 7 persons in 1 room
> Six cases of   6 persons in 1 room
> Twenty-five cases of 5 persons in 1 room

One case of 9 persons in 2 rooms
One case of 16 persons in 3 rooms
One case of 13 persons in 3 rooms
One case of 11 persons in 3 rooms

As said before, this is probably something under the real truth, although perhaps not greatly so. The figures show considerable overcrowding, but not nearly as much as is often the case in other cities. This is largely due to the character of Philadelphia houses, which are small and low, and will not admit many inmates. Five persons in one room of an ordinary tenement would be almost suffocating. The large number of one-room tenements with two persons should be noted. These 572 families are for the most part young or childless couples, sub-renting a bedroom and working in the city.[19]

Sections and Wards. The spread of Negro population in the city during the nineteenth century is worth studying.

The historic centre of Negro settlement in the city can be seen to be at Sixth and Lombard. From this point it moved north, as is indicated for instance by the establishment of Zoar Church in 1794. Immigration of foreigners and the rise of industries, however, early began to turn it back and it found outlet in the alleys of Southwark and Moyamensing. For a while about 1840 it was bottled up here, but finally it began to move west. A few early left the mass and settled in West Philadelphia; the rest began a slow steady movement along Lombard street. The influx of 1876 and thereafter sent the wave across Broad street to a new centre at Seventeenth and Lombard. There it divided into two streams; one went north and joined remnants of the old settlers in the Northern Liberties and Spring Garden. The other went south to the Twenty-sixth, Thirtieth and Thirty-sixth Wards. Meantime the new immigrants poured in at Seventh and Lombard, while Sixth and Lombard down to the Delaware was deserted to the Jews, and Moyamensing partially to the Italians. The Irish were pushed on beyond Eighteenth to the Schuylkill, or emigrated to the mills of Kensington and elsewhere.

This migration explains much that is paradoxical about Negro slums, especially their present remnant at Seventh and Lombard.

Many people wonder that the mission and reformatory agencies at work there for so many years have so little to show by way of results. One answer is that this work has new material continually to work upon, while the best classes move to the west and leave the dregs behind. The parents and grandparents of some of the best families of Philadelphia Negroes were born in the neighborhood of Sixth and Lombard at a time when all Negroes, good, bad and indifferent, were confined to that and a few other localities. With the greater freedom of domicile which has since come, these slum districts have sent a stream of emigrants westward. There has, too, been a general movement from the alleys to the streets and from the back to the front streets. Moreover it is untrue that the slums of Seventh and Lombard have not greatly changed in character; compared with 1840, 1850 or even 1870 these slums are much improved in every way. More and more every year the unfortunate and poor are being sifted out from the vicious and criminal and sent to better quarters.

And yet with all the obvious improvement, there are still slums and dangerous slums left.

To take a typical case:

Gillis' Alley, famed in the Police Court, is a narrow alley, extending from Lombard street through to South street, above Fifth street, cobbled and without sewer connections. Houses and stables are mixed promiscuously. Buildings are of frame and of brick. No.— looks both outside and in like a Southern Negro's cabin. In this miserable place four colored families have their homes. The aggregate rent demanded is $22 a month, though the owner seldom receives the full rent. For three small dark rooms in the rear of another house in this alley, the tenants pay, and have paid for thirteen years, $11 a month. The entrance is by a court not over two feet wide. Except at midday the sun does not shine in the small open space in the rear that answers for a yard. It is safe to say that not one house in this alley could pass an inspection without being condemned as prejudicial to health.

The general characteristics and distribution of the Negro population at present in the different wards can only be indicated in general terms. The wards with the best Negro population are parts of the Seventh, Twenty-sixth, Thirtieth and Thirty-sixth, Fourteenth,

Fifteenth, Twenty-fourth, Twenty-seventh and Twenty-ninth. The worst Negro population is found in parts of the Seventh, and in the Fourth, Fifth and Eighth. In the other wards either the classes are mixed or there are very few colored people. The tendency of the best migration to-day is toward the Twenty-sixth, Thirtieth and Thirty-sixth Wards, and West Philadelphia.

7

THE BLACK NORTH IN 1901: NEW YORK

I

The negro problem is not the sole property of the South. To be sure, it is there most complicated and pressing. Yet north of Mason and Dixon's line there live to-day three-quarters of a million men of negro lineage. Nearly 400,000 of these live in New England and the Middle Atlantic States, and it is this population that I wish especially to study in a series of papers.

The growth of this body of negroes has been rapid since the war. There were 150,000 in 1860, 225,000 in 1880, and about 385,000 to-day. It is usually assumed that this group of persons has not formed to any extent a "problem" in the North, that during a century of freedom they have had an assured social status and the same chance for rise and development as the native white American, or at least as the foreign immigrant.

This is not true. It can be safely asserted that since early Colonial times the North has had a distinct race problem. Every one of these States had slaves, and at the beginning of Washington's Administration there were 40,000 black slaves and 17,000 black freemen in this section. The economic failure of slavery as an investment here gave the better conscience of Puritan and Quaker a chance to be heard, and processes of gradual emancipation were begun early in the nineteenth century.

Some of the slaves were sold South and eagerly welcomed there. Most of them stayed in the North and became a free negro population.

Reprinted from W.E.B. Du Bois, *The Black North in 1901: A Social Study* (1901; New York: Arno Press, 1969), pp. 1-18.

They were not, however, really free. Socially they were ostracized. Strict laws were enacted against intermarriage. They were granted rights of suffrage with some limitations, but these limitations were either increased or the right summarily denied afterward.

North as well as South the negroes have emerged from slavery into a serfdom of poverty and restricted rights. Their history since has been the history of the gradual but by no means complete breaking down of remaining barriers.

To-day there are many contrasts between Northern and Southern negroes. Three-fourths of the Southern negroes live in the country districts. Nine-tenths of the Northern negroes live in cities and towns. The Southern negroes were in nearly all cases born South and of slave parentage.

About a third of the Northern negroes were born North, partly of free negro parentage, while the rest are Southern immigrants. Thus in the North there is a sharper division of the negroes into classes and a greater difference in attainment and training than one finds in the South.

From the beginning the Northern slaves lived in towns more generally than the Southern slaves, being used largely as house servants and artisans. As town life increased, the urban negro population increased. Here and there little villages of free negroes were to be found in the country districts of the North tilling the soil, but the competition of the great West soon sent them to town along with their white brothers, and now only here and there is there a negro family left in the country districts and villages of New England and of the Middle States.

From the earliest settlement of Manhattan, when the Dutch West India Company was pledging itself to furnish the new settlers with plenty of negroes, down to 1900, when the greater city contained 60,000 black folk, New York has had a negro problem. This problem has greatly changed from time to time. Two centuries ago it was a question of obtaining "hands" to labor. Then came questions of curbing barbarians and baptizing heathen. Long before the nineteenth century citizens were puzzled about the education of negroes, and then came negro riots and negro crime and the baffling windings of the color line.

At the beginning of the eighteenth century there were 1,500 negroes in New York City. They were house servants and laborers, and often were hired out by their masters, taking their stand for this purpose at the foot of Wall Street. By the middle of the century the population had doubled, and by the beginning of the nineteenth century it was about 9,000, five-sixths of whom were free by the act of gradual emancipation.

In 1840 the population was over 16,000, but it fell off to 12,500 in 1860 on account of the competition of foreign workmen and race riots. Since the war it has increased rapidly to 20,000 in 1880 and to 36,000 on Manhattan Island in 1900. The annexed districts raise this total to 60,666 for the whole city.

The distribution of this population presents many curious features. Conceive a large rectangle through which Seventh Avenue runs lengthwise. Let this be bounded on the south by a line near Sixteenth Street and on the north by Sixty-fourth or Sixty-fifth Street. On the east let the boundary be a wavering line between Fourth and Seventh Avenues and on the west the river.

In this quadrangle live over 20,000 negroes, a third of the total population. Ten thousand others live around the north end of the park and further north, while 18,000 live in Brooklyn. The remaining 10,000 are scattered here and there in other parts of the city.

The migration of the black population to its present abode in New York has followed the growth of the city. Early in the eighteenth century negroes lived and congregated in the hovels along the wharves and of course in the families of the masters. The centre of black population then moved slowly north, principally on the east side, until it reached Mulberry Street, about 1820. Crossing Broadway, a generation later the negroes clustered about Sullivan and Thompson Streets until after the war, when they moved northward along Seventh Avenue.

From 1870 to 1890 the population was more and more crowded and congested in the negro districts between Twenty-sixth and Sixty-third Streets. Since then there has been considerable dispersion to Brooklyn and the Harlem districts, although the old centres are still full.

The migration to Brooklyn began about 1820 and received its

great impetus from the refugees at the time of the draft riots. In 1870 there were 5,000 negroes in Brooklyn. Since then the population has increased very rapidly, and it has consisted largely of the better class of negroes in search of homes and seeking to escape the contamination of the Tenderloin.

In 1890 the Brooklyn negroes had settled chiefly in the Eleventh, Twentieth, and Seventh Wards. Since then they have increased in those wards and have moved to the east in the Twenty-third, Twenty-fourth, and Twenty-fifth Wards and in the vicinity of Coney Island.

Let us now examine any peculiarities in the colored population of Greater New York. The first noticeable fact is the excess of women. In Philadelphia the women exceed the men six to five. In New York the excess is still larger—five to four—and this means that here even more than in Philadelphia the demand for negro housemaids is unbalanced by a corresponding demand for negro men.

This disproportion acts disastrously to-day on the women and the men. The excess of young people from eighteen to thirty years of age points again to large and rapid immigration. The Wilmington riot alone sent North thousands of emigrants, and as the black masses of the South awaken or as they are disturbed by the violence this migration will continue and perhaps increase.

The North, therefore, and especially great cities like New York, has much more than an academic interest in the Southern negro problem. Unless the race conflict there is so adjusted as to leave the negroes a contented, industrious people, they are going to migrate here and there. And into the large cities will pour in increasing numbers the competent and the incompetent, the industrious and the lazy, the law abiding and the criminal.

Moreover, the conditions under which these new immigrants are now received are of such a nature that very frequently the good are made bad and the bad made professional criminals. One has but to read Dunbar's "Sport of the Gods" to get an idea of the temptations that surround the young immigrant. In the most thickly settled negro portion of the Nineteenth Assembly District, where 5,000 negroes live, the parents of half of the heads of families were country bred. Among these families the strain of city life is immediately seen when we find that 24 per cent. of the mothers are widows—a percentage only exceeded by the Irish, and far above the Americans, (16.3.)

In these figures lie untold tales of struggle, self-denial, despair, and crime. In the country districts of the South, as in all rural regions, early marriage and large families are the rule. These young immigrants to New York cannot afford to marry early. Two-thirds of the young men twenty to twenty-four years of age are unmarried, and five-eighths of the young women.

When they do marry it is a hard struggle to earn a living. As a race the negroes are not lazy. The canvass of the Federation of Churches in typical New York tenement districts has shown that while nearly 99 per cent. of the black men were wage earners, only 92 per cent. of the Americans and 90 per cent. of the Germans were at work.

At the same time the work of the negroes was least remunerative, they receiving a third less per week than the other nationalities. Nor can the disabilities of the negroes be laid altogether at the door of ignorance. Probably they are even less acquainted with city life and organized industry than most of the foreign laborers. In illiteracy, however, negroes and foreigners are about equal—five-sixths being able to read and write.

The crucial question, then, is: What does the black immigrant find to do? Some persons deem the answer to this question unnecessary to a real understanding of the negro. They say either that the case of the negro is that of the replacing of a poor workman by better ones in the natural competition of trade or that a mass of people like the American negroes ought to furnish employment for themselves without asking others for work.

There is just enough truth in such superficial statements to make them peculiarly misleading and unfair. Before the civil war the negro was certainly as efficient a workman as the raw immigrant from Ireland or Germany. But whereas the Irishmen found economic opportunity wide and daily growing wider, the negro found public opinion determined to "keep him in his place."

As early as 1824 Lafayette, on his second visit to New York, remarked "with astonishment the aggravation of the prejudice against the blacks," and stated that in the Revolutionary War "the black and white soldiers messed together without hesitation." In 1836 a well-to-do negro was refused a license as a drayman in New York City, and mob violence was frequent against black men who pushed forward beyond their customary sphere.

Nor could the negro resent this by his vote. The Constitution of 1777 had given him full rights of suffrage, but in 1821 the ballot, so far as blacks were concerned, was restricted to holders of $250 worth of realty—a restriction which lasted until the war, in spite of efforts to change it, and which restricted black laborers but left white laborers with full rights of suffrage.

So, too, the draft riots of 1863 were far more than passing ebullitions of wrath and violence, but were used as a means of excluding negroes all over the city from lines of work in which they had long been employed. The relief committee pleaded in vain to have various positions restored to negroes. In numerous cases the exclusion was permanent and remains so to this day.

Thus the candid observer easily sees that the negro's economic position in New York has not been determined simply by efficiency in open competition, but that race prejudice has played a large and decisive part. Probably in free competition ex-slaves would have suffered some disadvantages in entering mechanical industries. When race feeling was added to this they were almost totally excluded.

Again, it is impossible for a group of men to maintain and employ itself while in open competition with a larger and stronger group. Only by co-operation with the industrial organization of the Nation can negroes earn a living. And this co-operation is difficult to effect. One can easily trace the struggle in a city like New York. Seventy-four per cent. of the working negro population are common laborers and servants.

From this dead level they have striven long to rise. In this striving they have made many mistakes, have had some failures and some successes. They voluntarily withdrew from bootblacking, barbering, table waiting, and menial service whenever they thought they saw a chance to climb higher, and their places were quickly filled by foreign whites.

Some of the negroes succeeded in their efforts to rise, some did not. Thus every obstacle placed in the way of their progress meant increased competition at the bottom. Twenty-six per cent. of the negroes have risen to a degree and gained a firmer economic foothold. Twelve per cent. of these have gone but a step higher; these are the porters, packers, messengers, draymen, and the like—a select class of laborers, often well paid and more independent than the old class of upper house servants before the war, to which they in some respects correspond.

Some of this class occupy responsible positions, others have some capital invested, and nearly all have good homes.

Ten per cent. of the colored people are skilled laborers—cigarmakers, barbers, tailors and dressmakers, builders, stationary engineers, &c. Five and one-half per cent. are in business enterprises of various sorts. The negroes have something over a million and a half dollars invested in small business enterprises, chiefly real estate, the catering business, undertaking, drug stores, hotels and restaurants, express teaming, &c. In the sixty-nine leading establishments $800,000 is invested—$13,000 in sums from $500 to $1,000 and $269,000 in sums from $1,000 to $25,000.

Forty-four of the sixty-nine businesses were established since 1885, and seventeen others since the war. Co-operative holders of real estate—i.e., hall associations, building and loan associations, and one large church, which has considerable sums in productive real estate—have over half a million dollars invested. Five leading caterers have $30,000, seven undertakers have $32,000, two saloons have over $50,000, and four small machine shops have $27,000 invested.

These are the most promising enterprises in which New York negroes have embarked. Serious obstacles are encountered. Great ingenuity is often required in finding gaps in business service where the man of small capital may use his skill or experience.

One negro has organized the cleaning of houses to a remarkable extent and has an establishment representing at least $20,000 of invested capital, some ten or twelve employees, and a large circle of clients.

Again, it is very difficult for negroes to get experience and training in modern business methods. Young colored men can seldom get positions above menial grade, and the training of the older men unfits them for competitive business. Then always the uncertain but ever present factor of racial prejudice is present to hinder or at least make more difficult the advance of the colored merchant or business man, in new or unaccustomed lines.

In clerical and professional work there are about ten negro lawyers in New York, twenty physicians, and at least ninety in the civil service as clerks, mail carriers, public school teachers, and the like. The competitive civil service has proved a great boon to young aspiring negroes, and they are being attracted to it in increasing numbers. Already in the public schools there are one Principal, two special teachers, and about thirty-five classroom teachers of negro blood. So far no complaint of the work and very little objection to their presence has been heard.

In some such way as this black New York seeks to earn its daily bread, and it remains for us to ask of the homes and the public institutions just what kind of success these efforts are having.

II

Taking all available data into consideration we may conclude that of the 60,000 negroes in New York about 15,000 are supported by workers who earn a good living in vocations above domestic service and common labor. Some thirty thousand are kept above actual want by the wages of servants and day laborers. This leaves a great struggling, unsuccessful substratum of 15,000, including "God's poor, the devil's poor, and the poor devils," and, also, the vicious and criminal classes. These are not all paupers or scamps, but they form that mass of men who through their own fault or through the fault of conditions about them have not yet succeeded in successfully standing the competition of a great city.

Such figures are of course largely conjectural, but they appear near the truth. So large a substratum of unsuccessful persons in a community is abnormal and dangerous. And yet it is certain that nothing could be more disgraceful than for New York to condemn 45,000 hard working and successful people, who have struggled up in spite of slavery, riot, and discrimination, on account of 15,000 who have not yet succeeded and whom New Yorkers have helped to fail.

In no better way can one see the effects of color prejudice on the mass of the negroes than by studying their homes. The work of the Federation of Churches in the Eleventh and Thirteenth Assembly Districts, where over 6,000 negroes live, found 19 per cent. living in one and two room tenements, 37 per cent. in three rooms, and 44 per cent. in four or more rooms. Had the rooms been of good size and the rents fair this would be a good showing; but 400 of the rooms had no access to the outer air and 655 had but one window. Moreover, for these accommodations the negroes pay from $1 to $2 a month more than the whites for similar tenements—an excess rent charge which must amount to a quarter of a million dollars annually throughout the city. One fourth of these people paid under $10 a month rent; two-thirds paid from $10 to $20.

We may say, then, that in the Tenderloin district, where the newer negro immigrants must needs go for a home, the average family occupies three small rooms, for which it pays $10 to $15 a month. If the family desires a home further from the vice and dirt of New York's most dangerous slum, it must go either to Brooklyn or, far from work, up town, or be prepared to pay exorbitant rents in the vicinity of Fifty-third Street.

More than likely the new-comer knows nothing of the peculiar dangers of this district, but takes it as part of the new and strange city life to which he has migrated. Finding work scarce and rent high, he turns for relief to narrow quarters and the lodging system. In the more crowded colored districts 40 per cent. of the families take lodgers and in only 50 per cent. of the cases are the lodgers in any way related to the families. Unknown strangers are thus admitted to the very heart of homes in order that the rent may be paid. And these homes are already weak from the hereditary influence of slavery and its attendant ills.

The very first movement of philanthropy in solving some of the negro problems of New York would be the separation of the decent and vicious elements, which the lodging system and high rent bring in such fatal proximity. Thus the movement of the City and Suburban Homes Company to build a model negro tenement on

Sixty-second Street is an act of far-seeing wisdom. To-day it is the intricate and close connection of misfortune and vice among the lower classes that baffles intelligent reform.

A great mass of people, bringing with them a host of unhealthful habits, living largely in tenements, with wretched sanitary appliances, and in poor repair—such a mass must necessarily have a higher death rate than the average among the whites. Before the war this excess was very great, and even this year the colored death rate is 28 per thousand, against 20 for the whites. Since 1870 the death rate of negroes has been:

> 1870, 36 per thousand.
> 1880, 37 per thousand.
> 1890, 38 per thousand.
> 1900, 28 per thousand.

The decrease in 1900 is due to the inclusion of the healthier negro districts of the greater city, as, e. g., Brooklyn, and the immigration of young people. In itself a death rate of 28 is not high; the death rate of the whole city was 29 in 1870. Nevertheless, the disparity between whites and blacks shows plainly that the difference is due primarily to conditions of life and is remediable.

The most sinister index of social degradation and struggle is crime. Unfortunately, it is extremely difficult to-day to measure negro crime. If we seek to measure it in the South we are confronted by the fact that different and peculiar standards of justice exist for black and white. If we take a city like New York we find that continual migration and concentration of negro population here make it unfair to attribute to the city or to the permanent negro population the crime of the new-comers. Then, again, it has been less than a generation since, even in this city, negroes stood on a different footing before the courts from whites, and received severer treatment. In interpreting figures from the past, therefore, we must allow something at least for this.

There was complaint of negro misdemeanors back in the seventeenth century, as, for example, in 1682, when the city was suffering "great inconvenyencys" from the "frequent meetings and gatherings of negroes," and the City Council passed ordinances against such disorder and gambling. There was continual fear of negro uprisings, and when, after the establishment of Nean's Negro School, in 1704, a family of seven were murdered by their slaves, a great outcry was raised against negro education.

In 1712 and 1741 there were negro conspiracies—the first a fierce dash for freedom, the second a combination of negro thieves, white women of evil repute and their aiders and abettors. The city on both these occasions was vastly scared, and took fearful vengeance on those whom they thought guilty, burning and hanging twenty-nine blacks in 1741.

No very exact data of negro crime are available until about seventy-five years ago. In 1827, 25 per cent. of the convicts in New York State were negroes, although the negroes formed but 1 per cent. of the population. Twenty years later the negroes, forming the same proportion of the population, furnished 257 of the 1,637 convicts, or more than 15 per cent. In 1870 the proportion had fallen to 6 per cent.

Since then we may use the arrests in New York City as a crude indication of negro crime. These indicate that from 1870 to 1885 the negroes formed about 2 per cent. of the arrests, the best record they have had in the city. From 1885 to 1895 the proportion rose to 2½ per cent., and since then it has risen to 3½ per cent. A part of this rise is accounted for by the increase in the proportion of negro to white population, which was 1 1–3 per cent. in 1870 and 1¾ per cent. in 1900. The larger proportion of the increase in arrests is undoubtedly due to migration—the sudden contact of new-comers with unknown city life. From the mere record of arrests one can get no very good idea of crime, and yet it is safe to conclude from the fact that in the State in 1890 every 10,000 negroes furnished 100 prisoners that there is much serious crime among negroes. And, indeed, what else should we expect?

What else is this but the logical result of bad homes, poor health, restricted opportunities for work, and general social oppression? That the present situation is abnormal all admit. That the negro under normal conditions is law-abiding and good-natured cannot be disputed. We have but to change conditions, then, to reduce negro crime.

We have so far a picture of the negro from without—his numbers, his dwelling place, his work, his health, and crime. Let us now, if possible, place ourselves within the negro group and by studying that inner life look with him out upon the surrounding world. When a white person comes once vividly to realize the disabilities under which a negro labors, the public contempt and thinly veiled private dislike, "the spurns that patient merit of the unworthy takes"— when once one sees this, and then from personal knowledge knows that sensitive human hearts are enduring this, the question comes, How can they stand it? The answer is clear and peculiar: They do not stand it; they withdraw themselves as far as possible from it into a world of their own. They live and move in a community of their own kith and kin and shrink quickly and permanently from those rough edges where contact with the larger life of the city wounds and humiliates them.

To see what this means in practice, let us follow the life of an average New York negro. He is first born to a colored father and mother. The mulattoes we see on the streets are almost invariably the descendants of one, two, or three generations of mulattoes, the infusion of white blood coming often far back in the eighteenth century. In only 3 per cent. of the New York marriages of colored people is one of the parties white. The child's neighbors, as he grows up, are colored, for he lives in a colored district. In the public school he comes into intimate touch with white children, but as they grow up public opinion forces them to discard their colored acquaintances, and they soon forget even the nod of recognition. The young man's friends and associates are therefore all negroes. When he goes to work he works alongside colored men in most cases; his social circle, his clubs and organizations throughout the city are all confined to his own race, and his contact with the whites is practically confined to economic relationships, the streets, and street cars, with occasionally some intercourse at public amusements.

The centre of negro life in New York is still the church, although its all-inclusive influence here is less than in a Southern city. There are thirty or forty churches, large and small, but seven or eight chief ones. They have strongly marked individuality, and stand in many cases for distinct social circles. The older families of well-to-do free negroes who count on unspotted family life for two centuries gather at St. Philip's Episcopal Church, on Twenty-fifth Street. This church is an offshoot of Trinity and the lineal descendant of Nean's Negro School early in the eighteenth century. The mass of middle-class negroes whose fathers were New Yorkers worship at Mother Zion, Tenth and Bleecker Streets. This church is far from the present centre of negro population, but it is a historic spot, where the first organized protest of black folk against color discrimination in New York churches took place. Up on Fifty-third Street, at Olivet, one finds a great Baptist church, with the newer immigrants from Georgia and Virginia, and so through the city.

Next to the churches come the secret and beneficial societies. The Colored Masons date from 1826; the Odd Fellows own a four-story hall on Twenty-ninth Street, where ninety-six separate societies meet and pay an annual rent of $5,000. Then there are old societies like the African dating back to 1808, and new ones like the Southern Beneficial with very large memberships. There is a successful building association, a hospital, an orphan asylum, and a home for the aged, all entirely conducted by negroes, and mainly supported by them. Public entertainments are continually provided by the various churches and by associations such as the Railway Porters' Union, the West Indian Benevolent Association, the Lincoln Literary, &c.

Here, then, is a world of itself, closed in from the outer world and almost unknown to it, with churches, clubs, hotels, saloons, and charities; with its own social distinctions, amusements, and ambitions. Its members are rarely rich, according to the standards of to-day. Probably less than ten negroes in New York own over $50,000 worth of property each, and the total property held may be roughly estimated as between three and four millions. Many homes have been bought in Brooklyn and the suburbs in the last ten years, so that there is a comfortable class of laborers.

The morality and education of this black world is naturally below that of the white world. That is the core of the negro problem. Nevertheless, it would be wrong to suppose here a mass of ungraded ignorance and lewdness. The social gradations toward the top are sharp and distinct, and the intelligence and good conduct of the better classes would pass muster in a New England village. As we descend the social distinctions are less rigid, and toward the bottom the great difficulty is to distinguish between the bad and the careless, the idle and the criminal, the unfortunate and the imposters.

8

THE NEGROES
OF DOUGHERTY COUNTY, GEORGIA

My first work [in studying small communities] was at Farmville, Virginia. What I did in that case was to go to a typical town and settle down there for a time. I made a census of the town personally, went to the house of each negro family in the town, and tried to find out as much as I could about the general situation of things in that town. Here I would like to present the results of a similar study done in Georgia.

There are more negroes in Georgia than any other State of the Union; the growth there of the negro population has usually been larger than the growth in general throughout the United States. There are today over 850,000 negroes in the state. Down in the southwestern part of the state there is a county called Dougherty County. I went down there in the summer of 1898 and spent 2 or 3 months there with 2 or 3 assistants. We visited nearly every colored family in the county. Most of them live out in the country districts. In the county there is a population of about 10,000 negroes and about 2,000 whites—to be exact, there are 10,231 negroes (that was in 1890) and 1,975 whites; it is a black-belt county. I have traveled 10 miles down there without seeing a white face. I think the disproportion between the negroes and the whites has not been kept up in the last decade, but that is my personal opinion. I think there are more whites in proportion than there were 10 years ago. The county was first laid out as Baker County, and part of that was

Reprinted from *Report of the Industrial Commission on Education* (Washington, D.C.: United States Industrial Commission Reports, 1900-1902) 15:159-175. This selection, originally titled "Testimony of Prof. W. E. Burghardt Du Bois," is an edited version of Du Bois' testimony to the United States Industrial Commission.

afterwards set aside and called Dougherty. You have there a chance to study a community of negroes with a rather interesting history. During the civil war negro slaves were driven down there for a place of refuge from Savannah, Macon, and other parts of Georgia; they were held there, and after the war they settled there. It was a sort of huddling for self-protection, a thing that has very often occurred in the South. It was not purely an economic movement because the negroes saw they could do better there. By huddling together they got a sort of protection that they otherwise could not get.

In Baker County and a few others in that section, even today, if a stranger should pass through he might be stopped anywhere on a crossroad and asked who he was and what his business was there. Baker is a county that had poor land and was settled by poor whites. They had very few dealings with the negroes, and vice versa; and the relationship between the two races is not at all pleasant. In Dougherty County the old master class and the negroes come in close contact and on the whole the relation between the two is very pleasant. Some of the descendants of the poor whites have come in and have formed a little disturbing element, but perhaps the largest disturbing element is one that is spoken of but little in the study of the South, and that is the Jewish merchant. I will speak a little later of what he has to do with the situation.

In that county I studied a total of 6,093 people. In the country districts there were about 3,000 males and about 3,000 females, a few more females than males. In the cities and a great many of the country districts there are more females than males in the negro population. The males go off where they can get more lucrative employment. They go to Florida and Alabama and work as waiters and hostlers, and at bartending and industries of that sort so you have a slight excess of females though not nearly as large as in cities like Baltimore and Philadelphia where the excess leads to many irregularities of life.

Regarding the age classification, there is one thing to be noticed here. There are more children under 10 years of age than there are in the United States generally or than there are in Germany. In the United States the proportion is 24.3 per cent under 10 and in Germany it is 24.2. Here in Dougherty County it was 27.2, showing a larger proportion under age 10. There is nothing else particularly to be noted in the age classification.

As to the conjugal condition, most of them marry early, but not as early, perhaps, as their fathers and mothers did, and yet a good deal earlier than in the country districts of the North today. Perhaps it would correspond to the country districts in New England 30 or 40 years ago. I might say, parenthetically, I was born in New England, and consequently had a chance of making some comparisons from that point of view. Practically all the people get married but there is some irregularity in marriage relations. There is the old custom among the lowest classes of staying with a wife for a while and then separating and getting another, and so on. Sometimes these co-habitations without the regular marriage ceremony are practically permanent so they amount to common-law marriages; but in other cases a man lives with one wife for perhaps 5 or 6 years and perhaps less. This is not as bad in this country as it is in some other districts, but I should say about 8 per cent of the families throughout the country districts were cases of this sort; the cohabitation was for a comparatively short period and was liable to be broken up in anywhere from 1 to 5 years.

Regarding illiteracy, of the persons 10 years of age and over, 73 per cent were illiterates; that is, they were totally illiterate or they could perhaps read a very little, but could not write. I counted them all as illiterate because it is very difficult in collecting these statistics about illiteracy to make any really good distinction between those who can not read or write and those who can read but can not write; and those who can read and not write are practically as illiterate. Only 27 per cent can read and write. The percentage of illiterates is somewhat less under age 20; that is, about 60 per cent are illiterate. Those under 20 show the results of the common school system though the schools in Dougherty County are very poor. I saw only one schoolhouse there that would compare in any way with the worst schoolhouses I ever saw in New England. That was a board house equipped with rude benches, without desks, no glass in the windows, with no sort of furniture except a blackboard and three boards put together for a teacher's desk. Most of the schoolhouses were either old log huts or were churches. In the town they do have some very good teachers. They have an academy supported by the American Missionary Association where they have good teachers, but in the country there are very few school facilities. The superintendents are paid very little, and this has led, in some cases, to hiring a teacher who will help to increase the income of the superintendent. For instance, a man is put down for $30 a month as teacher of a school. It is not always certain if he had made a contract with somebody, either the superintendent or somebody else, to pay a part of it for the privilege of being appointed. The result is that worse men get appointed than would be the case if the superintendent could make enough by his ordinary salary. I do not know how far this goes and I do not know that it is peculiarly true of Dougherty County.

The most important thing about the people in Dougherty County is their occupation. The great mass of them are farmers and laborers. In the United States those persons over 10 years of age engaged in actual occupations form about 48 per cent. The rest form the leisure class, the housewives at home, the old people, and the children who are going to school. In Dougherty County 96 per cent are engaged in gainful occupations. That index shows the character of the population. There is no one left to really make homes. There is no time left for any afternoon of life—everybody is working but I do not mean that they are all working hard.

Among the men 20 years and over, there were 1,319 farmers and farm laborers, and 179 engaged in other occupations. You see a great preponderance of farmers. And among the women it is practically the same—1,341 farmers and laborers and only 216 in other occupations. Of those between the ages of 10 and 20 the disproportion was even larger.

I have these occupations in detail but I will use just those of the men between 20 and 40. Farmers and farm laborers, 696; laborers in mills and cotton compresses, on railroads, wood cutters, etc., 31; watchmen, porters, and teamsters, 12; servants, 8; artisans, carpenters, blacksmiths, shoemakers, machinists, and engineers, 11; merchants and tailors, 6; teachers, 3; ministers, 10. These data give an idea of how the men work in the prime of life.

Regarding the social classes, about one-half of one per cent are recipients of charity. They are mostly old people who usually live out in the country in houses that some person has furnished them rent free; they work a little on a small plot of ground but are practically supported by the charity of some neighbor. To some extent they are supported by colored neighbors but mostly by the whites. Above these are some 10 per cent who are croppers. I put these two groups together, the 10 per cent and the one-half per cent, and call them the *submerged tenth*. They are below the horizon, so to speak. Then comes the great mass of the *laborers*, those who work on the share system, receiving part of the receipts—metayers—39 per cent. Then come the wage laborers who work for a fixed money wage; then the *wage laborers* who have houses furnished to them. Of the wage laborers there are 21 per cent, and of the wage laborers with houses, 18 per cent. That is the mass of the population. Above these come the people who have emerged—who have gotten out of the mire altogether and are really making and having made an advance. They are the renters and the owners. The renters are 4.6 per cent and the owners are 5.7 per cent.

The croppers are the lowest in the economic scale outside of the charity recipients. They are negroes who live on the plantations and are entirely without capital. They furnish the labor and the owner furnishes the land, tools, seed, and everything. The crop is divided with the owner getting from one-half to two-thirds. If he has advanced supplies that is taken out of the cropper's share. About one-tenth of the negroes labor in this way which is not satisfactory to either party. The owner incurs a large responsibility and has only limited power over the labor. The laborer has nothing to lose and is not spurred to work under this system of advances, and the result is dissatisfaction on both sides. That system is being very rapidly changed to the metayer system of sharing crops and charges. It is interesting to see how a man falls into one class one year and climbs up and gets into another class another year.

Under the metayer system a man goes to a landowner and makes a contract with him to take a certain piece of land. The laborer furnishes some capital. He usually furnishes a mule and some tools and something for subsistance, and the owner, on the other hand, furnishes the land. Just after the war he used to furnish the land and also took care to see that the man who was working for him got his food and clothing, but the storekeeper came in and took that from him. He drove the landlord out of the business of furnishing the laborer, and he drove him out because he could offer inducements to the laborer. He had a store in town and the laborers wanted to get to town. The man that has come in and taken the place of the white landowner, then, is the merchant; in Dougherty County he is in most cases a Jewish merchant. Some of them are Russian Jews, some German Jews, but most of them are Polish Jews. They have come there with their thrift and their idea of driving a hard bargain, and they do a great many things that the white men of the South would not do. They have no objection at all to calling the negro "mister," they are pleasant to him, and they never find any particular fault with him unless he is in debt. They keep the things he wants in the store and the result is they obtain the business of these colored laborers. Their prices are anywhere from 30 to 100 per cent above the cash price.

For the land that the colored farmer hires he usually pays a rent in cotton. For 20 acres and a house he would pay from 300 to 500 pounds of lint cotton. The average farm, usually 40 acres, is called a one-mule farm, and they pay anywhere from 350 to 2,000 pounds of cotton depending on where the land is with regard to market and how good the land is.

He starts out, therefore, furnishing a mule and some of the tools, and the landowner furnishing the land and perhaps some of the tools, and he goes to work to put in his crop. Just as soon as the crop is up, and sometimes before the crop is up, he goes to town and gets credit from the merchant in town and the merchant takes a mortgage. They give him a regular mortgage and usually there are several little things put in that mortgage. In the first place, there is in Georgia, of course, the homestead exemption. There are certain things you can not sell if a man goes into bankruptcy just as there are in other States. It is a pretty large list in Georgia—a very respectable list. But the man that makes a crop mortgage nearly always promises not to take advantage of that reservation so he signs away his right to keep anything. If you go down to Albany almost any Saturday morning you will find out in front of the courthouse bedsteads, bureaus, stands, looking-glasses, and clocks, and all sorts of articles of household furniture being sold. Some metayer has gone into bankruptcy and the storekeeper has seized his crop and his household goods. He has probably told him that it would be cheaper not to go to the sheriff and have to pay the sheriff's fee, and the negro has learned it will not pay; so he just brings his things to town and they sell them at auction. The man starts in as a cropper the next year with no capital at all. If cotton goes up and he is successful, next year he is a metayer again; if not, he sinks still lower and goes to town and joins the loafers, or goes to another county and gets some other sort of work. Of 475 metayers who held land in this way 281 had 40 acre farms, 82 had 80 acre farms, and 6 tilled from 400 to 1,600 acres.

Regarding the rent, I tried to figure out what proportion of the crops that these men raised went in rent. Of 50 farmers who made from 1 to 5 bales of cotton the actual total was 240-1/2 bales. Their total rent was 75-1/2 bales; so their rent was 32 per cent of their income. There were 18 farmers who made from 5 to 10 bales, and about 21 per cent of their income went as rent. There were 21 farmers who made 10 bales and over, and about 16 per cent went as rent. Of 161 farmers who made over 1,000 bales in the year 1898 they paid 241 of those bales as rent; that is, 22 per cent. Of course that is very high rent, and when you add to that the interest that they pay on goods they have bought on credit you can see in a bad year there is practically nothing left for them.

Above the metayers come the laborers who are working for a fixed wage. They may be divided into two classes: (1) The semimetayers, or those who receive houses and rations: that is, they have houses to live in and receive meat and meal and a small wage of from $4 to $8 a month. They are usually called contract hands and work through the season for one landowner. Most of the white resident owners cultivate their land in this way. (2) The regular laborers usually furnish their own houses. They always furnish their own food and receive 30 to 50 cents a day on an average. They are usually young persons who have not enough to marry on so that if they do marry they become metayers. As long as they work for wages they can keep up and do not have to set up an establishment. When they need a regular income they have to go to renting on shares.

The money renters I have called the first of the emerging classes; that is, the first which in the struggle for existence have made a distinct forward step. The fixed money rental calls for a good deal of foresight on the part of the man making a contract. It requires in nearly all cases that a man shall furnish himself with his supplies; he can usually make a better contract and get better land if he can pay an actual sum of money down but there is a good deal of risk about it. In 1898 the money renters had come out rather badly because cotton had gone down and they were left with the same money rental; while on the other hand, those renting on the share system when the price went down, the same amount of cotton paid their rent.

Of those who paid money rent there were 19 who had farms under 40 acres; 8 who had farms between 40 or 50; 5 between 50 and 100 acres; 1 from 100 to 150 acres; 2 from 150 up. For the 19 farms under 40 acres the total rent was $352. That was an average of about $18.50 per farm. Those from 40 to 50 acres the rent averaged $41 a farm; from 50 to 100 acres it was $72 a farm; from 100 to 150 it was $100 a farm; and those over that $175 a farm.

There were also 57 families who owned land in Dougherty County. I followed that back to 1875 so I got an account of the negro landowners for the years, 1875, 1880, 1884, 1890, 1891, 1893, and 1898. I had to skip some of these years because the data were not there, and I had to get what I could but they were somewhere near periods of 5 years. There have been 185 colored men who have owned land in Dougherty County since 1875. Of these 1 held his land 25 years, 4 held their land 20 years, 12 held their land 15 years, 12 held their land 10 years, 41 held their land 5 years, and 115 held their land 1 year. Of course most of those who have held their land for short periods are still there and they may hold it longer. I do not mean they have stopped holding land but up to 1898 that was the record.

The record of their landowning is interesting. In 1870 blacks practically owned nothing or if they did it was in the name of white men. There was some land and property owning in Augusta and Savannah but it was all held in the name of white men. There was some land and property owning in Georgia before the war and it is rather interesting to know about it. In 1875 they owned in Dougherty County 752 acres of land; in 1880 this had gone up to 2,456 acres; in 1884 to 6,607 acres; in 1890, 9,238 acres; in 1891, 9,676, and finally in 1898 they owned 14,988 acres. The value of that land is $63,000. The total value of all property owned by negroes in Dougherty County is $194,000.

' As to the way in which these people live, the great mass of them live in 1-room cabins. I have indicated it this way: seven hundred and sixty-one families live in 1-room cabins, 560 live in 2-room cabins, 93 live in 3-room cabins, and 60 live in cabins with 4 or more rooms. The 1-room cabin is an abomination in every way and the 2-room cabin is not very much better. Of course they live outdoors most of the time. If it were not for that you could prove more crowding in Dougherty County than in the worst of the tenement districts of New York. For instance, in this county there are over 25 persons for every 10 rooms of house accommodation. In the tenement districts of New York it does not go above 22 usually. They live outdoors most of the time, but as far as their house room is concerned, and in the winter, it is very bad indeed. Of course the moral effect on these 761 families is very bad indeed.

While I was going through the country I tried to grade the people, and for that purpose I used a system of gradation which I had used in other places in Virginia. In the first grade I put people who correspond to the ordinary middle class of people in New England—good honest people who are getting along well, who are thrifty and thoroughly honest and without any trace of any immorality of any sort. In the second grade were those who were getting on well but usually did not own their homes but were at the same time honest and upright people. In the third grade I put the mass of laborers—all the laborers that had no criminal tendencies and were not distinctly lewd. Of course, there were some I put in that third grade who as to morality would not pass in New England, but they were not bad people and lewdness was not conspicuous. There were some of those I put in the third class, those that were cohabiting without marriage ceremony but cohabitation was practically permanent. In the fourth class I put all the rest; that is, the lowest grade of the loafers and a lot of laborers who change here and there—migrate here and there—and those that live in all sorts of loose relationships. Of the whole 6,000 in Dougherty County there were 8-1/2 per cent I put in the fourth or lowest grade. The great mass of the people I put in the third grade; that is, 83 per cent—poor people, but fairly honest. Then in the second grade I put 5-1/2 per cent—people getting on well who usually did not own their own homes—and 3 per cent I put in the first grade. That was about as definite a picture of the conditions of the people there as I could make.

As to the outcome of these persons after years of toil in every case where I could I got an exact statement of just what the men had taken in and had paid out during the year. Naturally I could not get that from all of them. There were 1,300 families and I got from nearly 300 families a statement of the income and expenditures which seemed reliable. It was based partly on written accounts and it seemed to me it was worth taking. After 12 months work there were 3 of these families of farm tenants who were bankrupt and were sold out by the sheriff, 163 who ended in debt, 53 who cleared nothing— came out even but cleared nothing; the rest cleared something as follows: twenty-seven cleared less than $10; 15 cleared from $10 to $25; 13 cleared from $25 to $50; 13 cleared $50 and over. These are the tenant families, not those that own the land, but this is the outcome of a year's work of 300 families.

As to the laws, the whole question of local government in Georgia, the way things are, and what should be done to make the laws better is a hard question to get information on because it verges on political matters. Certain crop-lien laws ought to be changed. They are made now entirely in the interests of the merchants and it gives them a grasp on men so that it is not at all an exaggeration to say that in the Gulf States in general most of the negro farm laborers are in an economic slavery which keeps just about as fast a hold on them as the slavery they came out of; that is, if a man once gets in debt he is bound under and can't leave the place. If he is in debt to a man and leaves the place he is arrested. The negro never evades a debt. If they try and live up to their obligations the laws are so fixed that it is very hard for anyone to know just exactly what is fair. It might very well be possible to say that a great majority of the men who hire them are fair; only a minority are not fair. The accounts are kept almost entirely by the storekeepers and the negro has practically nothing to do with his crop. If his cotton crop is mortgaged he dare not touch it in any way. The merchants who have the crop liens are spending nearly all the time riding around the country and watching the crops. When it is gathered it is taken to the warehouse and the warehousemen and the merchants make the settlement then pay the negro what is left; that is, the negro does not appear as the principal anywhere. And then, of course, he must raise cotton. There is no use of talking to him about diversifying his crop. He can't. If he is in debt cotton is the only thing the merchant will take from him to pay his debt.

As to crime in this country, there were from April 1, 1898, to April 1, 1899, 191 arrests. There is no way of separating the white and colored arrests but the sheriff assured me that nine-tenths of them were colored, and I think you can practically ignore the white race; that is, probably 191—nearly all of them—were colored. These 191 arrests were disposed of as follows: bonded to compel them to keep the peace, released on bonds, not tried during that year, 44; 42 were found not guilty; 17 went to the chain gain; 16 were fined; and 5 cases were settled out of court. For a community as large as this, and as largely under colored control, as most of the people have to be, this is a small showing for crime. The most serious crimes were 28 burglaries—that is, arrests for that—some were proved not guilty; 16 assults to murder, and 1 assault to rape. The others were miscellaneous—fights and things of that sort.

9

THE NEGROES
OF FARMVILLE, VIRGINIA

For many reasons it would appear that the time is ripe for
undertaking a thorough study of the economic condition of the
American Negro. Under the direction of the United States Com-
missioner of Labor the present study was made during July and
August, 1897, as the first of a series of investigations of small,
well-defined groups of Negroes in various parts of the country.

In this work there has been but the one object of ascertaining,
with as near an approach to scientific accuracy as possible, the real
condition of the Negro.

PRINCE EDWARD COUNTY

Prince Edward County is a small irregular quadrangle of about 300
square miles, situated in the middle country of Virginia, between the
Piedmont region and tide water, about 57 miles southwest of
Richmond, and midway between Petersburg and Lynchburg. This
county is thus near the geographical center of the State, and is also
in the center of a district that produces seven-eighths of the tobacco
crop of Virginia. The county seat is Farmville, a market town of
2,500 inhabitants, situated on the upper waters of the Appomattox.
This county has had an interesting history as regards its population.
A century ago it had a population of 8,000, evenly divided between
whites and blacks; to-day it has a population of over 14,000, but the
increase is almost entirely among the blacks, the number of whites
still remaining under 5,000.

Abridged from the *Bulletin of the Department of Labor*, no. 14 (January 1898),
pp. 1–38.

Of the total population of the county, less than one-third live in towns of 25 or more inhabitants, leaving the great mass of the people thoroughly rural and agricultural. Before the late war more than 75 per cent of the farms were of 100 acres or over, and were worked by gangs of from 10 to 50 slaves. By 1870 these farms had become so broken up that nearly 40 per cent of them were less than 50 acres in size. Since then something of a reaction has taken place and more waste land brought under cultivation, so that in 1890 31 per cent of the farms were less than 50 acres in size.

Agriculture is the chief occupation of the inhabitants of the county, tobacco being the leading product. Corn, wheat, oats, and potatoes are also raised, together with diary products and poultry.

In addition to this agricultural exhibit there is a little manufacturing, and there are three lines of railway crossing the county and bringing it into touch with the markets.

The total assessed valuation of real estate and personal property in the county was $2,397,007 in 1890, and on this was raised by taxation the sum of $24,281, making a tax rate of $10.13 per $1,000 of valuation. The money raised was distributed as follows: To the State, $7,192; to the county, $7,191; to the towns, $5,104; to the schools, $4,794.

Turning to the Negroes of this county, we find that in 1895 the 9,924 Negroes therein owned 17,555 acres of land, which, together with buildings, was assessed at $132,189. The whites of the county, in the same year, owned 202,962 acres, and the assessed value of their lands and buildings was $1,064,180.

Situated in the geographic center of an historic slave State, near the economic center of its greatest industry, tobacco culture, and also in the black belt of the State, i.e., in the region where a decided majority of the inhabitants are of Negro blood, Prince Edward County is peculiarly suited to an investigation into Negro development. The few available statistics serve to indicate how vast a revolution this region has passed through during the last century. They show the rise and fall of the plantation-slave system; the physical upheaval of war in a region where the last acts of the great civil war took place, and the moral and economic revolution of emancipation in a county where the slave property was worth at least

$2,500,000. They indicate, finally, the ensuing economic revolution brought about by impoverished lands, changes in the commercial demand for tobacco and the methods of handling it, the competition of the West in cereals and meat, the growing importance of manufactures which call workers to cities, and the social weight of a mass of ignorant freedmen.

The present study does not, however, concern itself with the whole county, but merely with the condition of the Negroes in its metropolis and county seat, Farmville, where its social, political, and industrial centers, where its agricultural products are marketed, and where its development is best epitomized and expressed.

FARMVILLE

Farmville is in the extreme northern part of Prince Edward County. It is thoroughly Virginian in character—easy-going, gossipy, and conservative, with respect for family traditions and landed property. It would hardly be called bustling, and yet it is a busy market town, with a long, low main street full of general stores, and branching streets with tobacco warehouses and tobacco factories, churches, and substantial dwellings. Of public buildings there is an opera house, a normal school for white girls, an armory, a court-house and jail, a bank, and a depot. The air is good, and there is an abundance of lithia and sulphur waters, which now and then attract visitors.

Farmville is the trading center of six counties. Here a large proportion of the tobacco of these counties is marketed, and some of it manufactured into strips; here are a half-dozen or more commission houses which deal in all sorts of agricultural products; and here, too, is the center for distributing agricultural implements, clothing, groceries, and household wares. On Saturday, the regular market day, the town population swells to nearly twice its normal size from the influx of country people—mostly Negroes—some in carriages, wagons, and ox carts, and some on foot, and a large amount of trading is done.

Naturally such a town in the midst of a large farming district has a great attraction for young countrymen, on account of its larger life and the prospect of better wages in its manufacturing and trading establishments. A steady influx of immigrants thus adds annually to the population of the town. At the same time Farmville boys and girls are attracted by the large city life of Richmond, Norfolk, Baltimore, and New York. In this manner Farmville acts as a sort of clearing house, taking the raw country lad from the farm to train in industrial life, and sending north and east more or less well-equipped recruits for metropolitan life. This gives the town an atmosphere of change and unrest rather unusual in so small a place, and at the same time often acts as a check to schemes of permanent prosperity.

In 1880 the population of Farmville district, including Farmville town, was 3,310, of whom 1,120 were whites and 2,190 blacks; and in 1890 the population of the district was 3,684, of whom 1,246 were whites and 2,438 blacks.

The chief industries of the town are: The selling of tobacco and its storage in warehouses, which is done by stock companies composed of Negro as well as white stockholders; the manufacture of tobacco into strips, carried on by 7 white firms in 16 tobacco factories; woodworking by the Farmville Manufacturing Company; coopering by a firm; fruit canning by the South Side Canning Company; grinding of feed by the Farmville mills, and the running of 57 retail stores, etc., divided as follows: Eight clothing stores, 12 grocery stores, 4 general stores, 4 commission merchants with stocks of harness and hardware, 4 drug stores, 3 dry-goods stores, 3 meat stores, 3 millinery stores, 2 restaurants, 2 book and stationery stores, 3 hardware stores, 2 furniture and undertaking stores, 1 jewelry store, 1 confectionery and toy store, 1 stove and tinware store, 1 wagon store, 1 steam laundry, and 2 saloons.

The total valuation of the town for 1890 was $661,230—real estate $541,230, personal property $120,000—on which a total tax of $9,855 was raised, and distributed as follows: To the State $1,983, to the county $1,983, to the town $3,906, to the State school fund $661, and to the county and town school fund $1,322. In 1880 the town had a debt of $11,200, and in 1890 this had increased to $65,000.

About three-fifths of the inhabitants of Farmville, August 1, 1897, were of Negro descent, and it is with this part of the population that this study has to do. The investigator spent the months of July and August in the town; he lived with the colored people, joined in their social life, and visited their homes.[1] For the inquiry he prepared the following schedule of questions for each family and individual:

1. Number of persons in the family?
2. Relationship of this person to head of family?
3. Sex?
4. Age at nearest birthday?
5. Conjugal condition?
6. Place of birth?
7. Length of residence in Farmville?
8. Length of residence in this house?
9. Able to read?
10. Able to write?
11. Months in school during last year?
12. Usual occupations?
13. Usual wages per day, week, or month?
14. Weeks unemployed during year?
15. Mother of how many children (born living)?
16. Number of children now living?
17. Present whereabouts of such children?
18. Does the family own the home?
19. Do they own any land or houses?
20. Rent paid here per month?
21. Church attendance?

There was usually no difficulty experienced in getting the Negroes to answer these questions, so far as they could. The greatest uncertainty in the accuracy of answers was in connection with the first and fourth questions; the first on account of members of the family temporarily absent, and the fourth because in so many cases the age is unknown. Answers as to wages were of course more or less indefinite, although fairly good returns were obtained. The fifteenth question could be answered only when the mother herself was present, and then not always with sufficient accuracy. Only a few answers to this query were recorded. On the whole, the answers seem to approach the truth nearly enough to be of some considerable scientific value, although a large possible margin of error is admitted.

Age, Sex, and Birthplace of Negro Population

The total number of Negroes in Farmville who reported as to age and sex was 1,225. If 250, estimated as not reporting, be added to this number, the total in and about Farmville is found to be about 1,475. Subtracting from this total 125 who lived outside the corporation, we find that the Negro population of the corporation of Farmville was approximately 1,350 in 1897. As the corporation line, however, cuts off somewhat arbitrarily a considerable number of Negroes who really share the group life of Farmville, they have been included in the total, except when otherwise stated. Twenty-five people whose residence in Farmville was for such indefinite periods as to make their citizenship questionable have been omitted; they have families here, but themselves work mostly in the North. About 75 servants, mostly young women living in white families as servants and having no other town homes, were not interrogated at all, and consequently are not accounted for in these returns. Their number and the number of those otherwise omitted are estimated and not actually counted.

Conjugal Condition, Births, and Deaths

Relating to the conjugal condition of the Negroes of this community, it is found that of the 351 males over 15 years of age who returned answers 147, or 41.9 per cent, were single; 178, or 50.7 per cent, were married, and 14, or 4 per cent, were widowed. The remaining 12, or 3.4 per cent, were in no case regularly divorced, but were permanently separated from their wives and have been so scheduled. Of the 392 women, 126, or 32.1 per cent, were single; 178, or 45.4 per cent, were married; 76, or 19.4 per cent, were widowed, and 12, or 3.1 per cent, were permanently separated.

Comparing the conditions in Farmville with the conditions in foreign lands and in the United States, we find some very instructive indications.[2] In slavery days marriage or cohabitation was entered upon very early, and the first generation of freedmen did the same. The second generation, however, is postponing marriage largely for economic reasons, and is migrating to better its condition. Consequently we find, in a race young in civilization, that the percentage of single men over 15 would seem to be larger than in Great Britain, France, Germany, Hungary, or Italy, if the conditions in Farmville are generally true, and that the number of single women is larger than might be expected. This leads to two evils—illicit sexual intercourse and restricted influence of family life. When among any people a low inherited standard of sexual morals is coincident with an economic situation tending to prevent early marriage and to promote abnormal migrations to the irresponsibility and temptations of city life, then the inevitable result is prostitution and illegitimacy. Thus it is quite possible to see these evils increase among a people during a period when great general advance is being made. They are the evils inseparable from a transition period, and they will remain until the industrial situation becomes satisfactory, migration becomes normal, and moral standards become settled.

The records of births as kept by the county are far from complete, and therefore not to be relied upon. The birth rate among the Negroes is large, but apparently decreasing. The per cent of illegitimate births is, of course, still more difficult to determine. By careful inquiry it was ascertained that there were living in the town August 1, 1897, at least 44 illegitimate children under 10 years of age. The total number of children under 10 was 301, indicating, roughly, a rate of nearly 15 per cent of illegitimate births. Even this rate is, by universal testimony, a great improvement on conditions in the past.

The records of deaths in the town are better kept than those of births, but these, too, are probably incomplete. There were 33 deaths reported in Farmville in 1896, indicating a death rate of 13.5 per 1,000. This is too low, but the true death rate is not high. There is a large infant mortality, but otherwise the colored population seems fairly healthy. Their death rate, of course, exceeds that of the whites.

While facts bearing on miscegenation between whites and blacks are difficult to obtain and interpret, yet they are of interest. Of the 44 illegitimate children mentioned, 10 were, in all probability, children of white men; 4 of these belonged to one mother, who was openly known to be the concubine of a white man who had a white family; 2 of the children belonged to another mother, and there were four mothers each having 1 illegitimate child, making six mothers in all having such children. There is no doubt that this illicit intercourse has greatly decreased in recent years. Curiously enough, there are in the vicinity of the town two cases of intermarriage of colored men and white women, which are undisturbed, despite the law.

Some attempt was made to determine what proportion of the whole population was of mixed blood, but with only partial success. If, as is often assumed in such inquiries, all cases of intermingling were matters of a single generation, or of two, the investigation would be easier. But when a person is a descendant of people of mixed blood for four or five generations the matter becomes very difficult. A record was kept of the personal appearance of a majority of those Negroes of the town who were met by the investigator face to face. Of 705 Negroes thus met, 333 were apparently of unmixed Negro blood; 219 were brown in color and showed traces of white blood, and 153 were yellow or lighter, and showed considerable infusion of white blood. According to this, one-third to one-half the Negroes of the town are of mixed blood, and verifying this by observations on the street and in assemblies, this seemed a fair conclusion.

Occupations and Wages

The opportunities for employment in Farmville explain much as to the present condition of its Negro citizens, as, for example, the migration from country to town and from town to city, the postponement of marriage, the ownership of property, and the general relations between whites and blacks. If we divide the total colored population above 10 years of age according to the popular classification of pursuits, we have in professional occupations, 22; in domestic, 287; in commercial, 45; in agricultural, 15; in industrial, 282; not engaged in gainful occupations, 259, and not reported, 14.

Using a different classification, we have those working on their own account, 36; laboring class, 350; house service, 92; day service,

149; at home, unoccupied, and dependent, 259; professional and clerical, 24, and not reported, 14.

While the range of employment open to colored men is not large, that open to women is peculiarly restricted, so that most girls have only the choice between domestic service and housewifery. The different classes of employment are taken up in turn:

The Professions. There are no colored physicians or lawyers in the town, preachers and teachers being the only representatives of the learned professions. The position of preacher is the most influential of all positions among the Negroes, and brings the largest degree of personal respect and social prestige. The two leading preachers in the town receive, the one $480 and house rent; the other, $600 a year. Both are graduates of theological seminaries and represent the younger and more progressive element. They use good English and no scandal attaches to their private life, so far as the investigator could learn. Their influence is, on the whole, good, although they are not particularly spiritual guides, being rather social leaders or agents. Such men are slowly but surely crowding out the ignorant but picturesque and, in many particulars, impressive preacher of slavery days. Types of the latter are now to be found only in small churches, or in country districts where they care for two or three churches and receive salaries ranging from $75 to $300 a year.

The teacher stands next to the preacher in general esteem. An increasing number of these are now young women, and those in Farmville teach the schools of the surrounding country districts. The school terms are from four to six months, and in addition there is considerable private teaching done. The teachers earn from $100 to $250 a year by teaching, and sometimes they do other work during vacation.

The Extrepreneurs. The individual undertaker of business enterprise is a new figure among Negroes, and his rise deserves to be carefully watched, as it means much for the future of the race. The business enterprises in which Farmville Negroes are engaged on their own account are brickmaking, the grocery trade, barbering, restaurant keeping, furniture repairing, silversmithing and clock repairing, shoemaking, wood selling and whip making, steam laundering, contracting and building, painting, blacksmithing, wheelwrighting, hotel keeping, and farming, representing in all 32 separate enterprises conducted by 36 proprietors, and employing, besides, about 40 other persons.

The entire brickmaking business of Farmville and vicinity is in the hands of a colored man—a freedman, who bought his own and his family's freedom, purchased his master's estate, and eventually hired his master to work for him. He owns a thousand acres or more of land in Cumberland County and considerable Farmville property. In his brickyard he hires about 15 hands, mostly boys from 16 to 20 years of age, and runs five or six months a year, making from 200,000 to 300,000 brick. His men receive about $12 a month, and extra pay for extra work. Probably over one-half the brick houses in and near Farmville are built of brick made in his establishment, and he has repeatedly driven white competitors out of business.

The grocery store, as kept by the Negro, is a comparatively new venture in Farmville, and is quite successful, although most of the stores are naturally small and unpretentious affairs. There are seven grocery stores in the town conducted by Negroes. Of these, three are flourishing and do a business of from $50 to $100 a week. The three proprietors of these stores have been in business from five to eight years, are property holders, have a good common-school training, and apparently possess good business judgment. Their wives generally help in the stores, and only occasionally do they hire clerks. Two other stores are newer than these, and are doing fairly well, with prospects of better trade in future. They are kept by young men who got their capital by menial service in New York City. The proprietors of these five stores depend entirely on their business for support. The two other stores are conducted by women as side enterprises. They have only a small patronage. An eighth grocery store, not noted in the table of occupations, was started in August, 1897, during the progress of this investigation.

The barbering and restaurant businesses were the ones to which the freedmen most naturally turned after their training as house servants. On this account, they do not to-day enlist the best talent of the race, since they savor in some respect of the unpleasant past; yet they are still largely followed. The wealthiest Negro in the town is the leading barber, who is reported worth not far from $10,000. There are five barber shops altogether—three for whites and two for blacks—and all run by Negroes. This is rather too many for the trade of the town, and one at least is being forced out. The income of barbers varies largely; probably from $5 to $15 a week would be the average. There are five proprietors, and generally five assistants, who receive from $3 to $5 a week. There are two restaurants which do a good business, especially on Saturdays, with the farmers. They employ about four persons besides the proprietors. There is also a lunch business done by one of the grocery stores.

Two blacksmiths and a wheelwright do a good business, sometimes taking in from $5 to $8 a day. There are also four shoe makers and repairers and two furniture repairers. A silversmith, who is a good workman, learned his trade of his former master, and is kept busy. There are three contractors—one in painting and two in small building jobs. A colored contractor on a larger scale resides temporarily in the town, but belongs in Richmond. He is building a fine country mansion for the leading white tobacco merchant of the place.

The only stream laundry in the county is conducted by two young colored men, brothers, who also own one in Richmond. The Farmville laundry employs five or six persons besides one of the brothers and his wife. It is equipped with the latest machinery, and the proprietors own the premises. They probably do a business of $100 a week in summer.

The town jailer, a Negro, is also a wood merchant, whip maker, and farmer. He is assisted by his son, and owns, besides his farm, a pleasant home in town. The timely assistance of a son and of his former master enabled him first to become a property holder. He is now educating his younger daughters at the seminary in Lynchburg.

A new enterprise in the town is a bakery and hotel. It occupies a neat building on the main street, and is conducted by a Hampton graduate and her husband. The bakery so far is the more successful part, but the hotel feature has a chance to grow.

Farmers. Most of the Negroes have given up farming for the industrial chances of the town. Of those living in town, three—the brickmaker, the wood merchant, and one of the barbers—own large and well-conducted farms. Besides this, nearly every family has a vegetable garden, sometimes of considerable size, from which produce is sold. Many factory hands hire out as farm laborers during the spring and summer; they receive from 35 to 50 cents a day and board, or, if they work by the month, from $8 to $10.

Industries. The industries in which Negroes are employed are tobacco manufacturing, cooperage, wood working, fruit canning, feed grinding, railroading, and brickmaking.

The chief and all-absorbing industry, and the one that characterizes the town, is that of preparing tobacco strips—an industry in which Farmville ranks among the first cities of Virginia. There are in all 16 factories for this industry in the town; two firms operate 4 each; one operates 3; one 2, and three other firms 1 each. These factories are large barnlike structures of wood, 3 or 4 stories high, with many windows.

The manufacture of tobacco strips consists in ridding the dry tobacco leaf of the woody stem. The loose tobacco is taken to the factory and placed on the floor of a room in piles, according to grade, style, and quality. Enough of a certain grade to make a hogshed of strips is then taken to another room and sprinkled and steamed, a little at a time. The bundles are then ready to be stemmed, as the leaves are supple and pliant. Women and young men, assisted by children who untie the bundles and place them in position, dextrously draw out the stems, and the children tie the strips thus left into uniform bundles. The bundles are then weighed, stretched on sticks, and hung up in the drying room for from eight to twelve hours. When thoroughly dried and cooled the tobacco is again steamed as it hangs, and then cooled for two days. Finally, it is steamed a third time in a steam box, straightened, and quickly packed in hogsheads.

The women and young men who stem the tobacco get 50 cents for every hundred pounds of stemmed tobacco, and can, with the aid of children, stem from 100 to 300 pounds a day, thus earning from $2.50 to $9 a week or more, for from five to seven months in the year. Other women laborers receive 35 or 40 cents a day, while the men who prize, steam, and pack tobacco receive from 75 cents to $1 a day for eight or nine months. The better classes of women do not like to work in the factories, and the surroundings are said to be unsuitable for girls. Many children are kept from school all or part of the time to enable them to help in this factory work. An adjunct to the tobacco business is the making of hogsheads and tierces, in which colored coopers are employed. They earn from $6 to $8 a week for the major part of the year.

The "foundry," as it is called, formerly did some iron molding, but now is engaged in woodworking, chiefly the turning of plow handles. It employs ten colored and four white mechanics, and pays them from 75 cents to $1 a day, without discrimination. The feed mills employ a few Negroes, and the Norfolk and Western and Farmville and Powhatan railways have colored section hands and brakemen. The section hands receive $1 per day and the brakemen not much more. A canning establishment, which is at present canning tomatoes, employs many women and men. Women receive 2 cents a bucket for paring tomatoes, and can earn from 40 to 50 cents a day; men receive from 75 cents to $1 a day.

The Trades. Among the skilled trades Negroes are found as painters, shoemakers, cabinetmakers, coopers, blacksmiths, wheelwrights, brick masons, plasterers, carpenters, bakers, butchers, and whip makers. All of these have been alluded to before, save those in the building trades. There are 14 carpenters, 3 painters, and 3 masons who live in the town, besides several who live in the country and work in town. White and black mechanics are often seen working side by side on the same jobs, and get on without apparent friction, although there is some discrimination in wages. Colored carpenters get generally from 75 cents to $1 per day, and painters and masons not over $1. There are apparently more Negroes with trades than white men, but there is a dearth of young Negro apprentices, so that colored contractors often have to hire white mechanics.

Clerical Work. Very little clerical work of any kind is done by Negroes. There is one railway-mail clerk, who secured his position through civil-service examination. He has had one route for seven years. The wife of the laundry proprietor does his bookkeeping, and occasionally a temporary helper is needed in the colored grocery stores. Very often the colored porters in white business establishments do considerable clerical work; they are, however, paid as porters.

Common Laborers. There are 92 common laborers, including 17 porters and 3 janitors. The porters work in stores and commission houses, and are often old and trusted servants. They earn from $8 to $10 a month and board. Three laborers in the foundry receive 50 cents a day; 11 teamsters receive from 75 cents to $1 a day; the other 58 laborers do odd jobs of all sorts, work now and then on farms or in the tobacco factories, do chores about private houses, drive cows, keep gardens, etc. They receive from 30 to 75 cents a day.

Domestic Service. Twenty-two men and 65 women, among those who appear upon the schedules, and about 75 others, some of whom are residents of the town and some not, are wholly engaged in domestic service. The men receive from $8 to $10 a month. The women receive from $1 to $5, according to age and work; a general servant in an ordinary family receiving $4 a month; a nurse girl, from $1 to $3, and a cook, $5. Besides this they get good board, fair lodging, much cast-off clothing, and not a little training in matters of household economy and taste.

There is considerable dissatisfaction over the state of domestic service. The Negroes are coming to regard the work as a relic of slavery and as degrading, and only enter it from sheer necessity, and then as a temporary makeshift. Parents hate to expose their sons to the early lessons of servility, which are thus learned, and their daughters to the ever-possible fate of concubinage. Employers, on the other hand, find an increasing number of careless and impudent young people who neglect their work, and in some cases show vicious tendencies, and demoralize the children of the family. They pay low wages, partly because the Southern custom compels families, who ought to do their own work, to hire help, and they can not afford to pay much; partly, too, because they do not believe the service rendered is worth more. The servants, receiving less than they think they ought, are often careful to render as little for it as possible. They grow to despise the menial work they do, partly because their employers themselves despise it and teach their daughters to do the same.

This may not represent the open, conscious thought of the

community, but it is the unconscious tendency of the present situation, which makes one species of honorable and necessary labor difficult to buy or sell without loss of self-respect on one side or the other. One result of this situation is the wholesale emigration of the better class of servants to the North, where they can earn three and often four times the wages for less work. At the same time one curious modification of the domestic-service system is slowly taking place, which may mean much in the future, and that is the fact that Negroes themselves are beginning to hire servants. Ten families among Farmville Negroes regularly hire one servant each, and several others have a woman to help occasionally. This system is, however, very different from the hiring of Negroes by whites. The employers in this case in no respect despise common labor or menial duties, because they themselves have performed such work all their lives. Their servant, too, is a neighbor's daughter, whom they know and like and treat practically as a member of the family. Thus there grows up a system very much like that in New England or in parts of Germany to-day, where housework is honored. At the same time. the Negro employers learn to sympathize with the complaints of the whites as to inefficient servants. In this way, possibly, the one circumstance which more than all others serves to ruin domestic service in the South may be modified, namely, the making of the term "Negro" and "servant" synonymous. Even to day the economic importance of the black population of Farmville has brought many white men to say "mister" to the preacher and teacher and to raise their hats to their wives.

Day Service. Just as the field hand of slavery days developed into the metayer, so the house servant easily developed into the day worker. Thirty-three single women and 114 housewives go out regularly at day work in families or take family washing into their homes. The increased independence of the servant and the decreased responsibility of the employer make this a popular system. It is, however, poorly paid, being a subsidiary employment for most families; and in hard times, when the house servant would have to be retained, it is easy to cut off this sort of worker. Those who work in families are either paid like house servants, by the week, or if they work by the day, from 30 to 50 cents a day. Much neglect of their own household duties and of children, especially of growing girls, is a result of this absence of the mother from home. Those who take in washing receive from 50 to 75 cents for a family wash. The girls at the white normal school pay $1.25 a month each for their washing. In this way many a Farmville mother helps her husband support the family, or during dull times keeps them all above want.

The Unemployed. A considerable number of idlers and loafers shows that the industrial situation in Farmville is not altogether satisfactory and that the moral tone of the Negroes has room for great betterment. One of the principal causes of idleness is the irregular employment. A really industrious man who desires work is apt to be thrown out of employment from one-third to one-half of the year by the shutting up of the tobacco factories, the brickyard, or the cannery. If he wants to get on in the world or accumulate property, he often finds that he must seek better wages and steadier employment elsewhere; or if he can not himself go, he sends a son or a daughter. Fully one-half, if not two-thirds, of the property owned by Negroes in the town has been paid for in large part with money earned outside the town. On the other hand, if the man be of only ordinary caliber he easily lapses into the habit of working part of the year and loafing the rest. This habit is especially pernicious for half-grown boys, and leads to much evil. Undoubtedly the present situation prolongs some of the evils of the slave system, and is the cause of much of that apparent laziness and irresponsibility for which so many Negroes are justly criticised. It is also true that larger, better, and steadier industrial opportunities in a town like Farmville would in time be able to counteract the tendency of youth to emigrate, would build up a faithful and efficient laboring community, and would pay good dividends to the projectors of new enterprises. The great demand is for steady employment which is not menial, at fair wages.

The women, too, demand enlarged industrial opportunities outside of domestic service, and of a kind compatible with decency and self-respect. They are on the whole more faithful and are becoming better educated than the men, and they are capable of doing far better work than they have a chance to do. As it is they can only become servants, and if they must serve they prefer $12 a month in

New York to $4 in Farmville. This explains the growing excess of colored women over colored men in many Northern cities.

However, besides all these willing workers, or those capable of training, there is undoubtedly in Farmville the usual substratum of loafers and semicriminals who will not work. There are probably five or six regular prostitutes, who ply their trade chiefly on Saturday nights. There are also some able-bodied men who gamble, and fish, and drink. Then there are the men who work, but who spend their time and money in company with the lowest classes. These people live in a few crowded tenements, easily distinguished, and are regarded by whites and blacks as beneath notice. Occasionally serious crime is perpetrated by this class, but their depredations are generally petty and annoying rather than dangerous. During 1896, 13 Negroes were indicted for serious crimes in the whole county; 4, for housebreaking, received sentences varying from six months in jail to four years in the penitentiary; 3, for petty larceny and assault, received a few months in jail; 2, for infanticide and attempted murder, received three and eight years, respectively, in the penitentiary; 3, for highway robbery, received from five to fifteen years in the penitentiary, and 1 received ten years for horsestealing. In the town some ten years since, there was one case of lynching for rape; but it is now generally conceded that the female was a lewd character, and that the black boy was guilty of no crime.

The slum elements of Farmville are as yet small in number, but they are destined to grow with the town. They receive recruits from the lazy, shiftless, and dissolute of the country around; they send them on to Washington, Philadelphia, and Baltimore as fit candidates for the worst criminal classes of those cities. The problem of Negro crime, therefore, is best studied and solved in towns of this size.

ECONOMICS OF THE FAMILY

The question of the size of Negro families is important, but difficult to determine, on account of the varying meanings of the word "family." The economic family, i. e., those living together under conditions of family life, must obviously be the unit of a national census, but when it is used as the basis of a study of the fecundity of a certain part of the population the logic is dangerous. For this reason an attempt has been made to schedule the Negro families according to three conceptions of the word "family," viz:

1. The possible family, i. e., the parents and all children ever born to them living.

2. The real family, i. e., the parents and all children living at present.

3. The economic family, i. e., all persons, related and unrelated, living in one home under conditions of family life.

Statistics of the possible family are not complete, partly on account of the difficulty of obtaining reliable answers and partly because this question was inserted in the schedules after the canvass had begun. The answers to the other questions are fairly full.

The small number of cases makes the figures for the possible family of value only as vaguely indicating the extreme limit of Negro reproduction which the large infant mortality and the preventive check to reproduction (late marriages) keep from realization. This method of inquiry rightly pursued might make an interesting comment on Malthusianism. The size of the real family comes nearest to being a true test of the fecundity of the race under present conditions, while the economic family shows the results of the present economic conditions. The economic family in Farmville is the complement of the Negro family in a city like Philadelphia, and these two families are very often but parts of one family; for married couples going North often leave their children in Farmville, and single persons live alone in cities and are counted as families of one, etc. In this way the continual migration complicates the question of the size of Negro families. Nevertheless, when all allowances are made, there is no doubt that the average Negro family in Farmville, in Virginia, and probably throughout the country is gradually decreasing in size. This is natural and salutary, and is due to-day not so much to a large death rate—for that is a factor which has always been reckoned upon and was undoubtedly more powerful in the past than now—but to the comparatively sudden application of the preventive check to population, viz, late marriages. This view receives further confirmation if we compare various sizes of families among Farmville Negroes with the sizes of families in the whole United States and in the North Atlantic States. This comparison is shown in the following table:

PER CENT OF NEGRO FAMILIES OF FARMVILLE AND OF TOTAL FAMILIES OF THE
UNITED STATES AND OF THE NORTH ATLANTIC STATES IN EACH GROUP, BY
SIZE OF FAMILY
[The figures for Farmville are from schedules; those for the United States are
from the census of 1890]

Size of family	Negroes of Farm- ville	United States	North Atlantic States
1 member	4.96	3.63	3.23
2 to 6 members	72.90	73.33	78.05
7 to 10 members	19.47	20.97	17.00
11 members or over	2.67	2.07	1.72

The houses which the 262 Negro families of Farmville occupy vary from 1 to 9 rooms each in size, but have generally 2 or 3 rooms.

The one-room cabin is rapidly disappearing from the town. Nearly all the 17 one-room dwellings are old log cabins, although there are a few frame tenements of this size. Such houses have one or two windows, a door, and usually a stone fireplace. They are from 15 to 20 feet square. The 134 two-room homes are mostly tenements. A large cheaply built frame house is constructed so as to contain two such tenements. In such houses the kitchen, by a very sensible arrangement of the tenants, is usually upstairs and the living room on the first floor. The rooms are from 15 to 18 feet square and have two windows. The staircase in many instances is open, so that there is no way to shut off the upper room. Three-room houses are generally owned by their occupants, and are neater and more tasteful than the tenements. They are usually tiny, new frame structures, with two rooms, one above the other, at the front, and a small one-story addition, for the kitchen, in the rear. To this a small veranda is often added. Four-room houses are similar, with a room above the kitchen, or are built similar to the double tenement houses. The large houses generally follow the plan of the old

Virginia mansion, with a wide hall and rooms on either side in both stories. Few of the houses have cellars and many are poorly built. Nearly all, however, are in healthful locations, with good water near by and a garden spot.

Of the 262 families, 6.5 per cent occupied one-room homes; 51.1 per cent, two-room homes; 17.2 per cent, three-room homes; 11.8 per cent, four-room homes, and 13.4 per cent, homes of five or more rooms. On an average there were 1.61 persons to a room and 2.9 rooms to a family. There are about 240 separate houses occupied by Negroes.

Of the 262 families, 114, or 43.5 per cent, own the homes they occupy, and 148 families, or 56.5 per cent, rent. The following table shows the number of families owning and renting homes by size of dwellings:

FAMILIES OWNING AND RENTING HOMES BY NUMBER OF ROOMS TO A DWELLING

Tenure	Families occupying dwellings of—								Total families
	1 room	2 rooms	3 rooms	4 rooms	5 rooms	6 rooms	7 rooms	8 or 9 rooms	
Owners	3	25	31	22	18	8	3	4	114
Renters	14	109	14	9	1			1	148
Total families	17	134	45	31	19	8	3	5	262

Of these 148 tenants, 15 rent from Negroes and 133 from whites. Several of the tenants own land.

The total annual income of the 262 families is naturally very difficult to fix with accuracy. Written accounts are seldom kept, and many families could not answer if they would. However, wages do not vary much in the town, and by taking into account the usual wages received, the months employed during the year, the total wage earners in the family, and the general style of living, the accompanying estimate has been made, which seems to give a fair indication of the truth, although the possibility of error is considerable.

Such figures are better understood when they are read in con-

NUMBER OF FAMILIES, BY SIZE OF FAMILY AND ANNUAL INCOME

Annual Income	Families of—									Total families
	1 member	2 members	3 members	4 members	5 members	6 members	7 members	8 members	9 to 11 members	
$50 or less	3		1		1					5
$50 to $75	5	4	1	1						11
$75 to $100	1	6		3		1				11
$100 to $150	1	7	6		2	2	1			19
$150 to $200		8	4	5	4	3	3	2		29
$200 to $250	1	14	5	9	3	4	2		2	40
$250 to $350		10	7	12	5	7	6	1	5	53
$350 to $500		1	7	13	7	1	4	5	6	44
$500 to $750		2	1	3	6	7	3	8	5	35
$750 or over					1				5	6
Not reported	2		2	2	2	1				9
Total families	13	52	34	48	31	26	19	16	23	262

nection with figures as to the cost and scale of living in the community.

In this connection the following budgets, estimated by the three leading colored grocers of Farmville, are given. The budgets relate to the yearly incomes and expenditures of three families, each consisting of 5 persons.

These budgets are not the actual written accounts of particular families, because it is difficult in an unlettered community to obtain such accounts, but are based, as mentioned above, on the estimates of the three leading colored grocers, and represent the accounts of various families who trade at their stores. As such they possess considerable value. In the light of these budgets, and from actual observation, the investigator has concluded that of the 262 families, about 29 live in poverty with less than suffices for ordinary comfort, 128 are in moderate circumstances, 63 are comfortable, and 42 well-to-do according to the standard of the town.

With fairly steady employment, and perhaps the aid of a grown

ESTIMATED ANNUAL INCOME AND EXPENDITURE OF FAMILY OF 5 PERSONS IN
MODERATE CIRCUMSTANCES

Income		Expenditure	
Items	Amount	Items	Amount
Head of family:		Food per week: 1 bag flour, 35	
24 weeks labor in tobacco fac-		cents; 3 pounds meat, 25 cents;	
tory, at 75 cents per day	$108.00	3 pounds sugar, 18 cents; 1	
16 weeks laobr on farm, at 40		pound coffee, 15 cents; 3	
cents per day	38.40	pounds lard, 25 cents; soap,	
Housewife:		etc., 8 cents; starch, 8 cents;	
50 weeks labor on three family		milk, butter, eggs, and vege-	
washings, at $1.50 per week	75.00	tables, 30 cents. 52 weeks, at	
		$1.64 per week	$85.28
		Fuel and lighting: 1 load of wood	
		per week for 20 weeks and	
		1 1/2 loads per week for 32	
		weeks, at 40 cents per load,	
		$27.20; oil, etc., 52 weeks, at	
		10 cents per week, $5.20	32.40
		Clothing	50.00
		Rent	36.00
		Miscellaneous	15.00
		Total	218.68
		Surplus	2.72
Total	221.40	Total	221.40

son or daughter, an ordinary colored family finds it possible to buy a
lot for from $50 to $100, and build a three-room house thereon at a
cost of from $300 to $500. A building association composed of both
colored and white shareholders, but largely conducted by the whites,
has greatly facilitated the buying of property by Negroes. Ex-masters
and white friends also have often helped. On the other hand, there
have been flagrant cases of cheating the ignorant freedmen, and
sometimes of making them pay twice for the same land.

ESTIMATED ANNUAL INCOME AND EXPENDITURE OF FAMILY OF 5 PERSONS
IN POOR CIRCUMSTANCES

Income		Expenditure	
Items	Amount	Items	Amount
Head of family:		Food, 52 weeks, at $1.50 to $2	
24 weeks of common labor, at		per week	$91.00
50 cents per day	$72.00	Fuel and lighting, 52 weeks, at	
Odd jobs	30.00	40 cents to 50 cents per week	23.40
Housewife:		Clothing: 1 suit, 2 pairs of pants,	
20 weeks' work in canning fac-		and 2 pairs of shoes, for man,	
tory, at 40 cents per day	48.00	$12; clothes for woman, $9;	
Boy:		clothes for children, $4.	25.00
12 months in service, at $2 per		Rent	24.00
month	24.00	Miscellaneous	10.00
		Total	173.40
		Surplus	.60
Total	174.00	Total	174.00

ESTIMATED ANNUAL INCOME AND EXPENDITURE OF FAMILY OF 5 PERSONS
OWNING HOME AND IN MODERATE CIRCUMSTANCES

Income		Expenditure	
Items	Amount	Items	Amount
Head of family:		Food per week: Flour, 30 cents;	
32 weeks' work as carpenter, at		meal, 12 cents; sugar, 12	
75 cents per day	$144.00	cents; coffee, 15 cents; lard,	
Housewife and boy:		16 cents; meat, 50 cents; soap,	
20 weeks' work as stemmers in		5 cents; butter, 10 cents; mis-	
tobacco factory, at $7 per		cellaneous, 50 cents, 52	
week	140.00	weeks, at $2 to $2.50 per week	$117.00
		Fuel	30.00
		Clothing	60.00
		Taxes	8.00
		Miscellaneous	30.00
		Total	245.00
		Surplus	39.00
Total	284.00	Total	284.00

A SIDE LIGHT: ISRAEL HILL

By the will of John Randolph, of Roanoke, his slaves were emancipated at his death in 1833. By a similar act on the part of another member of the Randolph family a number of slaves were emancipated and given a tract of land in the district of Farmville called Israel Hill, and situated about 2 miles west of the town. The descendants of these slaves still live here, and their peculiar situation together with the smallness of this farming community makes a brief study of its conditions valuable for the light it throws on Farmville conditions.

In this community many disturbing factors in Negro development are eliminated. Race antagonism is in its lowest terms, because there is but one white family near the community. The land question is partly settled, because nearly all the farmers own their land. One economic problem, however, remains unsettled, and that is the problem of sufficient paying employment for men and women. This economic demand, and its attempted settlement by wholesale emigration to a neighboring industrial center, receives curious illustration in the case of Israel Hill and Farmville.

August 1, 1897, Israel Hill had a population of 123 inhabitants. The numbers are too small to warrant positive conclusions, and yet it is noticeable what a gap the emigration of the young men and women has left. Only a fourth of the total population reporting as to age are between the ages of 20 and 50, although under normal conditions this part of a community is about 40 per cent of the whole.

The economic stress is also exemplified in the conjugal condition of the group. Only one person under 30 years of age of those reporting is married. Of all the men reporting who were above 20 years of age, two-fifths are bachelors, and of the women 4 out of 26 are unmarried.

Some newcomers have disturbed the calm of this sleepy village. Of the 98 inhabitants of Israel Hill who reported their place of birth, 57 persons, or 58 per cent, were born in the settlement, 11 persons were born in Prince Edward County outside of Israel Hill, and all of the others, except 1 born in Kentucky, were born in adjoining counties.

Those who have come from elsewhere have generally come through marriage. Twenty-five did not report their birthplaces.

Of the 25 families 22 own their homes. The other 3 rent of colored landlords, and 1 of the renters owns land. The holdings of land vary from 4.5 to 35.5 acres, and the farms and buildings are assessed at sums ranging from $40 to $300, the total assessed value of the community's real estate being about $2,500 or $3,000.

Seven of the 25 families live in one-room log cabins; 9 live in two-room log cabins, i. e., cabins with a lower room and a loft for sleeping purposes; 3 live in neat three-room frame houses, and 6 live in houses of four rooms or more. The average size of the families is 4.9 members. The real family, i. e., parents and all living children, is much larger than this. There are 13 families of five or more members, 4 of four members, 2 of three, 5 of two, and 1 of one member. There are about 2 persons to a room and 2.5 rooms to a family.

On the whole, this little hamlet presents two pictures in strange juxtaposition—one of discouragement, stagnation, and retrogression, the other of enterprise and quiet comfort. The key to the situation is the migration of the youth. Where a prospect of profitable employment has kept them at home the community has correspondingly prospered; but where they have been compelled, or thought themselves compelled, to seek work elsewhere and have left the farm and the old folks and children and gone to Farmville or farther their homes have fallen generally into decay.

GROUP LIFE

The Negroes of Farmville, Israel Hill, and the neighboring county districts form a closed and in many respects an independent group life. They live largely in neighborhoods with one another, they have their own churches and organizations and their own social life, they read their own books and papers, and their group life touches that of the white people only in economic matters. Even here the strong influence of group attraction is being felt, and Negroes are beginning to patronize either business enterprises conducted by themselves or those conducted in a manner to attract their trade. Thus, instead of the complete economic dependence of blacks upon whites, we see growing a nicely adjusted economic interdependence of the two races, which promises much in the way of mutual forbearance and understanding.

The most highly developed and characteristic expression of Negro group life in this town, as throughout the Union, is the Negro church. The church is, among American Negroes, the primitive social group of the slaves on American soil, replacing the tribal life roughly disorganized by the slave ship, and in many respects antedating the establishment of the Negro monogamic home. The church is much more than a religious organization; it is the chief organ of social and intellectual intercourse. As such it naturally finds the free democratic organizations of the Baptists and Methodists better suited to its purpose than the stricter bonds of the Presbyterians or the more aristocratic and ceremonious Episcopalians. Of the 262 families of Farmville, only 1 is Episcopalian and 3 are Presbyterian; of the rest, 26 are Methodist and 218 Baptist. In the town of Farmville there are 3 colored church edifices, and in the surrounding country there are 3 or 4 others.

The chief and overshadowing organization is the First Baptist Church of Farmville. It owns a large brick edifice on Main street. The auditorium, which seats about 500 people, is tastefully finished in light wood with carpet, small organ, and stained glass windows. Beneath this is a large assembly room with benches. This building is really the central clubhouse of the community, and in greater degree than is true of the country church in New England or the West. Various organizations meet here, entertainments and lectures take place here, the church collects and distributes considerable sums of money, and the whole social life of the town centers here. The unifying and directing force is, however, religious exercises of some sort. The result of this is not so much that recreation and social life have become stiff and austere, but rather that religious exercises have acquired a free and easy expression and in some respects serve as amusement-giving agencies. For instance, the camp meeting is simply a picnic, with incidental sermon and singing; the rally of country churches, called the "big meeting," is the occasion of the pleasantest social intercourse, with a free barbecue; the Sunday-school convention and the various preachers' conventions are occasions of reunions and festivities. Even the weekly Sunday service serves as a pleasant meeting and greeting place for working people who find little time for visiting during the week.

From such facts, however, one must not hastily form the conclusion that the religion of such churches is hollow or their spiritual influence bad. While under present circumstances the Negro church can not be simply a spiritual agency, but must also be a social, intellectual, and economic center, it nevertheless is a spiritual center of wide influence; and in Farmville its influence carries nothing immoral or baneful. The sermons are apt to be fervent repetitions of an orthodox Calvinism, in which, however, hell has lost something of its terrors through endless repetition; and joined to this is advice directed against the grosser excesses of drunkenness, gambling, and other forms disguised under the general term "pleasure" and against the anti-social peccadillos of gossip, "meanness," and undue pride of position. Very often a distinctly selfish tone inculcating something very like sordid greed and covetousness is, perhaps unconsciously, used; on the other hand, kindliness, charity, and sacrifice are often taught. In the midst of all, the most determined, energetic, and searching means are taken to keep up and increase the membership of the church, and "revivals," long-continued and loud, although looked upon by most of the community as necessary evils, are annually instituted in the August vacation time. Revivals in Farmville have few of the wild scenes of excitement which used to be the rule; some excitement and screaming, however, are encouraged, and as a result nearly all the youth are "converted" before they are of age. Certainly such crude conversions and the joining of the church are far better than no efforts to curb and guide the young.

The Methodist church, with a small membership, is the second social center of Farmville, and there is also a second Baptist church, of a little lower grade, with more habitual noise and shouting.

Next to the churches in importance come the secret and beneficial organizations, which are of considerable influence. Their real function is to provide a fund for relief in cases of sickness and for funeral expenses. The burden which would otherwise fall on one person or family is, by small, regular contributions, made to fall on the group. This business feature is then made attractive by a ritual, ceremonies, officers, often a regalia, and various social features. On the whole, the societies have been peculiarly successful when we remember that they are conducted wholly by people whose greatest weakness is lack of training in business methods.

The oldest society is one composed of 40 or 50 women—the Benevolent Society—which has been in existence in Farmville for over twenty years. There is a local lodge of Odd Fellows with about 35 members, which owns a hall. The Randolph Lodge of Masons has 25 members, and holds its sessions in a hired hall, together with the Good Samaritans, a semireligious secret order, with 25 local members. One of the most remarkable orders is that of the True Reformers, which has headquarters in Richmond, conducts a bank there, and has real estate all over Virginia. There are two "fountains" of this order in Farmville, with perhaps 50 members in all.

There have lately been some interesting attempts at cooperative industrial enterprises, and some capital was collected. Nothing tangible has, however, as yet resulted.

There is a genial and pleasant social life maintained among the Farmville Negroes, clustering chiefly about the churches. Three pretty distinctly differentiated social classes appear. The highest class is composed of farmers, teachers, grocers, and artisans, who own their own homes, and do not usually go out to domestic service; the majority of them can read and write, and many of the younger ones have been away to school. The investigator met this class in several of their social gatherings; once at a supper given by one of the grocers. The host was a young man in the thirties, with good common school training. There were eight in his family—a mother-in-law, wife, five children, and himself. The house, a neat two-story frame, with 6 or 8 rooms, was on Main street, and was recently purchased of white people at a cost of about $1,500. There was a flower and vegetable garden, cow and pigs, etc. The party consisted of a mail clerk and his wife; a barber's wife, the widowed daughter of the wood merchant; a young man, an employee in a tobacco factory, and his wife, who had been in service in Connecticut; a middle aged woman, graduate of Hampton, and others. After a preliminary chat, the company assembled in a back dining room. The host and hostess did not seat themselves, but served the company with chicken, ham, potatoes, corn, bread and butter, cake, and ice cream. Afterwards the company went to the parlor and talked, and sang—mostly hymns—by the aid of a little organ, which the widow played. At another time there was a country picnic on a farm 20 miles from town. The company started early and arrived at 10 o'clock on a fine old Virginia plantation, with manor house, trees, and lawn. The time was passed in playing croquet, tossing the bean bag, dancing, and lunching.

Again, a considerable company was invited to a farm house about a mile from town, near Israel Hill, where an evening was passed in eating and dancing.[3] Often the brickmaker opened his hospitable door and entertained with loaded tables and games of various sorts.

Among this class of people the investigator failed to notice a single instance of any action not indicating a thoroughly good moral tone. Thee was no drinking, no lewdness, no questionable conversation, nor was there any one in any of the assemblies against whose character there was any well-founded accusation. The circle was, to be sure, rather small, and there was a scarcity of young men. It was particularly noticeable that three families in the town, who, by reason of their incomes and education would have naturally moved in the best circle, were rigidly excluded. In two of these there were illegitimate children, and in the third a wayward wife. Of the Farmville families about 4—possibly fewer—belonged to this highest class.

Leaving the middle class for a moment, let us turn to the Farmville slums. There are three pretty well-defined slum districts— one near the railroad, one on South street, and one near the race track. In all, there would appear to be about 45 or 50 families of Negroes who are below the line of ordinary respectability, living in loose sexual relationship, responsible for most of the illegitimate children, chief supporters of the two liquor shops, and furnishing a half-dozen street walkers and numerous gamblers and rowdies. It is the emigration of this class of people to the larger cities that has recently brought to notice the large number of Negro criminals and the development of a distinct criminal class among them. Probably no people suffer more from the depredations of this class than the mass of colored people themselves, and none are less protected against them, because the careless observer overlooks patent social differences and attributes to the race excesses indulged in by a distinctly differentiated class. These slum elements are not particularly vicious and quarrelsome, but rather shiftless and debauched. Laziness and promiscuous sexual intercourse are their besetting sins. Considerable whisky and cider are consumed, but there is not much open drunkenness. Undoubtedly this class severely taxes the patience of the public authorities of the town.

The remaining 170 or more families, the great mass of the population, belong to a class between the two already described, with tendencies distinctly toward the better class rather than toward the worse. This class is composed of working people, domestic servants, factory hands, porters, and the like; they are a happy minded, sympathetic people, teachable and faithful; at the same time they are not generally very energetic or resourceful, and, as a natural result of long repression, lack "push." They have but recently become used to responsibility, and their moral standards have not yet acquired that fixed character and superhuman sanction necessary in a new people. Here and there their daughters have fallen before temptation, or their sons contracted slothful or vicious habits. However, the effort to maintain and raise the moral standard is sincere and continuous. No black woman can to-day, in the town of Farmville, be concubine to a white man without losing all social position—a vast revolution in twenty years; no black girl of the town can have an illegitimate child without being shut off from the best class of poeple and looked at askance by ordinary folks. Usually such girls find it pleasanter to go North and work at service, leaving their children with their mothers.

Finally, it remains to be noted that the whole group life of Farmville Negroes is pervaded by a peculiar hopefulness on the part of the people themselves. No one of them doubts in the least but that one day black people will have all rights they are now striving for, and that the Negro will be recognized among the earth's great peoples. Perhaps this simple faith is, of all products of emancipation, the one of the greatest social and economic value.

CONCLUSION

A study of a community like Farmville brings to light facts favorable and unfavorable, and conditions good, bad, and indifferent. Just how the whole should be interpreted is perhaps doubtful. One thing, however, is clear, and that is the growing differentiation of classes among Negroes, even in small communities. This most natural and encouraging result of 30 years' development has not yet been sufficiently impressed upon general students of the subject, and leads to endless contradiction and confusion. For instance, a visitor might tell us that the Negroes of Farmville are idle, unreliable, careless with their earnings, and lewd; another visitor, a month later, might say that Farmville Negroes are industrious, owners of property, and slowly but steadily advancing in education and morals. These apparently contradictory statements made continually of Negro groups all over the land are both true to a degree, and become mischievous and misleading only when stated without reservation as true of a whole community, when they are in reality true only of certain classes in the community. The question then becomes, not whether the Negro is lazy and criminal, or industrious and ambitious, but rather what, in a given community, is the proportion of lazy to industrious Negroes, of paupers to property holders, and what is the tendency of development in these classes. Bearing this in mind, it seems fair to conclude, after an impartial study of Farmville conditions, that the industrious and property accumulating class of the Negro citizens best represents, on the whole, the general tendencies of the group. At the same time, the mass of sloth and immorality is still large and threatening.

How far Farmville conditions are true elsewhere in Virginia the present investigator has no means of determining. He sought by inquiry and general study to choose a town which should in large degree typify the condition of the Virginia Negro to-day. How far Farmville fulfills this wish can only be determined by further study.

III

BLACK CULTURE AND CREATIVITY

In the selections included in this section, Du Bois describes some of
the forms of social organization which especially give rise to affective
and creative aspects of social interaction. In the first selection,
excerpted from *The Negro American Family* (1908), Du Bois notes
the great internal differentiation of social conditions among Negro
Americans with regard to most forms of organization. To illustrate
the differentiation with regard to family structure and activities, the
essay contains sections on Negro country families, the social life of
the country, and a study of five select homes representing mostly the
upper class of Negroes.

In the next essay, "The Religion of the American Negro" (1900),
Du Bois points out that the black church was the first social
institution which the Negro created after arriving in America; it
antecedes the Afro-American family by many decades. The church
remains as the center of Negro life, and in it one sees "in microcosm,
all that great world from which the Negro is cut off by color
prejudice and social condition." The church is "the most characteristic expression of African character," being a continuation of the
slave church which invented and integrated sociocultural com-
ponents: the preacher, the music, and the "frenzy."

In the third essay, "The Problem of Amusement" (1897), Du Bois
calls attention to a "phase of development in the organized life of
American Negroes which has hitherto received scant notice ... the
question of the amusements of Negroes." Specifically, he discusses
the dominance of the church in organizing recreation, the negative
attitude toward amusements that are outside of the church, and the

197

growing demand, especially among young adults, for increased amusements. His answer to a rhetorical question about the legitimacy of amusements outside of the Church deserves repetition: "for what is true amusement, true diversion, but the recreation of energy which we may sacrifice to noble ends, to higher ideals, while without proper amusements we waste or dissipate our mightiest powers."

In the fourth essay, "The Conservation of Races" (1897), which is here excerpted, Du Bois calls for racial solidarity and its attendant creativity. Elsewhere he had defined race as "a vast family of human beings, generally of common blood and language, always of common history, traditions, and impulses, who are both voluntarily and involuntarily striving together for the accomplishment of certain more or less vividly conceived ideals of life." He identified eight distinct major racial groups, including the Negro of Africa and America, but he emphasized that the real distinction between races is not physical, but is something to be discovered in their "cohesiveness and continuity." In this essay, Du Bois points to the unique and substantial contributions which black Americans have already made to American culture and says that their potential contribution to civilization would be realized if there were continued black solidarity and resistance to assimilation into Anglo-Saxon culture. Solidarity and creativity necessitate the cooperation of all black organizations—schools, newspapers, and businesses—and artists, and "an intellectual clearing house, for all these products of the Negro mind, which we may call a Negro Academy."

10

THE NEGRO AMERICAN FAMILY

MARRIAGE

The Scope of this Study

This essay is an attempt to study the family among Negro-Americans—its formation, its home, its economic organization and its daily life. Such a study is at once faced by a lamentable dearth of material. There is comparatively little exact information on many important points. Nevertheless there is perhaps enough to give a tentative outline which more exact research may later fill in. In each case an attempt has been made to connect present conditions with the African past. This is not because Negro-Americans are Africans, or can trace an unbroken social history from Africa, but because there is a distinct nexus between Africa and America which, though broken and perverted, is nevertheless not to be neglected by the careful student. It is, however, exceedingly difficult and puzzling to know just where to find the broken thread of African and American social history. Accurate scientific inquiry must trace the social history in the seventeenth and eighteenth centuries of such Negro tribes as furnished material for the American slave trade. This inquiry is unfortunately impossible. We do not know accurately which tribes are represented in America, and we have but chance pictures of Negro social conditions in those times. Assuming, however, that the condition of Negro tribes in the nineteenth century reflected much of their earlier conditions, and that central and west Africa furnished most of the slaves, some attempt has been made to picture in broad outline the social evolution of the Negro in his family relations. For past American conditions the chief printed

Abridged from *The Negro American Family*, Atlanta University Publications (1909; New York: Arno Press, 1968), pp. 9–10; 127–152. Reprinted with permission of Trevor Arnett Library, Atlanta University.

sources of information must be sought for in the vast literature of slavery. It is difficult to get a clear picture of the family relations of slaves, between the Southern apologist and his picture of cabin life, with idyllic devotion and careless toil, and that of the abolitionist with his tale of family disruption and cruelty, adultery and il-legitimate mulattoes. Between these pictures the student must steer carefully to find a reasonable statement of the average truth.

For present conditions there are, in printed sources, only the Census reports, the eight studies of the United States Bureau of Labor, the previous studies of this series, and a few other sources noted in the bibliography. To supplement this, sixteen students of the college department of Atlanta University have made a study of 32 families. These studies are based on first-hand knowledge, and are unusually accurate. They do not, however, represent properly the proportion of different types among the mass of Negroes. Most of the families studied belong to the upper half of the black population. Finally, to repeat, this study is but a sketch with no pretense toward attempting to exhaust a fruitful subject. The main cause of its limitation is lack of material.

THE FAMILY GROUP

Differentiation of Classes

Few modern groups show a greater internal differentiation of social conditions than the Negro American, and the failure to realize this is the cause of much confusion. In looking for differentiation from the past in Africa and slavery, few persons realize that this involves extreme differentiation in the present. The forward movement of a social group is not the compact march of an army, where the distance covered is practically the same for all, but is rather the strag-gling of a crowd, where some of whom hasten, some linger, some turn back; some reach far-off goals before others even start, and yet the crowd moves on. The measure of the advancement of such a throng is a question at once nice and indefinite. Measured by the rear guard there may be no perceptible advance. Measured by the advance guard the transformation may be miraculous. Yet neither of these are reasonable measurements, but rather the point which one might call the center of gravity of the mass is the true measuring point, and the determination of this point in the absence of exact measurements may be for a long time a matter of opinion rather than proof. So with the Negro American. It is easy to prove the degradation of thousands of Negroes on the back plantations of Mississippi and the alleys of Washington; it is just as easy to prove the accomplishments of the graduates of Atlanta University, or the members of St. Thomas Church, Philadelphia. The point is where, between these manifest extremes, lies today the cultural center of gravity of the race. It is begging and obscuring this question to harp on ignorance and crime among Negroes as though these were unexpected; or to laud exceptional accomplishments as though it was typical. The real crucial question is: What point has the mass of the race reached which can be justly looked upon as the average accomplishment of the group?

The exact location of this point is impossible to locate beyond doubt. Yet certain facts about it are certain: it is moving forward rapidly; this is proven by the decrease of illiteracy and the increase of property holding, both on such a scale, covering so long a period of years as to be incontrovertible evidence.

The Negro Families of Dougherty County, Georgia

The plantations of Dougherty in slavery days were not so imposing as those of Virginia. The Big House was smaller and one-storied, and the slave cabins set closer to it. Today the laborers' cabins are in form and disposition the same as in slavery days. They are sprinkled in little groups all over the land clustering about some dilapidated Big House where the head-tenant or agent lives. Out of fifteen hundred homes of Negroes only fifteen have five or more rooms; the mass live in one or two-room homes. The one-room cabin is painfully frequent—now standing in the shadow of the Big House, now staring at the dusty road, now rising dark and sombre amid the green of the cotton-fields. Rough-boarded, old and bare, it is neither plastered nor ceiled, and light and ventilation comes from the single door and perhaps a square hole in the wall. Within is a fireplace, black and smoky, unsteady with age; a bed or two, high, dark and fat; a table, a wooden chest and chairs or stools. On the wall is a stray showbill or a newspaper for decoration.

It is not simply in the tenement abominations of cities like New

York that the world's flesh is crowded and jammed together, sometimes twenty-two persons to every ten rooms; here in Dougherty county there are often over twenty-five persons to every ten rooms of house accommodation. To be sure, the rooms are large—fifteen to twenty-five feet square. And there is the fresh air and sunshine of all outdoors to take refuge in. Still I met one family of eleven eating and sleeping in one room, and thirty families of eight or more. Why should there be such wretched tenements in the Black Belt? Timber is rotting in the forest, land is running to waste and labor is literally cheaper than dirt. Over nine-tenths of the cabins belong to the landlords yet nearly all of them let the quarters stand and rot in rude carelessness. Why? First, because long custom born in slavery days, has assigned this sort of house to Negroes. If the landlord should hire white men he would not hesitate to erect cosy three-room cottages such as cluster around the Carolina cotton-mills. Small wonder that the substitution of white for Negro labor is often profitable, since the white being better paid and better cared for often responds by doing better work. Again, the Negroes themselves, as a mass, do not demand better homes; those who do, buy land and build their own homes, roomy and neat. But the rest can scarcely demand what they have seldom thought of. As their fathers lived so they live, and the standard of the slave still lowers the standard of the quasi-freeman. In the third place, the landlords fail to see that in an increasingly large number of cases it would be a distinctly good investment to raise the standard of living among the black laborers; that a man who demands three rooms and fifty cents a day may in the end be much cheaper than a listless, discouraged toiler herding in one room at thirty cents a day. Lastly, amid such conditions of life there is little to inspire the laborer to become a better farmer. If he is ambitious, he moves to town or tries other kinds of labor; as a tenant-farmer his outlook in the majority of cases is hopeless, and following it as a makeshift or in grim necessity, he takes its returns in shelter, meat and bread, without query or protest.

That we may see more clearly the working out of these social forces, let us look within the home and scan more nearly the family that lives there. The families are large and small: you will find many families with hosts of babies, and many young couples, but few families with half-grown boys and girls. The whole tendency of the labor system is to separate the family group—the house is too small for them, the young people go to town or hire out on a neighboring farm. Thus single, lone persons are left here and there. Away down at the edge of the woods will live some grizzle-haired black man, digging wearily in the earth for his last crust; or a swarthy fat auntie, supported in comfort by an absent daughter, or an old couple living half by charity and half by odd jobs.

The boys and girls cannot afford to marry early, nor until most of the men are over twenty-five and the girls over twenty. There is little or no actual prostitution among these people and most of the families are honest, decent people, with a fairly good standard of family morals. Nevertheless the influence of the past is plain in customs of easy marriage and easy separation. In the old days Sam "took up" with Mary by leave of his master. No ceremony was necessary, and in the busy life of the great plantations of the Black Belt it was usually dispensed with. If the master needed Sam on another plantation, or was minded to sell him, Sam's married life with Mary was unceremoniously ended, and just as unceremoniously begun with Jane or Matilda elsewhere.

This widespread custom of two centuries has not disappeared in forty years. Between three and four per cent of the families are today separated, others have been and are remarried usually without the trouble of a divorce, while others will separate in the future. Here is the plague spot of the Negro's social relations, and when this inherited low standard of family life happens to be in the keeping of lustful whites, as it sometimes is, the result is bad indeed.

The Social Life of the Country

A sketch of the social life of Negroes in the rural districts of the South is almost like an essay on the snakes in Ireland: it is the lack of social life that tends to depopulate the rural black belt and does draw off its best blood.

There are, however, many occasions of meeting and intercourse which may be set down thus in the order of their importance.

1. *The Saturday Visit to Town.* Practically throughout the rural South the black laborers and farmers come to town on Saturday.

This is more than an occasion of marketing; it is a time of holiday, and is spent in chatting and loafing, with some liquor drinking. To thousands this forms the one glimpse of the larger world, and the merchants of many towns, indeed the towns themselves depend on the weekly pilgrimage. It reduces the working week of the rural South practically to five days save in very busy times.

2. *The Sunday Church Service.* The Negro Church is the only social institution of the Negroes which started in the African forest and survived slavery; under the leadership of priest or medicine-man, afterward the Christian pastor, the Church preserved in itself the remnants of African tribal life and became after emancipation the center of Negro social life. So that today the Negro population of the United States is virtually divided into church congregations which are the real units of race life. The typical Negro country church stands at some cross-roads and holds services once or twice a month. These meetings are great reunions and are the occasions of feasting, country gossip and preaching. The people gather from 9 a. m. to 1 p. m., and remain usually till late in the afternoon. Christenings and baptizing takes place at this time.

3. *"The Christmas."* The week between Christmas and New Year's, including both days, is the great time of social rejoicing among country Negroes. Historically it was the time when the master gave his slaves time and license. Today it is the time when the serf receives his annual accounting with his landlord and collects his small balance due in cash. This he often spends in carousing and drinking, to pay for the hard year's work. Many honest, hard-working sober men get drunk religiously and regularly every Christmas. There are always many parties, church entertainments and excursions, together with fights and quarrels.

Later years have of course brought improvement. A resident of New Orleans writes: "Possibly there is less idleness at Christmas in Louisiana at present than formerly. My impression is that the influence of our better ministers and graduates or students from our higher institutions of learning is gradually modifying the character of the festivities and conduct of the people at the Christmas season."

4. *The "Frolic."* The occasional party given at the cabin is often

called "the frolic"; it varies all the way from a pleasant little gathering with games and feasting as portrayed by Dunbar, to a scene of wild drinking and debauchery as is often the case in lumber camps.

5. *The Wedding and the Funeral.* The only distinctly family festivity is the wedding. This is celebrated with varying emphasis, being a ceremony only a generation old in the country districts. In the newer Southwest it seems to be more of a general occasion of rejoicing. A correspondent says:

> The two things that interrupt our community life more than anything else in the way of home duties are the weddings and funerals, both of which seem to give the people more actual happiness and joy than anything they enter into during the whole year, but I suppose these hardly come under the head of social life. We have in our community a good many of the quiltings which appeal to the hearts of the women and during the winter is our regular form of festivities for them. This is an all-day affair with a luncheon served at midday, and sometimes we hear of as many as three or four in a single week.

6. *The Revival.* Connected with the church services comes the revival. This is a recruiting of church membership, and usually takes place in the fall after the crops are "laid by." It consists of protracted nightly meetings and brings together large numbers.

7. *School-closing.* Where the country schools are good and regular, as in Texas, there is considerable social life connected with the closing of schools; often there are examinations on this day with a free spread and an "exhibition" at night which attract large numbers.

8. *The Circus*, which visits the county-seat once or twice a year, is largely attended. So much so that such exhibitions are taxed as high as $500 for each county.

9. *Secret Societies.* In parts of Virginia and Georgia and some other States the benevolent societies, with their halls, are fast becoming the chief centers of the rural Negroes' social life. The annual installations of officers are the great social events of the year.

10. *Miscellaneous.* Besides the occasions mentioned there are summer excursions by train which take those who can get to town,

the Methodist Conference and Baptist Convention which attract many to town, and a very few annual holidays like Emancipation Day, January 1st, which is often celebrated by a speech from some visiting celebrity. There are also some local celebrations, like those due to the influence of the Catholic Mardi Gras in Louisiana.

A STUDY OF FIVE FAMILIES

To illustrate this emergence of better classes, a careful description of [five] Negro families follows. Number one represents one of the lowest type of a country family, number [two] a common type of a country family, and number three a common type of city family. The other [two] are of the higher types of Negro families. The incomes are given by the families themselves and are probably exaggerated in some cases.

No. 1. *A country family living in two rooms, with an income of $700 per year.* The whole family is very ignorant and consists of twelve members. None have had the advantage of school. A few of the younger children can write their names. No books or papers can be seen in the house.

The parents are religious fanatics; they believe in praying night and morning. The father can be heard praying on a still night for two miles. The elder boys are rough characters. They get drunk and fight, especially at church. The older girls are not wholesome characters; the two eldest have had illegitimate children, one by a white man and the other by a Negro; both children were given to relatives. The entire family is given to petty thefts, and is especially high-tempered. They do not get along with the neighbors, but tattle and tell lies and carry news to white people and Negroes.

The family consists of father, age 62 years; mother, age 61 years; six sons, ages respectively 28, 26, 22, 20, 14, and 11 years; and four daughters, ages respectively 24, 18, 16 and 8 years.

The entire family work in the field. The mother and one of the daughters leave each day in time to cook dinner. They work from sunrise or earlier until twelve, and from one until dark. The heavy farming work is done by the men and boys, the light work by the girls. The girls work from February to August and from September to December. The men and boys work the year round. When there is no work to be done on the farm, they have to report to the landlord for something to do. When it rains the bell taps and all must report at the barns to see what "Cap" wants done. For this kind of service they get no pay. The house is near the pasture and is partly surrounded with woods. The landlord's house is 300 yards away. The yard is very small, with weeds growing in the summertime into the window on the back side. The water is brought from a spring in the pasture. The house is dirty within. The bed-clothes are dingy and the doors are black with dirt. They have no bathing facilities. All bathe in a washpan, about three-quarts size, once a week. A peculiar odor is prevalent in spring and summer. They dress in gaudy colors. Their clothes are fairly good, but not well made and do not fit properly. In fact, they do not know how to wear what they have and are very hard on clothes. Only a low class of people visit them. Any decent person visiting there is branded as bad. Four of the family are members of the Baptist church. The two older daughters are members but were expelled on account of conduct. The only property is one buggy, an organ and twenty-five chickens.

Both sides are of African descent. They are very black, and it is said that their forefathers were all similarly high-tempered and immoral. Both sides of the family were in slavery, and after the war were held in peonage twenty-two years. They are much different from other colored people around in the structure of head and mouth, and in general appearance. They have three meals: breakfast before sunrise, of biscuits, pork, syrup and coffee; dinner at noon, of cornbread, syrup and pork; supper after dark, of cornbread or biscuits, and syrup. The table is too small to accommodate the entire family—seven by three feet. Some take their meals in their hands—children especially—and sit in a chair and sometimes in the door. Some of the time the food is served from the table and at other times from the cooking vessels. The dishes are common china, with some tin plates and cups. There is no tablecloth. There are two benches the length of the table on each side of the table.

No. [2]. *A country family occupying 9 rooms, with an income of $2500 per year.* The eleven members of this family are especially intelligent. They consist of mother and father, ages 50 and 60 years respectively, two daughters, ages 15 and 19 years, and seven boys, ages 29, 27, 25, 23, 21, 11 and 8, respectively. The deceased members of the family are two sons and two daughters; all died soon after birth. The whole family is peaceful and agreeable. The father is head, and what he says is law. The entire family is subjected to a strict discipline. The boys are allowed to visit, but they must return by sundown; if late, an excuse must be given beforehand. The girls do not leave home unless accompanied by some male member of the family. Every one on Sunday must go to Sunday-school, but there is no family prayer. No swearing is allowed. All the members of the family work on the farm excepting the mother. The boys and father do all the cutting, plowing, sometimes hoeing, repair work, and ditching, etc. The girls do the light work, such as hoeing, picking cotton, housework in general, and laundering. The mother stays at home, cooks, and looks after the children. From July 28th to August 24th they do nothing. This is called "laying-by time." From August 24th to December 1st they gather cotton, corn, potatoes, etc. From December 1st to January 15th they do practically nothing except keep fires and hunt.

This family is situated in a peaceful community composed of white and colored people. About two hundred yards from the house on one side are woods. The house is built on a high spot with a splendid drainage. The entire yard is filled with flowers and shade trees. The barns are a convenient distance from the main building, and there is an orchard. The best people of the community visit these people, and some white people from town and the neighborhood. Everything about this house is neat and clean. Their clothes are plain and simple and well cared for. The father is a member of the Masonic order. All are members of C. M. E. Church and of all its societies. The property owned consists of 175 acres of land, 5 mules, 5 milk cows, 7 heads of cattle, 25 hogs and pigs, 3 wagons, 2 buggies, 1 syrup mill, 1 disc harrow, 1 mower and rake, and other tools; there are also 150 chickens, 8 turkeys and 12 guineas.

On the father's mother's side the descent is direct from Africa, without any mixing of blood; on the father's father's side there has been an intermingling of white blood somewhere which makes the father a shade between black and light brown, or a ginger-cake color. On the mother's side the grandfather was a white man and her father was yellow. The mother's mother had a strain of Indian blood in her, making her dark red. This makes the mother yellow. Both sides were in slavery except the mother's grandfather. Breakfast is usually about or before sunrise, with coffee, milk, butter, syrup, meat, grits or rice, chicken or beef on Sunday mornings and biscuits and eggs. Dinner comes at 12 o'clock, with boiled vegetables, cornbread, pies, syrup, milk, butter, biscuits, potatoes, etc., are served. Supper is a little after sundown, with cornbread syrup, meat, milk, butter, and cold vegetables from dinner. Of course these meals vary on different occasions, especially when company is present and on Sundays. All the members of the family assemble around one large table and the father and mother serve the food, which is put on the table before the meal. The knives, forks and spoons are made of plated silver. The dishes are china, plain, with glasses for milk and water.

No. [3]. *A city family living in 3 rooms, with an income of $200 per year.* There are three members in this family, a mother and two daughters. The mother is fifty-one years old and wholly illiterate; she is a washerwoman and not at all neat or clean in her dress; she looks like an Indian and is very quick-tempered. The elder daughter is twenty-two years of age, very slow in thought and action. She finished the grammar schools and got as far as the second year in high school. In summer she washes and irons, in winter she cooks for a white family. Her dress is sometimes clean and neat, and sometimes just the opposite. The younger daughter is thirteen years of age and goes to grammar school. She has a very even temperament and is usually clean. They own no property except the house and lot where they live. Both daughters belong to the church, but the mother does not. They belong to no societies, and have no social life to speak of. They usually go together, except that the younger girl has some young girl friends. The father is dead. The mother's father was a white farmer and her mother a slave. The father's father and mother were slaves. He had two brothers, one of whom is dead. They know of no other relatives.

Breakfast, consisting of coffee, wheat bread, meat, bacon, sometimes beef, is eaten at half-past six, and dinner, with cornbread, vegetables, now and then meats is eaten about eight at night; except on Sunday, when breakfast is eaten at nine o'clock and dinner at half past two or three o'clock. The meals are eaten from miscellaneous dishes. The table upon which the family eats has no tablecloth upon it. The food is taken from the cooking utensils and put on a plate—some of everything they have is put on a plate—and each member of the family takes her plate and sits to the table in the kitchen and eats. There are only two meals cooked. Between meals they eat what is left from the previous meal.

No. [4]. *A city family living in 3 rooms, with an income of $800 per year.* This family is seven in number: husband, aged 34; wife, aged 29, their two children, both girls, ages ten and six; the husband's mother, about seventy; husband's brother, aged eighteen, and a nephew of the husband, aged fourteen. The wife before being married was orphaned and reared by her sister. She has a grammar-school education; she is red brown in color. The husband, a brown man, got a little education and then came to town in search of work. He found employment with the railroad as hostler; he was at this employment until after marriage when, under the influence of his wife, he became a brickmason. The husband's mother lived in the country until her husband died and several children, after which she moved to the city with her youngest son, a boy of eighteen, and her orphaned grandson, a boy of fourteen. The duties of the wife and the mother are to keep the home in order. The children go to school. The boy of fourteen cuts wood, brings up coal and kindling, goes to school, and spends two hours in the service of a small dairy, delivering dairy products to the neighbors, for which he receives fifty cents a week. The boy of eighteen drives a furniture wagon for a local furniture store, receiving six dollars per week for his services. The husband works at his trade, averaging about five hundred dollars a year. There have been born into this family since marriage six children, four of whom died in infancy, two of whom were twins. The dress of this family is common city dress with nothing extra. The men's suits average fifteen dollars per suit; the women's clothes, averaging five dollars per suit, being made at home. All belong to the church, although to different ones; all attend very regularly. The husband is a Mason and the wife a True Reformer. The home is now being paid for. The family is very genial in disposition, and receives some company.

The staple foods are meat, grits, rice, syrup, butter and jelly. All of this is bought from stores except the jelly, which is made in the summer. At breakfast there is rice, grits, coffee, biscuit and some sort of steak, sausage or liver, bought from the near-by market. Red damask tablecloth covers the table, with china dishes. The food is served on appropriate dishes. Common napkins are used. The whole family eat at the same time. At dinner they have baked beans, or roast, together with white potatoes, rice, and wheat bread, coffee, and some sort of cheap dessert, like pie. At supper there is something fried from the market, wheat bread, grits, cheese, coffee and tea. Breakfast is at six in the morning, dinner at twelve, and supper at six in the evening.

No. [5]. *A city family living in 9 rooms, with an income of $1300 per year.* The father's father's birthplace and age is unknown. He was a slave of some wealth when freed. He belonged to a very good task-master and had considerable amount of cattle and other property. Some of his money he intrusted to his master for safety, but he died without ever getting it back again. The father's mother's birthplace is unknown. She had about three-fourths Indian blood, and was married three times. She was the mother of six children: five boys and one girl. One boy died while a very small child. The mother died in 1891. The father was born December 24, 1865, and is the oldest of the six children. He has been the main breadwinner for the family since the death of his father, when he was a boy, and has had a very little chance for schooling. He had to raise the four remaining children after his mother's death. He married at twenty years of age, and has farmed fourteen years. He owns a house and a four-acre lot at —— Texas. He moved from —— to —— Texas, in 1900, and was porter in a hardware store for three years, with wages at $9.00 per week. Since then he has been a porter at the depot, with wages at $35.00 per month. He has one child, a boy, age 22 years. He is now buying a quarter block at $1500. The wife was born near ——, Texas, July 13, 1867. Her father died before her birth. The mother's birthplace was in ——, Texas, and she is still living. The mother's mother has been married twice. First husband died soon after marriage; the second husband is still living. She is the mother of two children; both are married, and both girls. The mother sells vegetables, chickens and eggs, milk and butter, to neighbors, washes and irons and sometimes cooks. She had very little chance for education, and was married at eighteen years. Neither husband nor wife possessed any property at their marriage. The boy was born at ——, Texas, and he had been in school ever since he reached school age. Only works during the summer, averaging about $5 per week. Husband belongs to Odd Fellows Lodge, and has an accident life insurance policy of $1500.

No. 13. *A city family living in 7 rooms, with an income of $1344 per year.* There are eight members in the family; father, 53 years of age; mother, 49 years of age; grandmother on the father's side, 80 years of age; eldest daughter 21, eldest son 19, younger daughter 17, youngest son 15 and the youngest girl 12. The father is a railway mail clerk and has been for years. The mother only carries on the household affairs with the aid of the three girls. The grandmother attends to the cow and sells the milk. The eldest daughter teaches in one of the public schools of the city. The oldest son works in a barber shop. The younger son attends college in the winter and works as messenger boy in one of the factories in summer. The other two girls attend school and also assist in the house work.

During vacation three meals are served: breakfast at 7:30 a. m., and dinner at 12:00 p. m. and supper at 6 p. m. But when school begins only two meals are served: breakfast, and late dinner about 4:30 p. m. They raise none of the food, everything is bought. The meals are served by the girls of the family. The dishes used on the dining-room table are china, the knives and forks silver, but those used in the kitchen are not so expensive. The table used in this kitchen is comparatively small, being only for family use. But when there is company the larger dining-room is used.

For breakfast they always have some kind of cereal, biscuits, tea and coffee; either fried steak, ham, or the like, and home-made butter. For dinner they generally have something boiled, and dessert, either pies or pudding. They always dress well and are always very neat and clean. This family was once accustomed to spending Christmas day with the grandparents—the mother's parents—but since their death they spend the holidays at home. They attend church regularly, and the mother belongs to one of the largest Methodist churches of the city. The mother and father own quite a deal of property; the mother's was left to her by her parents, the father acquired his by his own labor.

Conclusion

Judging from family life and other conditions how far, is it fair to conclude, has the Negro American emerged into twentieth century civilization? The United States had, in 1900, 10.7% of illiteracy, 46.5% of home ownership, and perhaps 2% of illegitimate births. The Negro had, in 1900, 44.5% of illiteracy, 20.3% of home ownership and, probably though not certainly, 25% of illegitimacy.

These rough measurements would permit the following assumption: that in the Nation at large four-fifths of the citizens have at least common school training, two-thirds have reached a plane of economic independence, and nine-tenths are observing the monogamic sex *mores*. Among the Negroes probably one-third have at least common-school training, one-third have reached a plane of economic independence, and at least one-half are observing the monogamic sex *mores*.

11

THE RELIGION
OF THE AMERICAN NEGRO

It was out in the country, far from home, far from my foster home, on a dark Sunday night. The road wandered from our rambling log house up the stony bed of a creek, past wheat and corn, until we could hear dimly across the fields a rhythmic cadence of song,—soft, thrilling, powerful, that swelled and died sorrowfully in our ears. I was a country school teacher then, fresh from the East, and had never seen a southern Negro revival. To be sure, we in Berkshire were not perhaps as stiff and formal as they in Suffolk of olden time; yet we were very quiet and subdued, and I know not what would have happened those clear Sabbath mornings had some one punctuated the sermon with a wild scream, or interrupted the long prayer with a loud Amen! And so most striking to me, as I approached the village and the little plain church perched aloft, was the air of intense excitement that possessed that mass of black folk. A sort of suppressed terror hung in the air and seemed to seize us—a pythian madness, a demoniac possession, that lent terrible reality to song and word. The black and massive form of the preacher swayed and quivered as the words crowded to his lips and flew at us in singular eloquence. The people moaned and fluttered, and then the gaunt-cheeked brown woman beside me suddenly leaped straight into the air and shrieked like a lost soul, while round about came wail and groan and outcry, and a scene of human passion such as I had never conceived before.

Those who have not thus witnessed the frenzy of a Negro revival in the untouched backwoods of the South can but dimly realize the

Reprinted from *New World* 9 (December 1900): 614-25.

religious feeling of the slave; as described, such scenes appear grotesque and funny, but as seen they are awful. Three things characterized this religion of the slave—the Preacher, the Music and the Frenzy. The Preacher is the most unique personality developed by the Negro on American soil. A leader, a politician, an orator, a "boss," an intriguer, an idealist—all these he is, and ever, too, the centre of a group of men, now twenty, now a thousand in number. The combination of a certain adroitness with deep-seated earnestness, of tact with consummate ability, gave him his preëminence, and helps him maintain it. The type, of course, varies according to time and place, from the West Indies in the sixteenth century to New England in the nineteenth, and from the Mississippi bottoms to cities like New Orleans or New York.

The Music of Negro religion is that plaintive rhythmic melody with its touching minor cadences, which, despite caricature and defilement, still remains the most original and beautiful expression of human life and longing yet born on American soil. Sprung from the African forests, where its counterpart can still be heard, it was adapted, changed and intensified by the tragic soul-life of the slave, until, under the stress of law and whip, it became the one true expression of a people's sorrow, despair and hope.

Finally the Frenzy or "Shouting," when the Spirit of the Lord passed by, and, seizing the devotee, made him mad with supernatural joy, was the last essential of Negro religion and the one more devoutly believed in than all the rest. It varied in expression from the silent rapt countenance or the low murmur and moan to the mad abandon of physical fervor—the stamping, shrieking and shouting, the rushing to and fro and wild waving of arms, the weeping and laughing, the vision and the trance. All this is nothing new in the world, but old as religion, as Delphi and Endor. And so firm a hold did it have on the Negro that many generations firmly believed that without this visible manifestation of the god, there could be no true communion with the Invisible.

These were the characteristics of Negro religious life as developed up to the time of Emancipation. Since under the peculiar circumstances of the black man's environment, they were the one expression of his higher life, they are of deep interest to the student of his development, both socially and psychologically. Numerous are the attractive lines of inquiry that here group themselves. What did slavery mean to the African savage? What was his attitude toward the World and Life? What seemed to him good and evil—God and Devil? Whither went his longings and strivings, and wherefore were his heart-burnings and disappointments? Answers to such questions can come only from a study of Negro religion as a development, through its gradual changes from the heathenism of the Gold Coast to the institutional Negro church of Chicago.

Moreover, the religious growth of millions of men, even though they be slaves, cannot be without potent influence upon their contemporaries. The Methodists and Baptists of America owe much of their condition to the silent but potent influence of their millions of Negro converts. Especially is this noticeable in the South, where theology and religious philosophy are on this account a full half century behind the North, and where the religion of the poor whites is a plain copy of Negro thought and methods. The mass of "Gospel" hymns which has swept through American churches and well-nigh ruined our sense of song, consists largely of debased imitations of Negro melodies made by ears that caught the jingle but not the music, the body but not the soul, of the Jubilee songs. It is thus clear that the study of Negro religion is not only a vital part of the history of the Negro in America, but no uninteresting part of American history.

The Negro church of to-day is the social centre of Negro life in the United States, and the most characteristic expression of African character. Take a typical church in a small Virginian town: it is the "First Baptist"—a roomy brick edifice seating five hundred or more persons, tastefully finished in Georgia pine, with a carpet, a small organ and stained-glass windows. Underneath is a large assembly room with benches. This building is the central club-house of a community of a thousand or more Negroes. Various organizations meet here—the church proper, the Sunday-school, two or three insurance societies, women's societies, secret societies and mass meetings of various kinds. Entertainments, suppers and lectures are held beside the five or six regular weekly religious services. Considerable sums of money are collected and expended here, employment is found for the idle, strangers are introduced, news is disseminated and charity distributed. At the same time this social, intellectual and economic centre is a religious centre of great power. Depravity, Sin, Redemption, Heaven, Hell and Damnation are preached twice a Sunday with much fervor, and revivals take place every year after the crops are laid by; and few indeed of the community have the hardihood to withstand conversion. Back of this more formal religion, the Church stands as a real conserver of morals, a strengthener of family life, and the final authority on what is Good and Right.

Thus one can see in the Negro church to-day, reproduced in microcosm, all that great world from which the Negro is cut off by color prejudice and social condition. In the great city churches the same tendency is noticeable and in many respects emphasized. A great church like the Bethel of Philadelphia has 1104 members, an edifice seating 1500 persons and valued at $100,000, an annual budget of $5000 and a government consisting of a pastor with several assisting local preachers, an executive and legislative board, financial boards and tax collectors; general church meetings for making laws; subdivided groups led by class leaders, a company of militia, and twenty-four auxiliary societies. The activity of such a church is immense and far-reaching, and the bishops who preside over these organizations throughout the land are among the most powerful Negro rulers in the world.

Such churches are really governments of men, and consequently a little investigation reveals the curious fact that, in the South, at least, practically every American Negro is a church member. Some, to be sure, are not regularly enrolled, and a few do not habitually attend services; but, practically, a proscribed people must have a social centre, and that centre for this people is the Negro church. The census of 1890 showed nearly 24,000 Negro churches in the country, with a total enrolled membership of over two and a half millions, or ten actual church members to every twenty-eight persons, and in some Southern States one in every two persons. Besides these there is the large number who, while not enrolled as members, attend and take part in many of the activities of the church. There is an organized Negro church for every sixty black families in the nation, and in some States for every forty families, owning, on an average, $1000 worth of property each, or nearly $26,000,000 in all.

Such, then, is the large development of the Negro church since Emancipation. The question now is, What have been the successive steps of this social history and what are the present tendencies? First, we must realize that no such institution as the Negro church could rear itself without definite historical foundations. These foundations we can find if we remember that the social history of the Negro did not start in America. He was brought from a definite social environment—the polygamous clan life under the headship of the chief and the potent influence of the priest. His religion was nature-worship, with profound belief in invisible surrounding influences, good and bad, and his worship was through incantation and sacrifice. The first rude change in this life was the slave ship and the West Indian sugar-fields. The plantation organization replaced the clan and tribe, and the white master replaced the chief with far greater and more despotic powers. Forced and long-continued toil became the rule of life, the old ties of blood relationship and kinship disappeared, and instead of the family appeared a new polygamy and polyandry, which, in some cases, almost reached promiscuity. It was a terrific social revolution, and yet some traces were retained of the former group life, and the chief remaining institution was the Priest or Medicine-man. He early appeared on the plantation and found his function as the healer of the sick, the interpreter of the Unknown, the comforter of the sorrowing, the supernatural avenger of wrong, and the one who rudely but picturesquely expressed the longing, disappointment and resentment of a stolen and oppressed people. Thus, as bard, physician, judge and priest, within the narrow limits allowed by the slave system, rose the Negro preacher, and under him the first Afro-American institution, the Negro church. This church was not at first by any means Christian nor definitely organized; rather it was an adaptation and mingling of heathen rites among the members of each plantation, and roughly designated as Voodooism. Association with the masters, missionary effort and motives of expediency gave these rites an early veneer of

Christianity, and after the lapse of many generations the Negro church became Christian.

Two characteristic things must be noticed in regard to this church. First, it became almost entirely Baptist and Methodist in faith; secondly, as a social institution it antedated by many decades the monogamic Negro home. From the very circumstances of its beginning, the church was confined to the plantation, and consisted primarily of a series of disconnected units; although, later on, some freedom of movement was allowed, still this geographical limitation was always important and was one cause of the spread of the decentralized and democratic Baptist faith among the slaves. At the same time, the visible rite of baptism appealed strongly to their mystic temperament. To-day the Baptist Church is still largest in membership among Negroes, and has a million and a half communicants. Next in popularity came the churches organized in connection with the white neighboring churches, chiefly Baptist and Methodist, with a few Episcopalian and others. The Methodists still form the second greatest denomination, with nearly a million members. The faith of these two leading denominations was more suited to the slave church from the prominence they gave to religious feeling and fervor. The Negro membership in other denominations has always been small and relatively unimportant, although the Episcopalians and Presbyterians are gaining among the more intelligent classes to-day, and the Catholic Church is making headway in certain sections. After emancipation, and still earlier in the North, the Negro churches largely severed such affiliations as they had had with the white churches, either by choice or by compulsion. The Baptist churches became independent, but the Methodists were compelled early to unite for purposes of episcopal government. This gave rise to the great African Methodist Church, the greatest Negro organization in the world, to the Zion Church and the Colored Methodist, and to the black conferences and churches in this and other denominations.

The second fact noted, namely, that the Negro church antedates the Negro home, leads to an explanation of much that is paradoxical in this communistic institution and in the morals of its members.

But especially it leads us to regard this institution as peculiarly the expression of the inner ethical life of a people in a sense seldom true elsewhere. Let us turn then from the outer physical development of the church to the more important inner ethical life of the people who compose it. The Negro has already been pointed out many times as a religious animal—a being of that deep emotional nature which turns instinctively toward the supernatural. Endowed with a rich tropical imagination and a keen, delicate appreciation of Nature, the transplanted African lived in a world animate with gods and devils, elves and witches; full of strange influences—of Good to be implored, of Evil to be propitiated. Slavery, then, was to him the dark triumph of Evil over him. All the hateful powers of the Under-world were striving against him, and a spirit of revolt and revenge filled his heart. He called up all the resources of heathenism to aid,— exorcism and witchcraft, the mysterious Obi worship with its barbarous rites, spells and blood-sacrifice even, now and then, of human victims. Weird midnight orgies and mystic conjurations were invoked, the witch-woman and the voodoo-priest became the centre of Negro group life, and that vein of vague superstition which characterizes the unlettered Negro even to-day was deepened and strengthened.

In spite, however, of such success as that of the fierce Maroons, the Danish blacks and others, the spirit of revolt gradually died away under the untiring energy and superior strength of the slave masters. By the middle of the eighteenth century the black slave had sunk, with hushed murmurs, to his place at the bottom of a new economic system, and was unconsciously ripe for a new philosophy of life. Nothing suited his condition then better than the doctrines of passive submission embodied in the newly learned Christianity. Slave masters early realized this, and cheerfully aided religious propaganda within certain bounds. The long system of repression and degradation of the Negro tended to emphasize the elements in his character which made him a valuable chattel: courtesy became humility, moral strength degenerated into submission, and the exquisite native appreciation of the beautiful became an infinite capacity for dumb suffering. The Negro, losing the joy of this world, eagerly seized upon the offered conceptions of the next; the avenging Spirit of the Lord enjoining patience in this world, under sorrow and tribulation until the Great Day when He should lead His dark children home,—this became his comforting dream. His Preacher repeated the prophecy, and his bards sang:

Children, we all shall be free
When the Lord shall appear!

This deep religious fatalism, painted so beautifully in Uncle Tom, came soon to breed, as all fatalistic faiths will, the sensualist side by side with the martyr. Under the lax moral life of the plantation, where marriage was a farce, laziness a virtue, and property a theft, a religion of resignation and submission degenerated easily, in less strenuous minds, into a philosophy of indulgence and crime. Many of the worst characteristics of the Negro masses of to-day had their seed in this period of the slave's ethical growth. Here it was that the Home was ruined under the very shadow of the Church, white and black; here habits of shiftlessness took root, and sullen hopelessness replaced hopeful strife.

With the beginning of the abolition movement and the gradual growth of a class of free Negroes came a change. We often neglect the influence of the freedman before the war, because of the paucity of his numbers and the small weight he had in the history of the nation. But we must not forget that his chief influence was internal—was exerted on the black world, and that there he was the ethical and social leader. Huddled as he was in a few centres like Philadelphia, New York and New Orleans, his chief characteristic was intense earnestness and deep feeling on the slavery question. Freedom became to him a real thing and not a dream. His religion became darker and more intense, and into his ethics crept a note of revenge, into his songs a day of reckoning close at hand. The "Coming of the Lord" swept this side of Death, and came to be a thing to be hoped for in this day. Through fugitive slaves and irrepressible discussion this desire for freedom seized the black millions still in bondage, and became their one ideal of life. The black bards caught new notes, and sometimes even dared to sing:

Before I'll be a slave
I'll be buried in my grave,
And go home to my Jesus
And be saved.

For fifty years Negro religion thus transformed itself and identified itself with the dream of Abolition until that which was a radical
fad in the White North and an anarchistic plot in the White South
had become a religion to the Black world. Thus, when Emancipation
finally came, it seemed to the freedman a literal Coming of the Lord.
His fervid imagination was stirred, as never before, by the tramp of
armies, the blood and dust of battle and the wail and whirl of social
upheaval. He stood dumb and motionless before the whirlwind—
what had he to do with it? Was it not the Lord's doing and
marvelous in his eyes? Joyed and bewildered with what came, he
stood awaiting new wonders till the inevitable Age of Reaction swept
over the nation and brought the crisis of to-day.

It is difficult to explain clearly the present critical stage of Negro
religion. First, we must remember that living as the blacks do in
close contact with a great modern nation and sharing, although
imperfectly, the soul-life of that nation, they must necessarily be
affected more or less directly by all the religious and ethical forces
that are to-day moving the United States. These questions and
movements are, however, overshadowed and dwarfed by the all-
important question (to them) of their civil, political and economic
status. They must perpetually discuss the "Negro Problem"—live,
move, and have their being in it, and interpret all else in its light or
darkness. With this come, too, peculiar problems of their inner
life,—of the status of women, the maintenance of Home, the
training of children, the accumulation of wealth and the prevention
of crime. All this must mean a time of intense ethical ferment, of
religious heart-searching and intellectual unrest. From the double
life every American Negro must live, as a Negro and as an American,
as swept on by the current of the nineteenth while yet struggling in
the eddies of the fifteenth century,—from this must arise a painful
self-consciousness, an almost morbid sense of personality and a
moral hesitancy which is fatal to self-confidence. The worlds within
and without the Veil of Color are changing, and changing rapidly,

but not at the same rate, not in the same way; and this must produce a peculiar wrenching of the soul, a peculiar sense of doubt and bewilderment. Such a double life, with double thoughts, double duties and double social classes, must give rise to double words and double ideals, and tempt the mind to pretense or to revolt, to hypocrisy or to radicalism.

In some such doubtful words and phrases can one perhaps most clearly picture the peculiar ethical paradox that faces the Negro of to-day and is tingeing and changing his religious life. Feeling that his rights and his dearest ideals are being trampled upon, that the public conscience is even more deaf to his righteous appeal, and that all the reactionary forces of prejudice, greed and revenge are daily gaining new strength and fresh allies, the Negro faces no enviable dilemma. Conscious of his impotence, and pessimistic, he often becomes bitter and vindictive, and his religion, instead of a worship, is a complaint and a curse, a wail rather than a hope, a sneer rather than a faith. On the other hand, another type of mind, shrewder and keener and more tortuous too, sees in the very strength of the anti-Negro movement its patent weaknesses, and with Jesuitic casuistry is deterred by no ethical considerations in the endeavor to turn this weakness to the black man's strength. Thus we have two great and hardly reconcilable streams of thought and ethical strivings; the danger of the one lies in anarchy, that of the other in hypocrisy. The one type of Negro stands almost ready to curse God and die, and the other is too often found a traitor to right and a coward before force; the one is wedded to ideals remote, whimsical, perhaps impossible of realization; the other forgets that life is more than meat and the body more than raiment. But, after all, is not all this simply the writhing of the age translated into black? The triumph of the Lie which to-day, with its false culture, faces the hideousness of the anarchist assassin?

To-day the two groups of Negroes, the one in the North, the other in the South, represent these divergent ethical tendencies, the first tending toward radicalism, the other toward hypocritical compromise. It is no idle regret with which the white South mourns the loss of the old-time Negro—the frank, honest, simple old servant who stood for the earlier religious age of submission and humility. With all his laziness and lack of many elements of true manhood he was at least open-hearted, faithful and sincere. To-day he is gone, but who is to blame for his going? Is it not those very persons who mourn for him? Is it not the tendency born of Reconstruction and Reaction to found a society on lawlessness and deception, to tamper with the moral fibre of a naturally honest and straightforward people until the whites threaten to become ungovernable tyrants and the blacks criminals and hypocrites? Deception is the natural defense of the weak against the strong, and the South used it for many years against its conquerors; to-day it must be prepared to see its black proletariat turn that same two-edged weapon against itself. And how natural this is! The death of Nat Turner and John Brown proved long since to the Negro the present hopelessness of physical defense. Political defense is becoming less and less available, and economic defense is still only partially effective. But there is a patent defense at hand,—the defense of deception and flattery, of cajoling and lying. It is the same defense which the Jews of the Middle Age used and which left its stamp on their character for centuries. To-day the young Negro of the South who would succeed cannot be frank and outspoken, honest and self-assertive; but rather he is daily tempted to be silent and wary, politic and sly; he must flatter and be pleasant, endure petty insults with a smile, shut his eyes to wrong; in too many cases he sees positive personal advantage in deception and lying. His real thoughts, his real aspirations must be guarded in whispers; he must not criticise, he must not complain. Patience, humility and adroitness must, in these growing black youth, replace impulse, manliness and courage. With this sacrifice there is an economic opening, and perhaps peace and some prosperity. Without this there is riot, migration or crime. Nor is this situation peculiar to the southern United States—is it not rather the only method by which undeveloped races have gained the right to share modern culture? The price of culture is a Lie.

On the other hand, in the North the tendency is to emphasize the radicalism of the Negro. Driven from his birthright in the South by a situation at which every fibre of his more outspoken and assertive nature revolts, he finds himself in a land where he can scarcely earn a decent living amid the harsh competition and the color discrimination. At the same time, through schools and periodicals, discussions and lectures, he is intellectually quickened and awakened. The soul, long pent up and dwarfed, suddenly expanded in new-found freedom. What wonder that every tendency is to excess,—radical complaint, radical remedies, bitter denunciation or angry silence. Some sink, some rise. The criminal and the sensualist leave the church for the gambling hell and the bawdy-house, and fill the slums of Chicago and Baltimore; the better classes segregate themselves from the group-life of both white and black, and form an aristocracy, cultured but pessimistic, whose bitter criticism stings while it points out no way of escape. They despise the submission and subserviency of the Southern Negroes, but offer no other means by which a poor and oppressed minority can exist side by side with its masters. Feeling deeply and keenly the tendencies and opportunities of the age in which they live, their souls are bitter at the fate which drops the Veil between, and the very fact that this bitterness is natural and justifiable only serves to intensify it and make it more maddening.

Between the two extreme types of ethical attitude which I have thus sought to make clear, wavers the mass of the millions of Negroes North and South; and their religious life and activity partake of this social conflict within their ranks. Their churches are differentiating; now into groups of cold, fashionable devotees, in no way distinguishable from similar white groups save in color of skin; now into large social and business institutions catering to the desire for information and amusement of their members, warily avoiding unpleasant questions both within and without the black world and preaching in effect if not in word: *Dum vivimus, vivamus.*

But, back of this, still brood silently the deep religious feeling of the real Negro heart, the stirring, unguided might of powerful human souls who have lost the guiding star of the past and are seeking in the great night a new religious ideal. Some day the Awakening will come, when the pent-up vigor of ten million souls shall sweep irresistibly toward the Goal, out of the Valley of the Shadow of Death, where all that makes life worth living—Liberty, Justice and Right—is marked "For White People Only."

12

THE PROBLEM OF AMUSEMENT

I wish to discuss with you somewhat superficially a phase of development in the organized life of American Negroes which has hitherto received scant notice. It is the question of the amusements of Negroes—what their attitude toward them is, what institutions among them conduct the recreations, and what the tendency of indulgence is in amusements of various sorts. I do not pretend that this is one of the more pressing of the Negro problems, but nevertheless it is destined as time goes on to become more and more so; and at all times and in all places, the manner, method, and extent of a people's recreation is of vast importance to their welfare.

I have been in this case especially spurred to take under consideration this particular one of the many problems affecting the Negroes in cities and in the country because I have long noted with silent apprehension a distinct tendency among us, to depreciate and belittle and sneer at means of recreation, to consider amusement as the peculiar property of the devil, and to look upon even its legitimate pursuit as time wasted and energy misspent. I have heard sermon after sermon and essay after essay thunder warnings against the terrible results of pleasure and the awful end of those who are depraved enough to seek pleasure. I have heard such a fusillade of "don'ts" thrown at our young people: don't dance, don't play cards, don't go to the theatre, don't drink, don't smoke, don't sing songs, don't play kissing games, don't play billiards, don't play foot-ball, don't go on excursions—that I have not been surprised, gentlemen and ladies, to find in the feverish life of a great city, hundreds of

Reprinted from *The Southern Workman* 27 (September, 1897): 181–84.

Negro boys and girls who have listened for a life-time to the warning, "Don't do this or you'll go to hell," and then have taken the bit between their teeth and said, "Well, let's go to hell."

If you go out through the country side of Virginia, to the little towns and hamlets, the first thing you will note is the scarcity of young men and women. There are babies aplenty, and boys and girls up to fifteen, sixteen, and seventeen—then suddenly the supply seems to stop, and from eighteen to thirty there is a great gap. Where are these young people? They are in Norfolk, Richmond, Baltimore, Washington, Philadelphia and New York. In one ward of Philadelphia young people between the ages of sixteen and thirty form over a third of the population; the Negro population of the whole city of Philadelphia, which has increased fully one hundred per cent since 1860, has received its main element of increase from these young boys and girls. Why have they gone? Primarily, their migration is, of course, but a belated ripple of that great wave city-ward which is redistributing the population of England, France, Italy, Germany, and the United States, and draining the country districts of those lands of their bone and sinew. The whole movement is caused by that industrial revolution which has transferred the seat of human labor from agriculture to manufacturing and concentrated manufacturing in cities, thus by higher wages attracting the young people. This is the primary motive, but back of this is a powerful and in some cases even more deciding motive; and that is the thirst for amusement. You, who were born and reared amid the kaleidoscopic life of a great city, scarcely realize what an irresistible attraction city life has for one who has long experienced the dull, lifeless monotony of the country. When now that country life has been further shorn of the few pleasures usually associated with it, when the public opinion of the best class of Negroes in the country districts distinctly frowns, not only upon most of the historical kinds of amusements usual in a peasant community, but also to some extent upon the very idea of amusement as a necessary, legitimate pursuit, then it is inevitable that you should have what we are seeing to-day, a perfect stampede of young Negroes to the city.

When now a young man has grown up feeling the trammels of precept, religion, or custom too irksome for him, and then at the

most impressionable and reckless age of life, is suddenly transplanted to an atmosphere of excess, the result is apt to be disastrous.
In the case of young colored men or women, it is disastrous, and the
story is daily repeated in every great city of our land, of young men
and women who have been reared in an atmosphere of restricted
amusement, throwing off when they enter city life, not one restriction, not some restrictions, but almost all, and plunging into
dissipation and vice. This tendency is rendered stronger by two
circumstances peculiar to the condition of the American Negro: the
first is his express or tacit exclusion from the public amusements of
most great cities; and second, the little thought of fact that the chief
purveyor of amusement to the colored people is the Negro church,
which in theory is opposed to most modern amusements. Let me
make this second point clear, for much of the past and future
development of the race is misunderstood from ignorance of certain
fundamental historic facts. Among most people the primitive
sociological group was the family or at least the clan. Not so among
American Negroes: every vestige of primitive organization among
the Negro slaves was destroyed by the slave ship; in this country the
first distinct voluntary organization of Negroes was the Negro
church. The Negro church came before the Negro home, it antedates
their social life, and in every respect it stands to-day as the fullest,
broadest expression of organized Negro life.

We are so familiar with churches, and church work is so near to
us, that we have scarce time to view it in perspective and to realize
that in origin and functions the Negro church is a broader, deeper,
and more comprehensive social organism than the churches of white
Americans. The Negro church is not simply an organism for the
propagation of religion; it is the centre of the social, intellectual, and
religious life of an organized group of individuals. It provides social
intercourse, it provides amusements of various kinds, it serves as a
newspaper and intelligence bureau, it supplants the theatre, it
directs the picnic and excursion, it furnishes the music, it introduces
the stranger to the community, it serves as a lyceum, library, and
lecture bureau—it is, in fine, the central organ of the organized life
of the American Negro for amusement, relaxation, instruction, and
religion. To maintain its preeminence the Negro church has been

forced to compete with the dance hall, the theatre, and the home as an amusement-giving agency; aided by color proscription in public amusements, aided by the fact mentioned before, that the church among us is older than the home, the church has been peculiarly successful, so that of the ten thousand Philadelphia Negroes whom I asked, "Where do you get your amusements?" fully three-fourths could only answer, "From the churches."

The minister who directs this peculiar and anomalous institution must not be criticised with full knowledge of his difficult role. He is in reality the mayor, the chief magistrate of a community, ruling to be sure, but ruling according to the dictates of a not over-intelligent town council, according to time-honored custom and law; and above all, hampered by the necessities of his budget; he may be a spiritual guide, he must be a social organizer, a leader of actual men; he may desire to enrich and reform the spiritual life of his flock, but above all he must have church members; he may desire to revolutionize church methods, to elevate the ideals of the people, to tell the hard, honest truth to a people who need a little more truth and a little less flattery—but how can he do this when the people of this social organism demand that he shall take from the purely spiritual activities of his flock, time to minister to their amusement, diversion, and physical comfort; when he sees the picnic masquerading as a camp-meeting, the revival becoming the social event of the season, the day of worship turned into a day of general reception and dining out, the rival church organizations plunging into debt to furnish their houses of worship with an elegance that far outruns the financial ability of a poverty stricken people; when the church door becomes the trysting place for all the lovers and Lotharios of the community; when a ceaseless round of entertainments, socials, and necktie parties chase the week through—what minister can be more than most ministers are coming to be, the business managers of a picnic ground?

This is the situation of the Negro church today—I do not say of all Negro churches, but I mean the average church. It is rather the misfortune than the fault of the church. With the peculiar development we have had in this country, I doubt if the Negro church could have more nobly fulfilled its huge and multiform task; if it totters beneath its burden, it nevertheless demands respect as the first demonstrator of the ability of the civilized Negro to govern himself. Notwithstanding all this, the situation remains, and demands— peremptorily demands—reform. On the one hand we have an increasingly restless crowd of young people who are always demanding ways and means of recreation; and every moment it is denied them is a moment that goes to increase that growth of a distinct class of Negro libertines, criminals, and prostitutes which is growing among us day by day, which fills our jails and hospitals, which tempts and taints our brothers, our sisters, and our children, and which does more in a day to tarnish our good name than Hampton can do in a year to restore it. On the other hand we have the Negro church seeking to supply this demand for amusement—and doing so to the detriment and death of its true, divine mission of human inspiration.

Under such circumstances two questions immediately arise: first, Is this growing demand for amusement legitimate? and second, Can the church continue to be the centre of amusements?

Let us consider the first question; and ask, What is amusement? All life is rhythm—the right swing of the pendulum makes the pointer go round, but the left swing must follow it; the down stroke of the hammer welds the iron, and yet the hammer must be lifted between each blow; the heart must beat and yet between each beat comes a pause; the day is the period of fulfilling the functions of life and yet the prelude and end of day is night. Thus throughout nature, from the restless beating of yonder waves to the rhythm of the seasons and the whirl of comets, we see one mighty law of work and rest, of activity and relaxation, of inspiration and amusement. We might imagine a short sighted philosopher arguing strongly against the loss of time involved in the intermittent activities of the world—arguing against the time spent by the hammer in raising itself for the second blow, against the unnecessary alternate swing of the pendulum, against sleep that knits up the ravelled sleeve of care, against amusements that reinvigorate and recreate and divert. With such a philosophy the world has never agreed, the whole world today is organized for work and recreation. Where the balance between the two is best maintained we have the best civilization, the best culture; and that civilization declines toward barbarism where, on the one hand, work and drudgery so predominate as to destroy the very vigor which stands behind them, or on the other hand, where relaxation and amusement become dissipation instead of recreation.

I dwell on these simple facts because I fear that even a proverbially joyous people like the American Negroes are forgetting to recognize for their children the God-given right to play; to recognize that there is a perfectly natural and legitimate demand for amusement on the part of the young people, and that no people can afford to laugh at, sneer at, or forcibly repress the natural joyousness and pleasure-seeking prospensity of young womanhood and young manhood. Go into a great city today and see how thoroughly and wonderfully organized its avenues of amusements are; its parks and play grounds, its theatres and galleries, its music and dancing, its excursions and trolley rides represent an enormous proportion of the expenditure of every great municipality. That the matter of amusement may often be overdone in such centres is too true, but of all the agencies that contribute to its overdoing none are more potent than undue repression. Proper amusement must always be a matter of careful reasoning and ceaseless investigation, of nice adjustment between repression and excess; there is not a single means of amusement from church socials to public balls, or from checkers to horse racing that may not be carried to harmful excess; on the other hand it would be difficult to name a single amusement which if properly limited and directed would not be a positive gain to any society; take, for instance, in our modern American society, the game of billiards; I suppose, taken in itself, a more innocent, interesting, and gentlemanly game of skill could scarcely be thought of, and yet, because it is today coupled with gambling, excessive drinking, lewd companionship, and late hours, you can hear it damned from every pulpit from San Francisco to New York as the straight road to perdition; so far as present conditions are concerned the pulpit may be right, but the social reformer must ask himself: Are these conditions necessary? Was it not far sighted prudence for the University of Pennsylvania to put billiard tables in its students' club room? Is there any valid reason why the Y.M.C.A. at Norfolk should not have a billiard table among its amusements?

In other words, is it wise policy to surrender a charming amusement wholly to the devil and then call it devilish?

If now there is among rational, healthy, earnest people a legitimate demand for amusement, and if from its peculiar history and constitution the Negro church has undertaken to furnish this amusement to American Negroes, is it fairly to be supposed that the church can be successful in its attempt? Of the answer to this question there is one unfailing sign: if the young people are flocking into the church then the church has accomplished its double task; but as matter of fact the young people are leaving the church; in the forty Negro churches of Philadelphia I doubt if there are two hundred young men who are effective, active church members; there are to be sure, two thousand young men who meet their sweethearts there Sunday nights—but they are not pillars of the church. The young women are more faithful but they too are dropping away; in the country, this tendency is less manifest because the young people have no other place to go, but even there it is found increasingly difficult to reach the young people. This simply means that the younger generation of Negroes are tired of the limited and hackneyed amusements the church offers, and that the spiritual message of the church has been dulled by too indistinct and inopportune reiteration.

And then there is another reason, deeper and more subtle, and therefore more dangerous than these; and that is, the recoil of young, honest souls against a distinct tendency toward hypocrisy in the apparent doctrine and the practice of the Negro church. The Methodist and Baptist and nearly all the churches which the slaves joined, had at the time of their introduction into America, felt the full impulse of a spiritual recoil against excessive amusement. The dissipations of an age of debauchery, of display, of license, had led those churches to preach the earnestness of life, and the disgrace of mere pleasure-seeking as a life work. Transported to America this religion of protest became a wholesale condemnation of amusements, and a glorification of the ascetic ideal of self-inflicted misery. In this tongue the Negro church first began to lisp; its earliest teaching was that the Christian stood apart from and utterly opposed to a world filled with pleasures, and that to partake of those pleasures was sinful. When now in these days the church speaks in those same tones and invites healthy and joyous young people from the back seats to renounce the amusements of this world for a diet of fasting and prayer, those same young people in increasing numbers are positively, deliberately, and decisively declining to do any such thing; and they are pointing to the obvious fact that the very church that is preaching against amusement is straining every nerve to amuse them; they feel that there is an essential hypocrisy in this position of the church and they refuse to be hypocrites.

As a matter of fact you and I know that our church is not really hypocritical on this point; she errs only in using antiquated and unfortunate phraseology. What the Negro church is trying to impress upon young people is that Work and Sacrifice is the true destiny of humanity—the Negro church is dimly groping for that divine word of Faust:

"Entbehren sallst du, sollst entbehren."

"Thou shalt forego, shalt do without."

But in this truth, properly conceived, properly enunciated, there is nothing incompatible with wholesome amusement, with true re-creation—for what is true amusement, true diversion, but the re-creation of energy which we may sacrifice to noble ends, to higher ideals, while without proper amusement we waste or dissipate our mightiest powers? If the Negro church could have the time and the opportunity to announce this spiritual message clearly and truly; if it could concentrate its energy and emphasis on an encouragement of proper amusement instead of on its wholesale denunciation; if it could cease to dissipate and cheapen religion by incessant semi-religious activity then we would, starting with a sound religious foundation, be able to approach the real question of proper amusement. For believe me, my hearers, the great danger of the best class of Negro youth today is not that they will hesitate to sacrifice their lives, their money, and their energy on the altar of their race, but the danger is lest under continuous and persistent proscription, under the thousand little annoyances and petty insults and disappointments of a caste system, they lose the divine faith of their fathers in the fruitfulness of sacrifice; for surely no son of the nineteenth century has heard more plainly the mocking words of "Sorrow, cruel fellowship!"

There has been no time in the history of American Negroes when they had a more pressing need of spiritual guidance of the highest type; when amid the petty cares of social reform and moral reaction, there was wider place for a divine faith in the high destiny and marvelous might of that vast historic Negro race whose promise and first-fruits we of America are. There are creeping in among us low ideals of petty hatred, of sordid gain, of political theft, of place hunting and immodest self-praise, that must be stifled lest they sting to death our loftier and nobler sentiments.

Thus far I have sought to show; first, that the problem of proper amusement for our young people is rapidly coming to be a pressing one; second, that the Negro church, from its historic development has become the chief center of our amusements, and has been forced into the untenable position of seeming to deny the propriety of worldly amusements and dissipating at the same time its spiritual energy in furnishing them for its members.

I now wish to insist that the time has come when the activities of the Negro church must become differentiated and when it must surrender to the school and the home, and social organizations, those functions which in a day of organic poverty it so heroically sought to bear. The next social organism that followed the church among the Negroes was the school, and with the slow but certain upbuilding of the Negro home, we shall at last become a healthy society. Upon the school and the home must rest the burden of furnishing amusements for Negro youth. This duty must not be shirked—it must not be an after-thought—it must not be a spasmodic activity but a careful, rational plan. Take the boys and girls of the primary schools: I want to impress the fact upon every school teacher here who has children from six to thirteen under her care that oversight over the amusements of those children is just as important as oversight over their studies. And first of all, let the children sing, and sing songs, not hymns; it is bad enough on Sunday to hear the rude vigor and mighty music of the slave songs replaced by that combination of flippant music and mediocre poetry which we call gospel hymns. But for heaven's sake, let us not further tempt Providence by using these not only for hymns but for day-school purposes. Buy good song books—books that sing of earth and air and sky and sea, of lovers, birds, and trees, of every thing that makes God's world beautiful. Set the Southland to singing Annie Laurie, the Lorelei, Santa Lucia, and "My Heart's in the Hielands" let the children yodel, whistle, and clap their hands—they will get more real religion out of one healthy, wholesome folk-song than out of an endless repetition of hymns on all occasions, with sour faces, and forced reverence. Again, make the observance of recess as compulsory as that of work. In work time make the pupils work and work hard and continuously, and at recess time make them play and play hard and joyously; join in and direct their games, their "I Spy," and "King Consello" and "Grey Wolf" and the thousand and one good old games which are known from England to China. Watch that boy who after a morning's work will not play; he is not built right. Watch that girl who can mope and sleep at recess time; she needs a physician. In these schools of primary grade especial attention should be paid to athletic sports; boys and girls should be encouraged if not compelled to run, jump, walk, row, swim, throw and vault. The school picnic with a long walk over hill and dale and a romp under the trees in close communion with Mother Nature is sadly needed. In fine, here should be developed a capacity for pure, open-hearted enjoyment of the beautiful world about us, and woe to the teacher who is so bigoted and empty-headed as to suggest to innocent laughing hearts that play is not a divine institution which ever has and ever will, go hand in hand with work.

When the child grows up, in the momentous years from fourteen to eighteen, the problem of amusements becomes graver, and because it is graver it demands not less attention but more; generally the last thing that is thought of in the organization of a great school is: How are we to furnish proper amusement of these two or three hundred young people of all ages, tastes, and temperaments? And yet, unless that school does amuse, as well as instruct those boys and girls, and teach them how to amuse themselves, it fails of half its duty and it sends into the world men and women who can never stand up successfully in the awful moral battle which Negro blood is today waging for humanity. Here again athletic sports must in the future play a larger part in the normal and mission schools of the South, and we must rapidly come to the place where the man all brain and no muscle is looked upon as almost as big a fool as the man all muscle and no brain; and when the young woman who cannot walk a couple of good country miles will have few proposals of marriage. The crucial consideration at this age of life, between fourteen and eighteen, is really the proper social intercourse of the sexes; it is a grave question because its mistaken answer today coupled with an awful social history compels us to plead guilty to the shameful fact that sexual impurity among Negro men and Negro women of America is the crying disgrace of the American republic. The Southern school which can so train its sons and daughters that they can mingle in pure and chaste conversation, and thoroughly enjoy the natural love they have for each other's companionship; which can amuse and interest them and at the same time protect them with a high sense of honor and chastity—that school will be the greatest of Negro schools and the mightiest of American institutions. On the other hand, the school which seeks to build iron walls between the sexes, which discourages honest, open intercourse, which makes it a business to set the seal of disapproval upon sensible and joyous amusement, that school is filling the bawdy houses and gambling halls of our great cities with its most hopeless inmates.

I wish to take but one illustration to make clear my meaning in this crucial question; and I take two common amusements which bring the sexes together—dancing and accompanying young ladies home from church Sunday night. I never shall forget a dance I attended in Eisenach, Germany; contrary to my very elaborate expectation the young men did not accompany the girls to the dance; the girls went with their fathers and mothers; the boys went alone. In the pretty, airy hall the mothers seated themselves in a circle about the sides of the room and drew up their daughters beside them; fathers and elder brothers looked on from the doorway. Then we danced under the eyes of mothers and fathers, and we got permission to dance from those parents; we felt ourselves to be trusted guests in the bosom of families; three hours glided by in pure joyousness until, finally, long tables were brought in; we sat down, and cooled off and drank coffee and sang. Then the mothers took their daughters home, and the young men took themselves. I have had many good times in life, but not one to which I look back with more genuine pleasure and satisfaction. When now we compare the amusement thus conducted with the universal custom among us of allowing our daughters, unattended and unwatched, to be escorted at night, through great cities or country districts by chance acquaintances unknown to parents, with no rational diversion, but frivolous conversation and aimless nonsense, I have no hesitancy in saying I would rather have a daughter of mine dance her head off under her mother's eye, than to throw her unguarded and uncared for into the hands of unwatched strangers. The cases I have cited are of course extreme—all escorting of girls from church is not improper, and all dancing is not carried on as at Eisenach, but I wish to leave this one query with you. Is it not possible for us to rescue from its evil associations and conditions, so pleasant, innocent, and natural an amusement as dancing?

I have already talked too long and have but half exhausted a fertile and peculiarly interesting subject; the whole question of home pleasures and of diversions for older people remains untouched. I wish to leave you with a reiteration of what I desire to be the central thought of this paper, it is not a defense of particular amusements or a criticism of particular prohibitions, but an insistence on the fact that amusement is right, that pleasure is God-given, and that the people that seek to deny it and to shut the door upon it, simply open wide the door to dissipation and vice. I beg you to strive to change the mental attitude of the race toward amusement for the young, from a wholesale negative to an emphatic positive. Instead of warning young people so constantly against excess of pleasure, let us rather inspire them to unselfish work, and show them that amusement and recreation are the legitimate and necessary accompaniments of work, and that we get the maximum of enjoyment from them when they strengthen and inspire us for renewed effort in a great cause; and above all, let us teach them that there can be no greater cause than the development of Negro character to its highest and holiest possibilities.

13

THE CONSERVATION OF RACES

The American Negro has always felt an intense personal interest in discussions as to the origins and destinies of races: primariy because back of most discussions of race with which he is familiar, have lurked certain assumptions as to his natural abilities, as to his political, intellectual and moral status, which he felt were wrong. He has, consequently, been led to deprecate and minimize race distinctions, to believe intensely that out of one blood God created all nations, and to speak of human brotherhood as though it were the possibility of an already dawning to-morrow.

Nevertheless, in our calmer moments we must acknowledge that human beings are divided into races; that in this country the two most extreme types of the world's races have met, and the resulting problem as to the future relations of these types is not only of intense and living interest to us, but forms an epoch in the history of mankind.

It is necessary, therefore, in planning our movements, in guiding our future development, that at times we rise above the pressing, but smaller questions of separate schools and cars, wage-discrimination and lynch law, to survey the whole question of race in human philosophy and to lay, on a basis of broad knowledge and careful insight, those large lines of policy and higher ideals which may form our guiding lines and boundaries in the practical difficulties of every day. For it is certain that all human striving must recognize the hard limits of natural law, and that any striving, no matter how intense

Reprinted from the American Negro Academy, *Occasional Papers*, no. 2 (Washington, D.C. 1897), pp. 5–15.

and earnest, which is against the constitution of the world, is vain. The question, then, which we must seriously consider is this: What is the real meaning of Race; what has, in the past, been the law of race development, and what lessons has the past history of race development to teach the rising Negro people?

When we thus come to inquire into the essential difference of races we find it hard to come at once to any definite conclusion. Many criteria of race differences have in the past been proposed, as color, hair, cranial measurements and language. And manifestly, in each of these respects, human beings differ widely. They vary in color, for instance, from the marble-like pallor of the Scandinavian to the rich, dark brown of the Zulu, passing by the creamy Slav, the yellow Chinese, the light brown Sicilian and the brown Egyptian. Men vary, too, in the texture of hair from the obstinately straight hair of the Chinese to the obstinately tufted and frizzled hair of the Bushman. In measurement of heads, again, men vary; from the broad-headed Tartar to the medium-headed European and the narrow-headed Hottentot; or, again in language, from the highly-inflected Roman tongue to the monosyllabic Chinese. All these physical characteristics are patent enough, and if they agreed with each other it would be very easy to classify mankind. Unfortunately for scientists, however, these criteria of race are most exasperatingly intermingled. Color does not agree with texture of hair, for many of the dark races have straight hair; nor does color agree with the breadth of the head, for the yellow Tartar has a broader head than the German; nor, again, has the science of language as yet succeeded in clearing up the relative authority of these various and contradictory criteria. The final word of science, so far, is that we have at least two, perhaps three, great families of human beings— the whites and Negroes, possibly the yellow race. That other races have arisen from the intermingling of the blood of these two. This broad division of the world's races which men like Huxley and Raetzel have introduced as more nearly true than the old five-race scheme of Blumenbach, is nothing more than an acknowledgment that, so far as purely physical characteristics are concerned, the differences between men do not explain all the differences of their history. It declares, as Darwin himself said, that great as is the physical unlikeness of the various races of men their likenesses are greater, and upon this rests the whole scientific doctrine of Human Brotherhood.

Although the wonderful developments of human history teach that the grosser physical differences of color, hair and bone go but a short way toward explaining the different roles which groups of men have played in Human Progress, yet there are differences—subtle, delicate and elusive, though they may be—which have silently but definitely separated men into groups. While these subtle forces have generally followed the natural cleavage of common blood, descent and physical peculiarities, they have at other times swept across and ignored these. At all times, however, they have divided human beings into races, which, while they perhaps transcend scientific definition, nevertheless, are clearly defined to the eye of the Historian and Sociologist.

If this be true, then the history of the world is the history, not of individuals, but of groups, not of nations, but of races, and he who ignores or seeks to override the race idea in human history ignores and overrides the central thought of all history. What, then, is a race? It is a vast family of human beings, generally of common blood and language, always of common history, traditions and impulses, who are both voluntarily and involuntarily striving together for the accomplishment of certain more or less vividly conceived ideals of life.

Turning to real history, there can be no doubt, first, as to the widespread, nay, universal, prevalence of the race idea, the race spirit, the race ideal, and as to its efficiency as the vastest and most ingenious invention for human progress. We, who have been reared and trained under the individualistic philosophy of the Declaration of Independence and the laisser-faire philosophy of Adam Smith, are loath to see and loath to acknowledge this patent fact of human history. We see the Pharoahs, Caesars, Toussaints and Napoleons of history and forget the vast races of which they were but epitomized expressions. We are apt to think in our American impatience, that while it may have been true in the past that closed race groups made history, that here in conglomerate America *nous avons changer tout cela*—we have changed all that, and have no need of this ancient instrument of progress. This assumption of which the Negro people are especially fond, can not be established by a careful consideration of history.

We find upon the world's stage today eight distinctly differentiated races, in the sense in which History tells us the word must be used. They are, the Slavs of eastern Europe, the Teutons of middle Europe, the English of Great Britain and America, the Romance nations of Southern and Western Europe, the Negroes of Africa and America, the Semitic people of Western Asia and Northern Africa, the Hindoos of Central Asia and the Mongolians of Eastern Asia. There are, of course, other minor race groups, as the American Indians, the Esquimaux and the South Sea Islanders; these larger races, too, are far from homogeneous; the Slav includes the Czech, the Magyar, the Pole and the Russian; the Teuton includes the German, the Scandinavian and the Dutch; the English include the Scotch, the Irish and the conglomerate American. Under Romance nations the widely-differing Frenchman, Italian, Sicilian and Spaniard are comprehended. The term Negro is, perhaps, the most indefinite of all, combining the Mulattoes and Zamboes of America and the Egyptians, Bantus and Bushmen of Africa. Among the Hindoos are traces of widely differing nations, while the great Chinese, Tartar, Corean and Japanese families fall under the one designation—Mongolian.

The question now is: What is the real distinction between these nations? Is it the physical differences of blood, color and cranial measurements? Certainly we must all acknowledge that physical differences play a great part, and that, with wide exceptions and qualifications, these eight great races of to-day follow the cleavage of physical race distinctions; the English and Teuton represent the white variety of mankind; the Mongolian, the yellow; the Negroes, the black. Between these are many crosses and mixtures, where Mongolian and Teuton have blended into the Slav, and other mixtures have produced the Romance nations and the Semites. But while race differences have followed mainly physical race lines, yet no mere physical distinctions would really define or explain the deeper differences—the cohesiveness and continuity of these groups. The deeper differences are spiritual, psychical, differences—undoubtedly based on the physical, but infinitely transcending them. The forces that bind together the Teuton nations are, then, first, their race identity and common blood; secondly, and more important, a common history, common laws and religion, similar habits of thought and a conscious striving together for certain ideals of life. The whole process which has brought about these race differentiations has been a growth, and the great characteristic of this growth has been the differentiation of spiritual and mental differences between great races of mankind and the integration of physical differences.

The age of nomadic tribes of closely related individuals represents the maximum of physical differences. They were practically vast families, and there were as many groups as families. As the families came together to form cities the physical differences lessened, purity of blood was replaced by the requirement of domicile, and all who lived within the city bounds became gradually to be regarded as members of the group; *i. e.*, there was a slight and slow breaking down of physical barriers. This, however, was accompanied by an increase of the spiritual and social differences between cities. This city became husbandmen, this, merchants, another warriors, and so on. The *ideals of life* for which the different cities struggled were different. When at last cities began to coalesce into nations there was another breaking down of barriers which separated groups of men. The larger and broader differences of color, hair and physical proportions were not by any means ignored, but myriads of minor differences disappeared, and the sociological and historical races of men began to approximate the present division of races as indicated by physical researches. At the same time the spiritual and physical differences of race groups which constituted the nations became deep and decisive. The English nation stood for constitutional liberty and commercial freedom; the German nation for science and philosophy; the Romance nations stood for literature and art, and the other race groups are striving, each in its own way, to develope for civilization its particular message, its particular ideal, which shall help to guide the world nearer and nearer that perfection of human life for which we all long, that

"one far off Divine event."

This has been the function of race differences up to the present time. What shall be its function in the future? Manifestly some of the great races of today—particularly the Negro race—have not as yet given to civilization the full spiritual message which they are capable of giving. I will not say that the Negro race has as yet given no message to the world, for it is still a mooted question among scientists as to just how far Egyptian civilization was Negro in its origin; if it was not wholly Negro, it was certainly very closely allied. Be that as it may, however the fact still remains that the full, complete Negro message of the whole Negro race has not as yet been given to the world: that the messages and ideal of the yellow race have not been completed, and that the striving of the mighty Slavs has but begun. The question is, then: How shall this message be delivered; how shall these various ideals be realized? The answer is plain: By the development of these race groups, not as individuals, but as races. For the development of Japanese genius, Japanese literature and art, Japanese spirit, only Japanese, bound and welded together, Japanese inspired by one vast ideal, can work out in its fullness the wonderful message which Japan has for the nations of the earth. For the development of Negro genius, of Negro literature and art, of Negro spirit, only Negroes bound and welded together, Negroes inspired by one vast ideal, can work out in its fullness the great message we have for humanity. We cannot reverse history; we are subject to the same natural laws as other races, and if the Negro is ever to be a factor in the world's history—if among the gaily-colored banners that deck the broad ramparts of civilization is to hang one uncompromising black, then it must be placed there by black hands, fashioned by black heads and hallowed by the travail of 200,000,000 black hearts beating in one glad song of jubilee.

For this reason, the advance guard of the Negro people—the 8,000,000 people of Negro blood in the United States of America—must soon come to realize that if they are to take their just place in the van of Pan-Negroism, then their destiny is *not* absorption by the white Americans. That if in America it is to be proven for the first time in the modern world that not only Negroes are capable of evolving individual men like Toussaint, the Saviour, but are a nation stored with wonderful possibilities of culture, then their destiny is not a servile imitation of Anglo-Saxon culture, but a stalwart originality which shall unswervingly follow Negro ideals.

It may, however, be objected here that the situation of our race in America renders this attitude impossible; that our sole hope of salvation lies in our being able to lose our race identity in the commingled blood of the nation; and that any other course would merely increase the friction of races which we call race prejudice, and against which we have so long and so earnestly fought.

Here, then, is the dilemma, and it is a puzzling one, I admit. No Negro who has given earnest thought to the situation of his people in America has failed, at some time in life, to find himself at these cross-roads; has failed to ask himself at some time: What, after all, am I? Am I an American or am I a Negro? Can I be both? Or is it my duty to cease to be a Negro as soon as possible and be an American? If I strive as a Negro, am I not perpetuating the very cleft that threatens and separates Black and White America? Is not my only possible practical aim the subduction of all that is Negro in me to the American? Does my black blood place upon me any more obligation to assert my nationality than German, or Irish or Italian blood would?

It is such incessant self-questioning and the hesitation that arises from it, that is making the present period a time of vacillation and contradiction for the American Negro; combined race action is stifled, race responsibility is shirked, race enterprises languish, and the best blood, the best talent, the best energy of the Negro people cannot be marshalled to do the bidding of the race. They stand back to make room for every rascal and demagogue who chooses to cloak his selfish deviltry under the veil of race pride.

Is this right? Is it rational? Is it good policy? Have we in America a distinct mission as a race—a distinct sphere of action and an opportunity for race development, or is self-obliteration the highest end to which Negro blood dare aspire?

If we carefully consider what race prejudice really is, we find it, historically, to be nothing but the friction between different groups of people; it is the difference in aim, in feeling, in ideals of two different races; if, now, this difference exists touching territory, laws, language, or even religion, it is manifest that these people cannot live in the same territory without fatal collision; but if, on the other hand, there is substantial agreement in laws, language and religion; if there is a satisfactory adjustment of economic life, then there is no reason why, in the same country and on the same street, two or three great national ideals might not thrive and develop, that men of different races might not strive together for their race ideals as well, perhaps even better, than in isolation. Here, it seems to me, is the reading of the riddle that puzzles so many of us. We are Americans, not only by birth and by citizenship, but by our political ideals, our language, our religion. Farther than that, our American-ism does not go. At that point, we are Negroes, members of a vast historic race that from the very dawn of creation has slept, but half awakening in the dark forests of its African fatherland. We are the first fruits of this new nation, the harbinger of that black to-morrow which is yet destined to soften the whiteness of the Teutonic to-day. We are that people whose subtle sense of song has given America its only American music, its only American fairy tales, its only touch of pathos and humor amid its mad money-getting plutocracy. As such, it is our duty to conserve our physical powers, our intellectual endowments, our spiritual ideals; as a race we must strive by race organization, by race solidarity, by race unity to the realization of that broader humanity which freely recognizes differences in men, but sternly deprecates inequality in their opportunities of development.

For the accomplishment of these ends we need race organizations: Negro colleges, Negro newspapers, Negro business organizations, a Negro school of literature and art, and an intellectual clearing house, for all these products of the Negro mind, which we may call a Negro Academy. Not only is all this necessary for positive advance, it is absolutely imperative for negative defense. Let us not deceive ourselves at our situation in this country. Weighted with a heritage of moral iniquity from our past history, hard pressed in the economic world by foreign immigrants and native prejudice, hated here, despised there and pitied everywhere; our one haven of refuge is ourselves, and but one means of advance, our own belief in our great destiny, our own implicit trust in our ability and worth. There is no power under God's high heaven that can stop the advance of eight thousand thousand honest, earnest, inspired and united people. But—and here is the rub—they *must* be honest, fearlessly criticising their own faults, zealously correcting them; they must be *earnest.* No people that laughs at itself, and ridicules itself, and wishes to God it was anything but itself ever wrote its name in history; it *must* be inspired with the Divine faith of our black mothers, that out of the blood and dust of battle will march a victorious host, a mighty nation, a peculiar people, to speak to the nations of earth a Divine truth that shall make them free. And such a people must be united; not merely united for the organized theft of political spoils, not united to disgrace religion with whoremongers and ward-heelers; not united merely to protest and pass resolutions, but united to stop the ravages of consumption among the Negro people, united to keep black boys from loafing, gambling and crime; united to guard the purity of black women and to reduce that vast army of black prostitutes that is today marching to hell; and united in serious organizations, to determine by careful conference and thoughtful interchange of opinion the broad lines of policy and action for the American Negro.

This, is the reason for being which the American Negro Academy has. It aims at once to be the epitome and expression of the intellect of the black-blooded people of America, the exponent of the race ideals of one of the world's great races. As such, the Academy must, if successful, be

> *a.* Representative in character.
>
> *b.* Impartial in conduct.
>
> *c.* Firm in leadership.

It must be representative in character; not in that it represents all interests or all factions, but in that it seeks to comprise something of the *best* thought, the most unselfish striving and the highest ideals. There are scattered in forgotten nooks and corners throughout the land, Negroes of some considerable training, of high minds, and high motives, who are unknown to their fellows, who exert far too little influence. These the Negro Academy should strive to bring into touch with each other and to give them a common mouthpiece.

The Academy should be impartial in conduct; while it aims to exalt the people it should aim to do so by truth—not by lies, by honesty—not by flattery. It should continually impress the fact upon the Negro people that they must not expect to have things done for them—they MUST DO FOR THEMSELVES; that they have on their hands a vast work of self-reformation to do, and that a little less complaint and whining, and a little more dogged work and manly striving would do us more credit and benefit than a thousand Force or Civil Rights bills.

Finally, the American Negro Academy must point out a practical path of advance to the Negro people; there lie before every Negro today hundreds of questions of policy and right which must be settled and which each one settles now, not in accordance with any rule, but by impulse or individual preference; for instance: What should be the attitude of Negroes toward the educational qualification for voters? What should be our attitude toward separate schools? How should we meet discriminations on railways and in hotels? Such questions need not so much specific answers for each part as a general expression of policy, and nobody should be better fitted to announce such a policy than a representative honest Negro Academy.

All this, however, must come in time after careful organization and long conference. The immediate work before us should be practical and have direct bearing upon the situation of the Negro. The historical work of collecting the laws of the United States and of the various States of the Union with regard to the Negro is a work of such magnitude and importance that no body but one like this could think of undertaking it. If we could accomplish that one task we would justify our existence.

In the field of Sociology an appalling work lies before us. First, we must unflinchingly and bravely face the truth, not with apologies, but with solemn earnestness. The Negro Academy ought to sound a note of warning that would echo in every black cabin in the land: *Unless we conquer our present vices they will conquer us; we are* diseased, we are developing criminal tendencies, and an alarmingly large percentage of our men and women are sexually impure. The Negro Academy should stand and proclaim this over the housetops, crying with Garrison: *I will not equivocate, I will not retreat a single inch, and I will be heard.* The Academy should seek to gather about it the talented, unselfish men, the pure and noble-minded women, to fight an army of devils that disgraces our manhood and our womanhood. There does not stand today upon God's earth a race more capable in muscle, in intellect, in morals, than the American Negro, if he will bend his energies in the right direction; if he will

> Burst his birth's invidious bar
> And grasp the skirts of happy chance,
> And breast the blows of circumstance,
>   And grapple with his evil star.

In science and morals, I have indicated two fields of work for the Academy. Finally, in practical policy, I wish to suggest the following *Academy Creed:*

1. We believe that the Negro people, as a race, have a contribution to make to civilization and humanity, which no other race can make.

2. We believe it the duty of the Americans of Negro descent, as a body, to maintain their race identity until this mission of the Negro people is accomplished, and the ideal of human brotherhood has become a practical possibility.

3. We believe that, unless modern civilization is a failure, it is entirely feasible and practicable for two races in such essential political, economic and religious harmony as the white and colored people of America, to develop side by side in peace and mutual happiness, the peculiar contribution which each has to make to the culture of their common country.

4. As a means to this end we advocate, not such social equality between these races as would disregard human likes and dislikes, but such a social equilibrium as would, throughout all the complicated relations of life, give due and just consideration to culture, ability, and moral worth, whether they be found under white or black skins.

5. We believe that the first and greatest step toward the settlement of the present friction between the races—commonly called the Negro Problem—lies in the correction of the immorality, crime and laziness among the Negroes themselves, which still remains as a

heritage from slavery. We believe that only earnest and long continued efforts on our own part can cure these social ills.

6. We believe that the second great step toward a better adjustment of the relations between the races, should be a more impartial selection of ability in the economic and intellectual world, and a greater respect for personal liberty and worth, regardless of race. We believe that only earnest efforts on the part of the white people of this country will bring much needed reform in these matters.

7. On the basis of the foregoing declaration, and firmly believing in our high destiny, we, as American Negroes, are resolved to strive in every honorable way for the realization of the best and highest aims, for the development of strong manhood and pure womanhood, and for the rearing of a race ideal in America and Africa, to the glory of God and the uplifting of the Negro people.

CHANGING PATTERNS
OF RACIAL RELATIONS

Du Bois had always viewed the field of racial relations as requiring the dispassionate but skilled analysis of the trained sociologist. His analysis of racial relations, as presented in the four papers in this section, provides the reader with a sense of the accuteness of his observations and his ability to abstract these observations into concepts such as the social system, the color-line, and moral strain. In a 1901 paper, "The Relations of the Negroes to the Whites in the South," Du Bois points out how the color-line drastically restricts the comingling of the races with regard to the physical proximity of homes and dwelling areas, economic relationships, political relations, intellectual endeavors, and social interaction.

In the next paper, "The Social Evolution of the Black South" (1911), he describes how the color-line evolved over the previous half-century. The social system of the plantation during slavery initially consisted of a mass of socially undifferentiated field-hands who were unequivocably subordinated to the authority of the planter; it later consisted of field-hands, artisans, house servants, and the planter. With Emancipation, the social system became less inflexible as the freedmen gained the right to change employment and to migrate from the plantation to another plantation or to the city. But in time, as Du Bois notes, blacks in the urban South were increasingly subjected to social subordination. This contradiction of the intent of Emancipation induced in blacks and whites psychological states of "moral strain," which they sought to lessen through modes of rationalization: denial, resentment, and silence.

The third paper, "Problem of the Twentieth Century is the

Problem of the Color Line," published in 1950, traces changes in the racial situation in the United States since 1901, when Du Bois first made the prediction upon which the title is based. Substantial gains are noted in education, the right to vote, civil rights, employment, housing, the press, and social equality. But there are some disquieting signs within the moral fabric of black Americans themselves. In Du Bois' words, "The effort of Negroes to become Americans of equal status with other Americans is leading them to a state of mind by which they not only accept what is good in America, but what is bad and threatening so long as the Negro can share equally. This is peculiarly dangerous at this epoch in the development of world culture."

In the final paper, "Prospect of a World without Race Conflict," published in 1944, Du Bois described the world situation as it appeared to him. He did not envision, in the near future, the possibility of a world without racial conflict. The reason was that the United States, Great Britain, and other Western European nations continued to define Third World nations as socially inferior because of racial differences; yet, he noted, the world was silent about the subject of race and instead talked about the most serious problems as being those of employment, defense against aggression, health, poverty, population growth, and the like. But, said Du Bois, these world problems could not be discussed adequately while separated from the subject of race. What was necessary first was wide dissemination of the truth regarding race; secondly, "we need deliberate and organized action on the front where race fiction is being used to prolong economic inequality and injustice in the world."

14

THE RELATIONS OF THE NEGROES
TO THE WHITES IN THE SOUTH

In the discussion of great social problems it is extremely difficult for those who are themselves actors in the drama to avoid the attitude of partisans and advocates. And yet I take it that the examination of the most serious of the race problems of America is not in the nature of a debate but rather a joint endeavor to seek the truth beneath a mass of assertion and opinion, of passion and distress. And I trust that whatever disagreement may arise between those who view the situation from opposite sides of the color line will be rather in the nature of additional information than of contradiction.

The world-old phenomenon of the contact of diverse races of men is to have new exemplification during the new century. Indeed the characteristic of the age is the contact of European civilization with the world's undeveloped peoples. Whatever we may say of the results of such contact in the past, it certainly forms a chapter in human action not pleasant to look back upon. War, murder, slavery, extermination and debauchery—this has again and again been the result of carrying civilization and the blessed gospel to the isles of the sea and the heathen without the law. Nor does it altogether satisfy the conscience of the modern world to be told complacently that all this has been right and proper, the fated triumph of strength over weakness, of righteousness over evil, of superiors over inferiors. It would certainly be soothing if one could readily believe all this, and yet there are too many ugly facts, for everything to be thus easily explained away. We feel and know that there are many delicate

Reprinted from the *Annals of the American Academy of Political and Social Sciences* 18 (July 1901): 121–40.

differences in race psychology, numberless changes which our crude social measurements are not yet able to follow minutely, which explain much of history and social development. At the same time, too, we know that these considerations have never adequately explained or excused the triumph of brute force and cunning over weakness and innocence.

It is then the strife of all honorable men of the twentieth century to see that in the future competition of races, the survival of the fittest shall mean the triumph of the good, the beautiful and the true; that we may be able to preserve for future civilization all that is really fine and noble and strong, and not continue to put a premium on greed and impudence and cruelty. To bring this hope to fruition we are compelled daily to turn more and more to a conscientious study of the phenomena of race contact—to a study frank and fair, and not falsified and colored by our wishes or our fears. And we have here in the South as fine a field for such a study as the world affords: a field to be sure which the average American scientist deems somewhat beneath his dignity, and which the average man who is not a scientist knows all about, but nevertheless a line of study which by reason of the enormous race complications, with which God seems about to punish this nation, must increasingly claim our sober attention, study and thought. We must ask: What are the actual relations of whites and blacks in the South, and we must be answered not by apology or faultfinding, but by a plain, unvarnished tale.

In the civilized life of to-day the contact of men and their relations to each other fall in a few main lines of action and communication: there is first the physical proximity of homes and dwelling places, the way in which neighborhoods group themselves, and the contiguity of neighborhoods. Secondly, and in our age chiefest, there are the economic relations—the methods by which individuals co-operate for earning a living, for the mutual satisfaction of wants, for the production of wealth. Next there are the political relations, the co-operation in social control, in group government, in laying and paying the burden of taxation. In the fourth place there are the less tangible but highly important forms of intellectual contact and commerce, the interchange of ideas through conversation and conference, through periodicals and libraries, and above all the gradual formation for each community of that curious *tertium quid* which we call public opinion. Closely allied with this come the various forms of social contact in every-day life, in travel, in theatres, in house gatherings, in marrying and giving in marriage. Finally, there are the varying forms of religious enterprise, of moral teaching and benevolent endeavor.

These are the principal ways in which men living in the same communities are brought into contact with each other. It is my task this afternoon, therefore, to point out from my point of view how the black race in the South meets and mingles with the whites, in these matters of every-day life.

First as to physical dwelling, it is usually possible, as most of you know, to draw in nearly every Southern community a physical color line on the map, to the one side of which whites dwell and the other Negroes. The winding and intricacy of the geographical color line varies of course in different communities. I know some towns where a straight line drawn through the middle of the main street separates nine-tenths of the whites from nine-tenths of the blacks. In other towns the older settlement of whites has been encircled by a broad band of blacks; in still other cases little settlements or nuclei of blacks have sprung up amid surrounding whites. Usually in cities each street has its distinctive color, and only now and then do the colors meet in close proximity. Even in the country something of this segregation is manifest in the smaller areas, and of course in the larger phenomena of the black belt.

All this segregation by color is largely independent of that natural clustering by social grades common to all communities. A Negro slum may be in dangerous proximity to a white residence quarter, while it is quite common to find a white slum planted in the heart of a respectable Negro district. One thing, however, seldom occurs: the best of the whites and the best of the Negroes almost never live in anything like close proximity. It thus happens that in nearly every Southern town and city, both whites and blacks see commonly the worst of each other. This is a vast change from the situation in the past when through the close contact of master and house-servant in the patriarchal big house, one found the best of both races in close contact and sympathy, while at the same time the squalor and dull round of toil among the field hands was removed from the sight and hearing of the family. One can easily see how a person who saw slavery thus from his father's parlors and sees freedom on the streets of a great city fails to grasp or comprehend the whole of the new picture. On the other hand the settled belief of the mass of the Negroes that the Southern white people do not have the black man's best interests at heart has been intensified in later years by this continual daily contact of the better class of blacks with the worst representatives of the white race.

Coming now to the economic relations of the races we are on ground made familiar by study, much discussion and no little philanthropic effort. And yet with all this there are many essential elements in the co-operation of Negroes and whites for work and wealth, that are too readily overlooked or not thoroughly understood. The average American can easily conceive of a rich land awaiting development and filled with black laborers. To him the Southern problem is simply that of making efficient workingmen out of this material by giving them the requisite technical skill and the help of invested capital. The problem, however, is by no means as simple as this, from the obvious fact that these workingmen have been trained for centuries as slaves. They exhibit, therefore, all the advantages and defects of such training; they are willing and good-natured, but not self-reliant, provident or careful. If now the economic development of the South is to be pushed to the verge of exploitation, as seems probable, then you have a mass of working-men thrown into relentless competition with the workingmen of the world but handicapped by a training the very opposite to that of the modern self-reliant democratic laborer. What the black laborer needs is careful personal guidance, group leadership of men with hearts in their bosoms, to train them to foresight, carefulness and honesty. Nor does it require any fine-spun theories of racial differences to prove the necessity of such group training after the brains of the race have been knocked out by two hundred and fifty years of assiduous education in submission, carelessness and stealing. After emancipation it was the plain duty of some one to assume this group leadership and training of the Negro laborer. I will not stop here to inquire *whose* duty it was—whether that of the white ex-master who had profited by unpaid toil, or the Northern philanthropist whose persistence brought the crisis, or of the National Government whose edict freed the bondsmen—I will not stop to ask *whose* duty it was, but I insist it was the duty of *some one* to see that these workingmen were not left alone and unguided without capital, landless, without skill, without economic organization, without even the bald protection of law, order and decency; left in a great land not to settle down to slow and careful internal development, but destined to be thrown almost immediately into relentless, sharp competition with the best of modern workingmen under an economic system where every participant is fighting for himself, and too often utterly regardless of the rights or welfare of his neighbor.

For we must never forget that the economic system of the South to-day which has succeeded the old régime is not the same system as that of the old industrial North, of England or of France with their trade unions, their restrictive laws, their written and unwritten commercial customs and their long experience. It is rather a copy of that England of the early nineteenth century, before the factory acts, the England that wrung pity from thinkers and fired the wrath of Carlyle. The rod of empire that passed from the hands of Southern gentlemen in 1865, partly by force, partly by their own petulance, has never returned to them. Rather it has passed to those men who have come to take charge of the industrial exploitation of the New South—the sons of poor whites fired with a new thirst for wealth and power, thrifty and avaricious Yankees, shrewd and unscrupulous Jews. Into the hands of these men the Southern laborers, white and black, have fallen, and this to their sorrow. For the laborers as such there is in these new captains of industry neither love nor hate, neither sympathy nor romance—it is a cold question of dollars and dividends. Under such a system all labor is bound to suffer. Even the white laborers are not yet intelligent, thrifty and well trained enough to maintain themselves against the powerful inroads of organized capital. The result among them even, is long hours of toil, low wages, child labor, and lack of protection against usury and cheating. But among the black laborers all this is aggravated, first, by a race prejudice which varies from a doubt and distrust among the best element of whites to a frenzied hatred among the worst; and, secondly, it is aggravated, as I have said before, by the wretched economic heritage of the freedmen from slavery. With this training it is difficult for the freedman to learn to grasp the opportunities already opened to him, and the new opportunities are seldom given him but go by favor to the whites.

Left by the best elements of the South with little protection or oversight, he has been made in law and custom the victim of the worst and most unscrupulous men in each community. The crop-lien system which is depopulating the fields of the South is not simply the result of shiftlessness on the part of Negroes but is also the result of cunningly devised laws as to mortgages, liens and misdemeanors which can be made by conscienceless men to entrap and snare the unwary until escape is impossible, further toil a farce, and protest a crime. I have seen in the black belt of Georgia an ignorant, honest Negro buy and pay for a farm in installments three separate times, and then in the face of law and decency the enterprising Russian Jew who sold it to him pocketed money and deed and left the black man landless, to labor on his own land at thirty cents a day. I have seen a black farmer fall in debt to a white storekeeper and that storekeeper go to his farm and strip it of every single marketable article—mules, plows, stored crops, tools, furniture, bedding, clocks, looking-glass, and all this without a warrant, without process of law, without a sheriff or officer, in the face of the law for homestead exemptions, and without rendering to a single responsible person any account or reckoning. And such proceedings can happen and will happen in any community where a class of ignorant toilers are placed by custom and race prejudice beyond the pale of sympathy and race brotherhood. So long as the best elements of a community do not feel in duty bound to protect and train and care for the weaker members of their group they leave them to be preyed upon by these swindlers and rascals.

This unfortunate economic situation does not mean the hindrance of all advance in the black south, or the absence of a class of black landlords and mechanics who, in spite of disadvantages, are accumulating property and making good citizens. But it does mean that this class is not nearly so large as a fairer economic system might easily make it, that those who survive in the competition are handicapped so as to accomplish much less than they deserve to, and that above all, the personnel of the successful class is left to chance and accident, and not to any intelligent culling or reasonable methods of selection. As a remedy for this, there is but one possible procedure. We must accept some of the race prejudice in the South as a fact—deplorable in its intensity, unfortunate in results, and dangerous for the future, but nevertheless a hard fact which only time can efface. We cannot hope then in this generation, or for several generations, that the mass of the whites can be brought to assume that close sympathetic and self-sacrificing leadership of the blacks which their present situation so eloquently demands. Such leadership, such social teaching and example, must come from the blacks themselves. For sometime men doubted as to whether the Negro could develop such leaders, but to-day no one seriously disputes the capability of individual Negroes to assimilate the culture and common sense of modern civilization, and to pass it on to some extent, at least, to their fellows. If this be true, then here is the path out of the economic situation, and here is the imperative demand for trained Negro leaders of character and intelligence, men of skill, men of light and leading, college-bred men, black captains of industry and missionaries of culture. Men who thoroughly comprehend and know modern civilization and can take hold of Negro communities and raise and train them by force of precept and example, deep sympathy and the inspiration of common blood and ideals. But if such men are to be effective they must have some power—they must be backed by the best public opinion of these communities, and able to wield for their objects and aims such weapons as the experience of the world has taught are indispensable to human progress.

Of such weapons the greatest, perhaps, in the modern world is the power of the ballot, and this brings me to a consideration of the third form of contact between whites and blacks in the South—political activity.

In the attitude of the American mind toward Negro suffrage, can be traced with singular accuracy the prevalent conceptions of government. In the sixties we were near enough the echoes of the

French Revolution to believe pretty thoroughly in universal suffrage. We argued, as we thought then rather logically, that no social class was so good, so true and so disinterested as to be trusted wholly with the political destiny of their neighbors; that in every state the best arbiters of their own welfare are the persons directly affected, consequently it is only by arming every hand with a ballot—with the right to have a voice in the policy of the state—that the greatest good to the greatest number could be attained. To be sure there were objections to these arguments, but we thought we had answered them tersely and convincingly; if some one complained of the ignorance of voters, we answered: "Educate them." If another complained of their venality we replied: "Disfranchise them or put them in jail." And finally to the men who feared demagogues and the natural perversity of some human beings, we insisted that time and bitter experience would teach the most hardheaded. It was at this time that the question of Negro suffrage in the South was raised. Here was a defenseless people suddenly made free. How were they to be protected from those who did not believe in their freedom and were determined to thwart it? Not by force, said the North; not by government guardianship, said the South; then by the ballot, the sole and legitimate defense of a free people, said the Common Sense of the nation. No one thought at the time that the ex-slaves could use the ballot intelligently or very effectively, but they did think that the possession of so great power, by a great class in the nation would compel their fellows to educate this class to its intelligent use.

Meantime new thoughts came to the nation: the inevitable period of moral retrogression and political trickery that ever follows in the wake of war overtook us. So flagrant became the political scandals that reputable men began to leave politics alone, and politics consequently became disreputable. Men began to pride themselves on having nothing to do with their own government and to agree tacitly with those who regarded public office as a private perquisite. In this state of mind it became easy to wink at the suppression of the Negro vote in the South, and to advise self-respecting Negroes to leave politics entirely alone. The decent and reputable citizens of the North who neglected their own civic duties grew hilarious over the exaggerated importance with which the Negro regarded the franchise. Thus it easily happened that more and more the better class of Negroes followed the advice from abroad and the pressure from home and took no further interest in politics, leaving to the careless and the venal of their race the exercise of their rights as voters. This black vote which still remained was not trained and educated but further debauched by open and unblushing bribery, or force and fraud, until the Negro voter was thoroughly inoculated with the idea that politics was a method of private gain by disreputable means.

And finally, now, to-day, when we are awakening to the fact that the perpetuity of republican institutions on this continent depends on the purification of the ballot, the civic training of voters, and the raising of voting to the plane of a solemn duty which a patriotic citizen neglects to his peril and to the peril of his children's children—in this day when we are striving for a renaissance of civic virtue, what are we going to say to the black voter of the South? Are we going to tell him still that politics is a disreputable and useless form of human activity? Are we going to induce the best class of Negroes to take less and less interest in government and give up their right to take such an interest without a protest? I am not saying a word against all legitimate efforts to purge the ballot of ignorance, pauperism and crime. But few have pretended that the present movement for disfranchisement in the South is for such a purpose; it has been plainly and frankly declared in nearly every case that the object of the disfranchising laws is the elimination of the black man from politics.

Now is this a minor matter which has no influence on the main question of the industrial and intellectual development of the Negro? Can we establish a mass of black laborers, artisans and landholders in the South who by law and public opinion have absolutely no voice in shaping the laws under which they live and work. Can the modern organization of industry, assuming as it does free democratic government and the power and ability of the laboring classes to compel respect for their welfare—can this system be carried out in the South when half its laboring force is voiceless in the public councils and powerless in its own defense? To-day the black man of the South has almost nothing to say as to how much he shall be taxed, or how those taxes shall be expended; as to who shall make the laws and how they shall be made. It is pitiable that frantic efforts must be made at critical times to get lawmakers in some states even to listen to the respectful presentation of the black side of a current controversy. Daily the Negro is coming more and more to look upon law and justice not as protecting safeguards but as sources of humiliation and oppression. The laws are made by men who as yet have little interest in him; they are executed by men who have absolutely no motive for treating the black people with courtesy or consideration; and finally the accused lawbreaker is tried not by his peers but too often by men who would rather punish ten innocent Negroes than let one guilty one escape.

I should be the last one to deny the patent weaknesses and shortcomings of the Negro people; I should be the last to withhold sympathy from the white South in its efforts to solve its intricate social problems. I freely acknowledge that it is possible and sometimes best that a partially undeveloped people should be ruled by the best of their stronger and better neighbors for their own good, until such time as they can start and fight the world's battles alone. I have already pointed out how sorely in need of such economic and spiritual guidance the emancipated Negro was, and I am quite willing to admit that if the representatives of the best white southern public opinion were the ruling and guiding powers in the South to-day that the conditions indicated would be fairly well fulfilled. But the point I have insisted upon and now emphasize again is that the best opinion of the South to-day is not the ruling opinion. That to leave the Negro helpless and without a ballot to-day is to leave him not to the guidance of the best but rather to the exploitation and debauchment of the worst; that this is no truer of the South than of the North—of the North than of Europe—in any land, in any country under modern free competition, to lay any class of weak and despised people, be they white, black or blue, at the political mercy of their stronger, richer and more resourceful fellows is a temptation which human nature seldom has and seldom will withstand.

Moreover the political status of the Negro in the South is closely connected with the question of Negro crime. There can be no doubt that crime among Negroes has greatly increased in the last twenty years and that there has appeared in the slums of great cities a

distinct criminal class among the blacks. In explaining this unfortunate developement we must note two things, (1) that the
inevitable result of emancipation was to increase crime and criminals, and (2) that the police system of the South was primarily designed to control slaves. As to the first point we must not forget that
under a strict slave régime there can scarcely be such a thing as crime.
But when these variously constituted human particles are suddenly
thrown broadcast on the sea of life, some swim, some sink, and some
hang suspended, to be forced up or down by the chance currents of
a busy hurrying world. So great an economic and social revolution as
swept the South in '63 meant a weeding out among the Negroes of
the incompetents and vicious—the beginning of a differentiation of
social grades. Now a rising group of people are not lifted bodily from
the ground like an inert solid mass, but rather stretch upward like a
living plant with its roots still clinging in the mold. The appearance,
therefore, of the Negro criminal was a phenomenon to be awaited,
and while it causes anxiety it should not occasion surprise.

Here again the hope for the future depended peculiarly on careful
and delicate dealing with these criminals. Their offenses at first were
those of laziness, carelessness and impulse rather than of malignity
or ungoverned viciousness. Such misdemeanors needed discriminating treatment, firm but reformatory, with no hint of injustice
and full proof of guilt. For such dealing with criminals, white or
black, the South had no machinery, no adequate jails or reformatories and a police system arranged to deal with blacks alone, and
which tacitly assumed that every white man was *ipso facto* a member
of that police. Thus grew up a double system of justice which erred
on the white side by undue leniency and the practical immunity of
red-handed criminals, and erred on the black side by undue severity,
injustice and lack of discrimination. For, as I have said, the police
system of the South was originally designed to keep track of all
Negroes, not simply of criminals, and when the Negroes were freed
and the whole South was convinced of the impossibility of free Negro
labor, the first and almost universal device was to use the courts as a
means of re-enslaving the blacks. It was not then a question of crime
but rather of color that settled a man's conviction on almost any
charge. Thus Negroes came to look upon courts as instruments of

injustice and oppression, and upon those convicted in them as martyrs and victims.

When now the real Negro criminal appeared and, instead of petty stealing and vagrancy, we began to have highway robbery, burglary, murder and rape, it had a curious effect on both sides the color line; the Negroes refused to believe the evidence of white witnesses or the fairness of white juries, so that the greatest deterrent to crime, the public opinion of one's own social caste was lost and the criminal still looked upon as crucified rather than hanged. On the other hand the whites, used to being careless as to the guilt or innocence of accused Negroes, were swept in moments of passion beyond law, reason and decency. Such a situation is bound to increase crime and has increased it. To natural viciousness and vagrancy is being daily added motives of revolt and revenge which stir up all the latent savagery of both races and make peaceful attention to economic development often impossible.

But the chief problem in any community cursed with crime is not the punishment of the criminals but the preventing of the young from being trained to crime. And here again the peculiar conditions of the South have prevented proper precautions. I have seen twelve-year-old boys working in chains on the public streets of Atlanta, directly in front of the schools, in company with old and hardened criminals; and this indiscriminate mingling of men, women and children makes the chain-gangs perfect schools of crime and debauchery. The struggle for reformatories which has gone on in Virginia, Georgia and other states is the one encouraging sign of the awakening of some communities to the suicidal results of this policy.

It is the public schools, however, which can be made outside the homes the greatest means of training decent self-respecting citizens. We have been so hotly engaged recently in discussing trade schools and the higher education that the pitiable plight of the public school system in the South has almost dropped from view. Of every five dollars spent for public education in the State of Georgia the white schools get four dollars and the Negro one dollar, and even then the white public school system, save in the cities, is bad and cries for reform. If this be true of the whites, what of the blacks? I am becoming more and more convinced as I look upon the system of common school training in the South that the national government must soon step in and aid popular education in some way. To-day it has been only by the most strenuous efforts on the part of the thinking men of the South that the Negro's share of the school fund has not been cut down to a pittance in some half dozen states, and that movement not only is not dead but in many communities is gaining strength. What in the name of reason does this nation expect of a people poorly trained and hard pressed in severe economic competition, without political rights and with ludicrously inadequate common school facilities? What can it expect but crime and listlessness, offset here and there by the dogged struggles of the fortunate and more determined who are themselves buoyed by the hope that in due time the country will come to its senses?

I have thus far sought to make clear the physical, economic and political relations of the Negroes and whites in the South as I have conceived them, including for the reasons set forth, crime and education. But after all that has been said on these more tangible matters of human contact there still remains a part essential to a proper description of the South which it is difficult to describe or fix in terms easily understood by strangers. It is, in fine, the atmosphere of the land, the thought and feeling, the thousand and one little actions which go to make up life. In any community or nation it is these little things which are most elusive to the grasp and yet most essential to any clear conception of the group life, taken as a whole. What is thus true of all communities is peculiarly true of the South where, outside of written history and outside of printed law, there has been going on for a generation, as deep a storm and stress of human souls, as intense a ferment of feeling, as intricate a writhing of spirit as ever a people experienced. Within and without the sombre veil of color, vast social forces have been at work, efforts for human betterment, movements toward disintegration and despair, tragedies and comedies in social and economic life, and a swaying and lifting and sinking of human hearts which have made this land a land of mingled sorrow and joy, of change and excitement.

The centre of this spiritual turmoil has ever been the millions of black freedmen and their sons, whose destiny is so fatefully bound up with that of the nation. And yet the casual observer visiting the South sees at first little of this. He notes the growing frequency of dark faces as he rides on, but otherwise the days slip lazily on, the sun shines and this little world seems as happy and contented as other worlds he has visited. Indeed, on the question of questions, the Negro problem, he hears so little that there almost seems to be a conspiracy of silence; the morning papers seldom mention it, and then usually in a far-fetched academic way, and indeed almost every one seems to forget and ignore the darker half of the land, until the astonished visitor is inclined to ask if after all there *is* any problem here. But if he lingers long enough there comes the awakening: perhaps in a sudden whirl of passion which leaves him gasping at its bitter intensity; more likely in a gradually dawning sense of things he had not at first noticed. Slowly but surely his eyes begin to catch the shadows of the color line; here he meets crowds of Negroes and whites; then he is suddenly aware that he cannot discover a single dark face; or again at the close of a day's wandering he may find himself in some strange assembly, where all faces are tinged brown or black, and where he has the vague uncomfortable feeling of the stranger. He realizes at last that silently, resistlessly, the world about flows by him in two great streams. They ripple on in the same sunshine, they approach here and mingle their waters in seeming carelessness, they divide then and flow wide apart. It is done quietly, no mistakes are made, or if one occurs the swift arm of the law and public opinion swings down for a moment, as when the other day a black man and a white woman were arrested for talking together on Whitehall street, in Atlanta.

Now if one notices carefully one will see that between these two worlds, despite much physical contact and daily intermingling, there is almost no community of intellectual life or points of transferrence where the thoughts and feelings of one race can come with direct contact and sympathy with the thoughts and feelings of the other. Before and directly after the war when all the best of the Negroes were domestic servants in the best of the white families, there were bonds of intimacy, affection, and sometimes blood relationship between the races. They lived in the same home, shared in the family life, attended the same church often and talked and conversed with each other. But the increasing civilization of the Negro since has naturally meant the development of higher classes: there are increasing numbers of ministers, teachers, physicians, merchants, mechanics and independent farmers, who by nature and training are the aristocracy and leaders of the blacks. Between them, however, and the best element of the whites, there is little or no intellectual commerce. They go to separate churches, they live in separate sections, they are strictly separated in all public gatherings, they travel separately, and they are beginning to read different papers and books. To most libraries, lectures, concerts and museums Negroes are either not admitted at all or on terms peculiarly galling to the pride of the very classes who might otherwise be attracted. The daily paper chronicles the doings of the black world from afar with no great regard for accuracy; and so on throughout the category of means for intellectual communication; schools, conferences, efforts for social betterment and the like, it is usually true that the very representatives of the two races who for mutual benefit and the welfare of the land ought to be in complete understanding and sympathy are so far strangers that one side thinks all whites are narrow and prejudiced and the other thinks educated Negroes dangerous and insolent. Moreover, in a land where the tyranny of public opinion and the intolerence of criticism is for obvious historical reasons so strong as in the South, such a situation is extremely difficult to correct. The white man as well as the Negro is bound and tied by the color line and many a scheme of friendliness and philanthropy, of broad-minded sympathy, and generous fellowship between the two has dropped still-born because some busy-body has forced the color question to the front and brought the tremendous force of unwritten law against the innovators.

It is hardly necessary for me to add to this very much in regard to the social contact between the races. Nothing has come to replace that finer sympathy and love between some masters and house servants, which the radical and more uncompromising drawing of the color line in recent years has caused almost completely to disappear. In a world where it means so much to take a man by the hand and sit beside him; to look frankly into his eyes and feel his heart beating with red blood—in a world where a social cigar or a cup of tea together means more than legislative halls and magazine articles and speeches, one can imagine the consequences of the almost utter absence of such social amenities between estranged races, whose separation extends even to parks and street cars.

Here there can be none of that social going down to the people; the opening of heart and hand of the best to the worst, in generous acknowledgment of a common humanity and a common destiny. On the other hand, in matters of simple almsgiving, where there be no question of social contact, and in the succor of the aged and sick, the South, as if stirred by a feeling of its unfortunate limitations, is generous to a fault. The black beggar is never turned away without a good deal more than a crust, and a call for help for the unfortunate meets quick response. I remember, one cold winter, in Atlanta, when I refrained from contributing to a public relief fund lest Negroes should be discriminated against; I afterward inquired of a friend: "Were any black people receiving aid?" "Why," said he, "they were *all* black."

And yet this does not touch the kernel of the problem. Human advancement is not a mere question of almsgiving, but rather of sympathy and co-operation among classes who would scorn charity. And here is a land where, in the higher walks of life, in all the higher striving for the good and noble and true, the color line comes to separate natural friends and co-workers, while at the bottom of the social group in the saloon, the gambling hell and the bawdy-house that same line wavers and disappears.

I have sought to paint an average picture of real relations between the races in the South. I have not glossed over matters for policy's sake, for I fear we have already gone too far in that sort of thing. On the other hand I have sincerely sought to let no unfair exaggerations creep in. I do not doubt but that in some Southern communities conditions are far better than those I have indicated. On the other hand, I am certain that in other communities they are far worse.

Nor does the paradox and danger of this situation fail to interest and perplex the best conscience of the South. Deeply religious and intensely democratic as are the mass of the whites, they feel acutely the false position in which the Negro problems place them. Such an essentially honest-hearted and generous people cannot cite the caste-leveling precepts of Christianity, or believe in equality of opportunity for all men, without coming to feel more and more with each generation that the present drawing of the color line is a flat contradiction to their beliefs and professions. But just as often as they come to this point the present social condition of the Negro stands as a menace and a portent before even the most open-minded: if there were nothing to charge against the Negro but his blackness or other physical peculiarities, they argue, the problem would be comparatively simple; but what can we say to his ignorance, shiftlessness, poverty and crime: can a self-respecting group hold anything but the least possible fellowship with such persons and survive? and shall we let a mawkish sentiment sweep away the culture of our fathers or the hope of our children? The argument so put is of great strength but it is not a whit stronger than the argument of thinking Negroes; granted, they reply, that the condition of our masses is bad, there is certainly on the one hand adequate historical cause for this, and unmistakable evidence that no small number have, in spite of tremendous disadvantages, risen to the level of American civilization. And when by proscription and prejudice, these same Negroes are classed with, and treated like the lowest of their people simply *because* they are Negroes, such a policy not only discourages thrift and intelligence among black men, but puts a direct premium on the very things you complain of— inefficiency and crime. Draw lines of crime, of incompetency, of vice as tightly and uncompromisingly as you will, for these things must be proscribed, but a color line not only does not accomplish this purpose, but thwarts it.

In the face of two such arguments, the future of the South depends on the ability of the representatives of these opposing views to see and appreciate, and sympathize with each other's position; for the Negro to realize more deeply than he does at present the need of uplifting the masses of his people, for the white people to realize more vividly than they have yet done the deadening and disastrous effect of a color prejudice that classes Paul Lawrence Dunbar and Sam Hose in the same despised class.

It is not enough for the Negroes to declare that color prejudice is the sole cause of their social condition, nor for the white South to reply that their social condition is the main cause of prejudice. They both act as reciprocal cause and effect and a change in neither *alone* will bring the desired effect. Both must change or neither can improve to any great extent. The Negro cannot stand the present reactionary tendencies and unreasoning drawing of the color line much longer without discouragement and retrogression. And the condition of the Negro is ever the excuse for further discrimination. Only by a union of intelligence and sympathy across the color line in this critical period of the Republic shall justice and right triumph, and

"Mind and heart according well,
Shall make one music as before,
   But vaster."

15

THE SOCIAL EVOLUTION
OF THE BLACK SOUTH

I have worded the subject which I am going to treat briefly in this paper; "The Social Evolution of the Black South," and I mean by that, the way in which the more intimate matters of contact of Negroes with themselves and with their neighbors have changed in the evolution of the last half century from slavery to larger freedom. It will be necessary first in order to understand this evolution to remind you of certain well known conditions in the South during slavery. The unit of the social system of the south was the plantation, and the plantation was peculiar from the fact that it tended to be a monarchy and not an aristocracy.

In the early evolution of England we find men of noble and aristocratic birth continually rising and disputing with the monarch as to his arbitrary power and finally gaining, in the case of Magna Carta, so great influence as practically to bind the monarch to their will. In France on the other hand we find continually a tendency for monarchs like Louis XIV to gain such power that they forced even the aristocracy to be their sycophants, and men who, like the rest of the monarch's subjects had no rights which the monarch was bound to respect.

We must now remember that the little plantations which formed the unit of the social life in the South before the war tended continually to the French model of Louis XIV and went in many cases far beyond it, so that the ruler of the plantation was practically absolute in his power even to the matter of life and death, being seldom interfered with by the state. While, on the other hand, the

Reprinted from *American Negro Monographs* 1 (March 1911): 3–12.

mass of field hands were on a dead level of equality with each other and in their subordination to the owners power. This does not mean that the slaves were consequently unhappy or tyranized over in all cases, it means simply what I have said, they were at practically the absolute mercy of the owner. The real owner could be a beneficent monarch—and was in some cases in the South—or he might be the brutal, unbridled tyrant—and was in some cases in the South. Just where the average lay between these two extremes is very difficult to determine with any degree of accuracy but the experience of the world leads us to believe that abuse of so great power was in a very large number of cases inevitable.

Turning now to this great army of field hands we find them usually removed one or two degrees from the ear of the monarch by the power of the overseer and his assistants. Here again was a broad gate way for base and petty tyranny. The social life on the plantation, *that is*, the contact of slave with slave was necessarily limited. There was the annual frolic culminating in "the Christmas"; and there was usually a by-weekly or monthly church service. The frolic tended gradually to demoralization for an irregular period, longer or shorter, of dissipation and excess. Historically it was the American representative of the dance and celebration among African tribes with however, the old customary safeguards and traditions of leadership almost entirely gone. Only the dance and liquor usually remained. The church meeting on the plantation was, in its historical beginning, the same. Just as the Greek dance in the theatre was a species of a religious observance in its origin and indeed in its culmination so the African dance differentiated: Its fun and excesses went into the more or less hidden night frolics; while its tradition and ceremony was represented in the church services and veneered with more or less Christian elements. Of the distinctly family social life: The whole tendency of the plantation was to leave less and less.

Polygamy was established and to some extent encouraged into the West Indies and its opposite was not systematically frowned upon in America, and there was neither time nor place for family cere-monial. There was a common sleeping place more or less confined to a family; a common eating place but few family celebrations.

Sometimes there was a ceremony of marriage but this was an exception among the field hands. There was certainly no ceremony of divorce and little authority over children. The whole tendency of the plantation was toward communism of eating, children and property.—Facts which show their definite results among us to-day—some good and some bad. The beautiful hospitality, for instance, among our poorest Negroes and the willing adoption of orphan children is balanced against bad systems of eating and living and illegitimate births. In and over all these plantation organizations there must of course have arisen that thing so characteristic of monarchal power, namely, the tale bearer and the thief. The man who curries favor by telling on the neighbors, and the man who having no chance to earn what he wants, steals it. From tale-bearing and deception on the one hand and unusual ability and adaptability on the others there arose from the dead level of the plantation field hands two classes of incipient aristocracy, namely, the artisan and the house-servant. The artisan by natural and acquired manual and mental dexterity coupled with more or less keenness of mind became a slave of special value. On his ability the whole plantation to a large extent depended. He built the houses, he repaired them, made and repaired most of the tools, arranged the crops for market; manufactured the rolling stock. As the plantations increased and were systematized he became so valuable that he was an article of special barter and could by shrewdness himself dictate often the terms of his use. Many stringent laws were aimed against him to keep him from becoming too independent. Nevertheless he increased in numbers and sometimes bought his own freedom. In many cases he acquired property. He was demanded in large and larger numbers in the cities and he formed a growing problem of the slave system. He is the direct ancestor of the city Negro. Side by side with the slave mechanic and in some cases identical with him arose the house-servants; as the mechanic gained his power by ability and economic demand the house-servant gained a more tremendous and dangerous power by personal contact until on some plantations it was actually a question as to whether the master would rule his servants or his servants rule him, but when such a statement is made it must be interpreted as applying to the house-servant and the house-servants were but a small per cent of the total number of slaves; because the house servant gained very intimate knowledge and opportunity to serve the good will and even the affection of the master or to pander to his vices and because too from the house-servants the great amalgamation of the races took place so that the servant was often blood relative of the master. In this way the house-servant became even a more dangerous person than the mechanic.—More dangerous because he could command a more careful protection of his master a more intimate protection, and because he inevitably had chances for education which the mechanic did not. When therefore, emancipation came it found the cultured house-servant further on the road to civilization, followed by the less cultured but more effectual artisan and both dragged down by the great unnumbered weight of largely untouched field hands. The great change which freedom brought to the plantation was the right of emigration from one plantation to another but this right was conceded by no means everywhere and is not even until this very day. Gradually, however, large and larger numbers of field hands changed plantations or migrated to town. In the change of plantations they slowly but surely improved the rate of compensation and conditions of work, on the other hand, they remained and still remain so far as they stayed on the plantations, a backward uneducated class of servants except where they have been able to buy land. And even there they have become efficient, pushing and rising only in cases where they have education of some degree. Now it was the Negro that migrated to town that got a chance for education, both in early days and largely so to-day. In town he met the school and the results of the school, i. e., he himself learned to read and write and he came in more or less contact with the things and influence of men who had learned more than mere reading and writing. We must then if we would know the social condition of the Negro to-day turn our attention to this city group. No matter how much we may believe the country the place for the Southern Negro or stress its certain advantages to him there, the sad truth remains that the black man who can take advantage of these opportunities is represented in the country districts in very small numbers and cannot under present circumstances be represented by larger numbers save through conscientious, systematic group effort. It is the city group of Negroes, therefore that is the most civilized and advancing and it is that group whose social structure we need to study. It is in the south above all a segregated group, and this means that it is the group that lives to itself, works by itself worships alone and finds education and amusement among its own. This segregation is growing, and its growth involves two things true in all evolution processes, namely, greater differentiation and greater integration. Greater differentiation from the white group in, for instance, the schools of the city which it inhabits, the interests which attract it; the ideals which inspire it and the traditions which it inherits. On the other hand greater integration in the sense of stronger self consciousness, more harmonious working together with a broader field for such co-operation. We often compare the North and South with regard to these things and pointing to the tremendous co-operation of the southern city group we urge the Northern group to follow its foot-steps without stopping to think that tremendous and even harsh differentiation must precede and accompany all such integration and in so far as that differentiation is absent in the North, it is this absence here that it gives a chance for a slower but larger integration in the North which may in the long run, and already has, helped the smaller intenser integration of the black Southern group. Now to illustrate just what I mean by the integral life of the Southern group let me point the possibilities of a black man in a city like Atlanta to-day. He may arise in the morning in a house which a black man built and which he himself owns; it has been painted and papered by black men; the furniture was probably bought at a white store, but not necessarily, and if it was, it was brought to the house by a colored drayman; the soap with which he washes might have been bought from a colored drug store; his provisions are bought at a Negro grocery; for the most part his morning paper is delivered by a colored boy; he starts to work walking to the car with a colored neighbor and sitting in a part of the car surrounded by colored people; in most cases he works for white men but not in all, he may work for a colored man or a colored family; even if he works for a white man his fellow workmen with whom he comes in contact are all colored; with them he eats his dinner and returns home at night; once a week he reads a colored paper; he is insured in a colored insurance company; he patronizes a colored school with colored teachers, and a colored church with a colored preacher; he gets his amusements at places frequented and usually run by colored people; he is buried by a colored undertaker in a colored grave-yard. In his section of the city few or no white people live, consequently his children grow up with colored companions; in his home a white person seldom if ever enters; all the family meals, amusements and ceremonies are among his own people. Now such a situation means more than mere separation from white people; it means, as I have intimated before, not simply separation but organized provision for the service of this colored group. The group must see to it that religion, education, amusements, etc., are furnished its members, and while some of these things are left to chance more and more such groups are conscientiously exerting themselves to provide for themselves in these ways and this is what I mean by integration. The place, however, where the separation cannot be made perfect is in matters of work in economic co-operation and here the Negro in this city group occupies one of two very different positions: he may be and often is one of those who is engaged in service which the group as such demands, i. e., a teacher, a lawyer, a physician, a druggist, an artisan whose clients are colored or a servant for colored people. This group of employees are growing rapidly but it is a small group and a group naturally paid relatively small wages. On the other hand, the great mass of this city group are persons whose employment makes them a part of the whole economic organization of the South and Nation. These are the great mass of laborers, porters, servants and artisans. Their contact with the white group is considerable and constant and in that contact enters and necessitates continual existence of social inter-course. It is here that the great battle of the race question is being fought. But fought as you will perceive, not by the most highly educated and able members of the group but, usually, by the middle class workingman and very often too the tendency is rather to separate that group of men from its natural intellectual leaders; This in the Southern city group of yesterday was possible, but is to-day being made more and more impossible because these natural leaders are seeking economic improvement as leaders of the integrating forces of the race. They depend, therefore, for their enumeration upon this mass of workingmen and upon the loyalty with which this mass of workingmen co-operate in organization. They must, therefore, cater to the whims and likes and dislikes of the mass of the Negro people. This makes physicians and their kind, like teachers, preachers and lawyers drawn to the mass of their people by strong cords of self-interest because their bread and butter lies in the masses hands, while on the other hand, this same mass is tremendously dependent upon this intellectual aristocracy for such organization of their life as will make their life pleasant and endurable. Consequently there has grown up in the new South among the city groups certain well defined social classes with comparatively few social chasms. Roughly speaking, there is a large middle class of working people; an upper class of professional people and a lower class of the poor and semi-criminal. The upper class find their social intercourse among themselves and in contact with the mass of laborers whom they meet in church, in the lodge, in the school and neighborhood and in the streets. The middle class of laborers have most of their social contact with themselves, occasional contact with their town upper class and also a large semi-social contact with the whites through their occupations as house-servants, artisans, porters, etc. The last class of the very poor and semi-criminal have little or no contact with their own people outside their own class but a very large and a very intimate contact with certain classes of whites. Now these facts are perfectly real to one who knows the South and are true in some degree of Northern cities, but they lead to certain results to which few people give intelligent thought. Namely: in case the white group wishes to communicate with the Negro group its only method of communication is through the middle class of workingmen. The white people of Atlanta *do not know* the colored teachers, physicians, lawyers or merchants. They *do* know the servants, the porters and the artisans. They are therefore, continually led to assume that the Negroes whom they do not know or meet are either nonexistent or are quite a negligible quantity. They do not realize *first* that there is a group of greater education and ability than they have met right in their own midst and *secondly* they do not realize that that higher group is an organ unit with the mass of workingmen, and that consequently it is quite impossible to deal to-day with the mass of Negroes without taking this upper class into account. Then again the poor and semi-criminal class looms large in the eyes of the white community because of their dependence and their delinquencies, and when there comes the question of the reformation or proper punishment of this class the white community is at an utter loss as to where to appeal. They see with perfect justice that the Negro laborer although himself honest is not capable of bearing the burden of reforming his criminals. The whites themselves cannot do it because they lack the human contact and charity. They consequently make no trial and leave this class to be abused by the economic and social exploitation of their own worst white elements. This but inflames and degrades and makes worst the Negro criminal classes. On the other hand, the upper class of Negroes has no way of communicating with its white neighbors at any rate of speaking with sufficient authority, so that these whites will realize that they are at least the nucleus of the class who can deal with the problem of race contact and crime. This then in brief is the situation. What now is the mental attitude engendered by it?

The chief results among both black and whites is evidence of peculiar moral strain. A strain which does not always voice itself; indeed which finds it difficult to choose words, but a strain nevertheless which is manifested in a hundred different ways. Both white men and black men try to hide it. Ask a black man about conditions in the South and he is evasive; he speaks upon this and that pleasant point but of the whole situations of the general trend he does not wish to speak, or if he does speak his speech is difficult to understand. Precisely the same thing in differing ways is true of the white man, and it leaves the outside spectator peculiarly puzzled. The fact is that both black and white in the South endure the present pain and bitterness but see a wonderful vision. The black man endures segregation and personal humiliation but sees the development and unfolding of a human group, one of the most fascinating and inspiring of spectacles. The white man endures the moral contradiction of conscious injustice and meanness, but sees the vision of a white world without race problems where all men can really be brothers with an intense yearning for democracy but democracy upon certain terms. With them the evil and the vision, there must be among both black and white a daily and hourly *compromise*. The black man can daily balance things and say "Is the vision of a strongly developed race worth the present insult, or blow or discrimination?" The white man must say "Is the promise of a real democracy worth the present lie and deception and cruelty?" The necessity of these daily compromises leads to three sorts of mental attitudes among both races. The man who sees the situation clearly and lies about it; the man who sees the situation and resents it; and the man who does not clearly understand the circumstances and is silent and sensitive under the ruthless conditions.

Among the first of these three attitudes is the wily and oily orator who attends Northern chatauquas and tells of his love for his black mammy; the brutal hot-headed brawler and lyncher who wants to fight a desperate cause but takes it out in fighting the helpless; and finally the man who typifies what is called the "silent South". On the part of the Negro there are avowed also the three types: the wily and crafty man who tells the North and the Negro of the kindness of the South and advance of the black man; the fighter who complains or shoots or migrates; and the silent sensitive black man who suffers but says nothing. Now of these three types I am free to say that the one of whom I hope most is the white brawler and the black fighter; I mean by that not that lynching is not horrible and fighting terrible but I do mean that these are types of men of a certain rough honesty.

Your Tillmans and your Vardamans represent a certain disgusting but honest ignorance which acts upon its information and some day when it gets the right information it is going to act right. On the other hand, I believe that at the end of the devious way of the compromiser and liar lies moral death.

I do not believe that the systematic deception concerning the situation in the South either on the part of white men or black men will in the long-run help that situation a single particle. I sincerely hope, therefore, that out of the white silent South and from the ranks of the silent and sensitive Negroes will come men who will approach the lyncher and fighter with their barbaric honesty of purpose and will bring to the situation that large knowledge and moral courage which will enable them to say that *this is wrong* in the South and *that is right*, and *I am fighting for the right*; who will stoop, if necessary, but will let no man ever doubt but that they stoop to conquer.

16

THE PROBLEM OF THE TWENTIETH CENTURY IS THE PROBLEM OF THE COLOR LINE

We are just finishing the first half of the Twentieth Century. I remember its birth in 1901. There was the usual discussion as to whether the century began in 1900 or 1901; but, of course, 1901 was correct. We expected great things ... peace; the season of war among nations had passed; progress was the order ... everything going forward to bigger and better things. And then, not so openly expressed, but even more firmly believed, the rule of white Europe and America over black, brown and yellow peoples.

I was 32 years of age in 1901, married, and a father, and teaching at Atlanta University with a program covering a hundred years of study and investigation into the condition of American Negroes. Our subject of study at that time was education: the college-bred Negro in 1900, the Negro common school in 1901. My own attitude toward the Twentieth Century was expressed in an article which I wrote in the Atlantic Monthly in 1901. It said:

> The problem of the Twentieth Century is the problem of the color-line ... I have seen a land right merry with the sun, where children sing, and rolling hills lie like passioned women wanton with harvest. And there in the King's Highway sat, and sits, a figure veiled and bowed, by which the Traveler's footsteps hasten as they go. On the tainted air broods fair. Three centuries' thought have been the raising and unveiling of that bowed human soul; and now behold, my fellows, a century now for the duty and the deed! The problem of the Twentieth Century is the problem of the color-line.

Reprinted from the *Pittsburgh Courier*, January 14, 1950. © 1950 by the Pittsburgh Courier Publishing Co.

281

This is what we hoped, to this we Negroes looked forward; peace, progress and the breaking of the color line. What has been the result? We know it all too well ... war, hate, the revolt of the colored peoples and the fear of more war.

In the meantime, where are we; those 15,000,000 citizens of the United States who are descended from the slaves, brought here between 1600 and 1900? We formed in 1901, a separate group because of legal enslavement and emancipation into caste conditions, with the attendant poverty, ignorance, disease and crime. We were an inner group and not an integral part of the American nation; but we were exerting ourselves to fight for integration.

The burden of our fight was in seven different lines. We wanted education; we wanted particularly the right to vote and civil rights; we wanted work with adequate wage; housing, without segregation or slums; a free press to fight our battles, and (although in those days we dare not say it) social equality.

In 1901 our education was in perilous condition, despite what we and our white friends had done for thirty years. The Atlanta University Conference said in its resolutions of 1901:

> We call the attention of the nation to the fact that less than one million of the three million Negro children of school age are at present regularly attending school, and these attend a session which lasts only a few months. We are today deliberately rearing millions of our citizens in ignorance and at the same time limiting the rights of citizenship by educational qualifications. This is unjust.

More particularly in civil rights, we were oppressed. We not only did not get justice in the courts, but we were subject to peculiar and galling sorts of injustice in daily life. In the latter half of the Nineteenth Century, where we first get something like statistics, no less than 3,000 Negroes were lynched without trial. And in addition to that we were subject continuously to mob violence and judicial lynching.

In political life we had, for twenty-five years, been disfranchised by violence, law and public opinion. The 14th and 15th amendments were deliberately violated and the literature of the day in book, pamphlet and daily press, was widely of opinion that the Negro was not ready for the ballot, could not use it intelligently, and that no action was called for to stop his political power from being exercised by Southern whites like Tillman and Vardaman.

We did not have the right or opportunity to work at an income which would sustain a decent and modern standard of life. Because of a past of chattel slavery, we were for the most part common laborers and servants, and a very considerable proportion were still unable to leave the plantations where they worked all their lives for next to nothing.

There were a few who were educated for the professions and we had many good artisans; that number was not increasing as it should have been, nor were new artisans being adequately trained. Industrial training was popular, but funds to implement it were too limited, and we were excluded from unions and the new mass industry.

We were housed in slums and segregated districts where crime and disease multiplied, and when we tried to move to better and healthier quarters we were met by segregation ordinance if not by mobs. We not only had no social equality, but we did not openly ask for it. It seemed a shameful thing to beg people to receive us as equals and as human beings; that was something we argued "that came and could not be fetched." And that meant not simply that we could not marry white women or legitimize mulatto bastards, but we could not stop in a decent hotel, nor eat in a public restaurant nor attend the theatre, nor accept an invitation to a private white home, nor travel in a decent railway coach. When the "public" was invited, this did not include us and admission to colleges often involved special consideration if not blunt refusal.

Finally we had poor press . . . a few struggling papers with little news and inadequately expressed opinion, with small circulation or influence and almost no advertising.

This was our plight in 1901. It was discouraging, but not hopeless. There is no question but that we had made progress, and there also was no doubt but what that progress was not enough to satisfy us or to settle our problems.

We could look back on a quarter century of struggle which had its results. We had schools; we had teachers; a few had forced themselves into the leading colleges and were tolerated if not welcomed. We voted in Northern cities, owned many decent homes and were fighting for further progress. Leaders like Booker Washington had received wide popular approval and a Negro literature had begun to appear.

But what we needed was organized effort along the whole front, based on broad lines of complete emancipation. This came with the Niagara Movement in 1906 and the NAACP in 1909. In 1910 came the Crisis magazine and the real battle was on.

What have we gained and accomplished? The advance has not been equal on all fronts, nor complete on any. We have not progressed with closed ranks like a trained army, but rather with serried and broken ranks, with wide gaps and even temporary retreats. But we have advanced. Of that there can be no atom of doubt.

First of all in education; most Negro children today are in school and most adults can read and write. Unfortunately this literacy is not as great as the census says. The draft showed that at least a third of our youth are illiterate. But education is steadily rising. Six thousand Bachelor degrees are awarded to Negroes each year and Doctorates in philosophy and medicine are not uncommon. Nevertheless as a group, American Negroes are still in the lower ranks of learning and adaptability to modern conditions. They do not read widely, their travel is limited and their experience through contact with the modern world is curtailed by law and custom.

Secondly, in civil rights, the Negro has perhaps made his greatest advance. Mob violence and lynching have markedly decreased. Three thousand Negroes were lynched in the last half of the Nineteenth Century and five hundred in the first half of the Twentieth. Today lynching is comparatively rare. Mob violence also has decreased, but is still in evidence, and summary and unjust court proceedings have taken the place of open and illegal acts. But the Negro has established, in the courts, his legal citizenship and his right to be included in the Bill of Rights. The question still remains of "equal but separate" public accommodations, and that is being attacked. Even the institution of "jim-crow" in travel is tottering.

The infraction of the marriage situation by law and custom is yet to be brought before the courts and public opinion in a forcible way.

Third, the right to vote on the part of the Negro is being gradually established under the 14th and 15th amendments. It was not really until 1915 that the Supreme Court upheld this right of Negro citizens and even today the penalties of the 14th amendment have never been enforced. There are 7,000,000 possible voters among American Negroes and of these it is a question if more than 2,000,000 actually cast their votes. This is partly from the national inertia, which keeps half of all American voters away from the polls; but even more from the question as to what practical ends the Negro shall cast his vote.

He is thinking usually in terms of what he can do by voting to better his condition and he seldom gets a chance to vote on this matter. On the wider implications of political democracy he has not yet entered; particularly he does not see the economic foundations of present civilization and the necessity of his attacking the rule of corporate wealth in order to free the labor group to which he belongs.

Fourth, there is the question of occupation. There are our submerged classes of farm labor and tenants: our city laborers, washerwomen and scrubwomen and the mass of lower-paid servants. These classes still form a majority of American Negroes and they are on the edge of poverty, with the ignorance, disease and crime that always accompany such poverty.

If we measure the median income of Americans, it is $3,000 for whites and $2,000 for Negroes. In Southern cities, 7 per cent of the white families and 30 per cent of the colored families receive less than $1,000 a year. On the other hand the class differentiation by income among Negroes is notable: the number of semi-skilled and skilled artisans has increased or will as membership in labor unions. Professional men have increased, especially teachers and less notably, physicians, dentists and lawyers.

The number of Negroes in business has increased; mostly in small retail businesses, but to a considerable extent in enterprises like insurance, real estate and small banking, where the color line gives Negroes certain advantages and where, too, there is a certain element of gambling. Also beyond the line of gambling, numbers of Negroes have made small fortunes in anti-social enterprises. All this means that there has arisen in the Negro group a distinct stratification from poor to rich. Recently I polled 450 Negro families belonging to a select organization forty-five years old. Of these families 127 received over $10,000 a year and a score of these over $25,000; 200 families received from $5,000 to $10,000 a year and eighty-six less than $5,000.

This is the start of a tendency which will grow; we are beginning to follow the American pattern of accumulating individual wealth and of considering that this will eventually settle the race problem. On the other hand, the whole trend of the thought of our age is toward social welfare; the prevention of poverty by more equitable distribution of wealth, and business for general welfare rather than private profit. There are few signs that these ideals are guiding Negro development today. We seem to be adopting increasingly the ideal of American culture.

Housing, has, of course, been a point of bitter pressure among Negroes, because the attempt to segregate the race in its living conditions has not only kept the more fortunate ones from progress, but it has confined vast numbers of Negro people to the very parts of cities and country districts where they have fewest opportunities and least social contacts. They must live largely in slums, in contact with criminals and with fewest of the social advantages of government and human contact. The fight against segregation has been carried on in the courts and shows much progress against city ordinances, against covenants which make segregation hereditary.

Literature and art have made progress among Negroes, but with curious handicaps. An art expression is normally evoked by the conscious and unconscious demand of people for portrayal of their own emotion and experience. But in the case of the American Negroes, the audience, which embodies the demand and which pays sometimes enormous price for satisfaction, is not the Negro group, but the white group. And the pattern of what the white group wants does not necessarily agree with the natural desire of Negroes.

The whole of Negro literature is therefore curiously divided. We have writers who have written, not really about Negroes, but about the things which white people, and not the highest class of whites, like to hear about Negroes. And those who have expressed what the Negro himself thinks and feels, are those whose books sell to few, even of their own people; and whom most folk do not know. This has not made for the authentic literature which the early part of this century seemed to promise. To be sure, it can be said that American literature to-day has a considerable amount of Negro expression and influence, although not as much as once we hoped.

Despite all this we have an increasing number of excellent Negro writers who make the promise for the future great by their real accomplishment. We have done something in sculpture and painting, but in drama and music we have markedly advanced. All the world listens to our singers, sings our music and dances to our rhythms.

In science, our handicaps are still great. Turner, a great entomologist, was worked to death for lack of laboratory; just never had the recognition he richly deserved, and Carver was prisoner of his inferiority complex. Notwithstanding this, our real accomplishment in biology and medicine; in history and law; and in the social sciences has been notable and widely acclaimed. To this in no little degree is due our physical survival, our falling death rate and our increased confidence in our selves and in our destiny.

The expression of Negro wish and desire through a free press has greatly improved as compared with 1900. We have a half dozen large weekly papers with circulations of a hundred thousand or more. Their news coverage is immense, even if not discriminating. But here again, the influence of the American press on us has been devastating. The predominance of advertising over opinion, the desire for income rather than literary excellence and the use of deliberate propaganda, had made our press less of a power than it could be, and leaves wide chance for improvement in the future.

In comparison with other institutions, the Negro church during the Twentieth Century has lost ground. It is no longer the dominating influence that it used to be, the center of social activity and of economic experiment. Nevertheless, it is still a powerful institution in the lives of numerical majority of American Negroes if not upon the dominant intellectual classes. There has been a considerable increase in organized work for social progress through the church, but there has also been a large increase of expenditure for buildings, furnishings, and salaries; and it is not easy to find any increase in moral stamina or conscientious discrimination within church circles.

The scandal of deliberate bribery in election of Bishops and in the holding of positions in the churches without a hierarchy has been widespread. It is a critical problem now as to just what part in the future the church among Negroes is going to hold.

Finally there comes the question of social equality, which, despite efforts on the part of thinkers, white and black, is after all the main and fundamental problem of race in the United States. Unless a human being is going to have all human rights, including not only work, but friendship, and if mutually desired, marriage and children, unless these avenues are open and free, there can be no real equality and no cultural integration.

It has hitherto seemed utterly impossible that any such solution of the Negro problem in America could take place. The situation was quite similar to the problem of the lower classes of laborers, serfs and servants in European nations during the Sixteenth, Seventeenth and Eighteenth centuries. All nations had to consist of two separate parts and the only relations between them was employment and philanthropy.

That problem has been partly solved by modern democracy, but modern democracy cannot succeed unless the peoples of different races and religions are also integrated into the democratic whole. Against this large numbers of Americans have always fought and are still fighting, but the progress despite this has been notable. There are places in the United States, especially in large cities like New York and Chicago, where the social differences between the races has, to a large extent, been nullified and there is a meeting on terms of equality which would have been thought impossible a half century ago.

On the other hand, in the South, despite religion, education and reason, the color line, although perhaps shaken, still stands, stark and unbending, and to the minds of most good people, eternal. Here lies the area of the last battle for the complete rights of American Negroes.

Within the race itself today there are disquieting signs. The effort of Negroes to become Americans of equal status with other Americans is leading them to a state of mind by which they not only accept what is good in America, but what is bad and threatening so long as the Negro can share equally. This is peculiarly dangerous at this epoch in the development of world culture.

After two world wars of unprecendented loss of life, cruelty and destruction, we are faced by the fact that the industrial organization of our present civilization has in it something fundamentally wrong. It went to pieces in the first world war because of the determination of certain great powers excluded from world rule to share in that rule, by acquisition of the labor and materials of colonial peoples. The attempt to recover from the cataclysm resulted in the collapse of our industrial system, and a second world war.

In spite of the propaganda which has gone on, which represents America as the leading democratic state, we Negroes know perfectly well, and ought to know even better than most, that America is not a successful democracy and that until it is, it is going to drag down the world. This nation is ruled by corporate wealth to a degree which is frightening. One thousand persons own the United States and their power outweighs the voice of the mass of American citizens. This must be cured, not by revolution, not by war and violence, but by reason and knowledge.

Most of the world is today turning toward the welfare state; turning against the idea of production for individual profit toward the idea of production for use and for the welfare of the mass of citizen. No matter how difficult such a course is, it is the only course that is going to save the world and this we American Negroes have got to realize.

We may find it easy now to get publicity, reward, and attention by going along with the reactionary propaganda and war hysteria which is convulsing this nation, but in the long run America will not thank its black children if they help it go the wrong way, or retard its progress.

17

PROSPECT OF A WORLD
WITHOUT RACE CONFLICT

It is with great regret that I do not see after this war, or within any reasonable time, the possibility of a world without race conflict; and this is true despite the fact that race conflict is playing a fatal role in the modern world. The supertragedy of this war is the treatment of the Jews in Germany. There has been nothing comparable to this in modern history. Yet its technique and its reasoning have been based upon a race philosophy similar to that which has dominated both Great Britain and the United States in relation to colored people.

This philosophy postulates a fundamental difference among the greater groups of people in the world, which makes it necessary that the superior peoples hold the inferior in check and rule them in accordance with the best interest of these superiors. Of course, many of the usual characteristics were missing in this outbreak of race hate in Germany. There was in reality little of physical difference between German and Jew. No one has been able to accuse the Jews of inferiority; rather it was the superiority of the Jews in certain respects which was the real cause of conflict. Nevertheless, the ideological basis of this attack was that of fundamental biological difference showing itself in spiritual and cultural incompatibility. Another difference distinguishes this race war. Usually the cure for race persecution and subordination has been thought to be segregation, but in this case the chance to segregate the Jews, at least partially, in Palestine, has practically been vetoed by the British government.

Reprinted from *American Journal of Sociology* 49 (March 1944): 450–56.

In other parts of the world the results of race conflict are clear. The representative of Prime Minister Churchill presiding over the British war cabinet has been the prime minister of the Union of South Africa. Yet South Africa has without doubt the worst race problem of the modern world. The natives have been systematically deprived of their land, reduced to the status of a laboring class with the lowest of wages, disfranchised, living and working under caste conditions with only a modicum of education, and exposed to systematic public and private insult. There is a large population of mixed-bloods, and the poverty, disease, and crime throughout the Union of South Africa are appalling. Here in a land which furnishes gold and diamonds and copper, the insignia of the luxury and technique of modern civilization, this race hate has flourished and is flourishing. Smuts himself, as political leader of the Union of South Africa, has carried out much of the legislation upon which this race conflict is based; and, although from time to time he has expressed liberal ideas, he has not tried or succeeded in basically ameliorating the fundamental race war in that part of the world.

The situation in India is another case of racial conflict. The mass of people there are in the bondage of poverty, disfranchisement, and social caste. Despite eminent and widely known leadership, there has not come on the part of the British any effective attempt fundamentally to change the attitude of the governing country toward the subject peoples. The basic reason for this, openly or by inference, is the physical difference of race which makes it, according to British thought, impossible that these peoples should within any reasonable space of time become autonomous or self-governing. There have been promises, to be sure, from time to time, and promises are pending; but no one can doubt that if these people were white and of English descent, a way out of the present impasse would have long since been found.

There is no doubt but that India is a congeries of ignorant, poverty-stricken, antagonistic groups who are destined to go through all the hell of internal strife before they emancipate themselves. But it is just as true that Europe of the sixteenth century was no more ready for freedom and autonomy than India. But Europe was not faced and coerced by a powerful overlord who did not believe Europeans were men and was determined to treat them as serfs to minister to his own comfort and luxury.

In India we have the first thoroughgoing case of modern colonial imperialism. With the capitalism built on the African slave trade and on the sugar, tobacco, and cotton crops of America, investment in India grew and spread for three hundred years, until there exists the greatest modern case of the exploitation of one people by another. This exploitation has been modified in various ways: some education has been furnished the Indians, a great system of railroads has been installed, and industrialization has been begun. But nothing has been done to loosen to any appreciable degree the strangle hold of the British Empire on the destinies of four hundred million human beings. The prestige and profit of the control of India have made it impossible for the British to conceive of India as an autonomous land.

The greatest and most dangerous race problem today is the problem of relations between Asia and Europe: the question as to how far "East is East and West is West" and of how long they are going to retain the relation of master and serf. There is in reality no difference between the reaction to this European idea on the parts of Japan and China. It is a question simply of the method of eliminating it. The idea of Japan was to invoke war and force—to drive Europe out of Asia and substitute the domination of a weak Asia by a strong Japan. The answer of China was co-operation and gradual understanding between Great Britain, France, America, and China. Chinese leaders are under no illusions whatever as to the past attitude of Europe toward Chinese. The impudence, browbeating, robbery, rape, and insult is one long trail of blood and tears, from the Opium War to the kowtowing before the emperor in Berlin. Even in this present war and alliance there has occurred little to reassure China: certain courtesies from the British and belated and meager justice on the part of the United States, after the Soong sister had swept in on us with her retinue, jade, and jewels. There has not only been silence concerning Hong Kong, Burma, and Singapore but there is the continued assumption that the subjugation of Japan is in the interest of Europe and America and not of

Asia. American military leaders have insisted that we must have in the Pacific after this war American bases for armed force. But why? If Asia is going to develop as a self-governing, autonomous part of the world, equal to other parts, why is policing by foreigners necessary? Why cannot Asia police itself? Only because of the deep-seated belief among Europeans and Americans that yellow people are the biological inferiors to the whites and not fit for self-government.

Not only does Western Europe believe that most of the rest of the world is biologically different but it believes that in this difference lies congenital inferiority; that the black and brown and yellow people are not simply untrained in certain ways of doing and methods of civilization; that they are naturally inferior and inefficient; that they are a danger to civilization as civilization is understood in Europe. This belief is so fundamental that it enters into the very reforms that we have in mind for the post-war world.

In the United States the race problem is peculiarly important just now. We see today a combination of northern investors and southern Bourbons desiring not simply to overthrow the New Deal but to plunge the United States into fatal reaction. The power of the southerners arises from the suppression of the Negro and poor-white vote, which gives the rotten borough of Mississippi four times the political power of Massachusetts and enables the South through the rule of seniority to pack the committees of Congress and to dominate it. Nothing can be done about this situation until we face fairly the question of color discrimination in the South; until the social, political, and economic equality of civilized men is recognized, despite race, color, and poverty.

In the Caribbean area, in Central and South America, there has been for four hundred years wide intermixture of Europeans, African, and Red Indian races. The result in one respect is widely different from that of Europe and North America; the social equality of Negroes, Indians, and mulattoes who were civilized was recognized without question. But the full results of this cultural liberalism were largely nullified by the economic control which Western Europe and North America held over these lands. The exploitation of cheap colored labor through poverty and low prices for materials was connived at as usual in the civilized world and the spoils shared with local white politicians. Economic and social prestige favored the whites and hindered the colored. A legend that the alleged backwardness of the South Americans was due to race mixture was so far stressed in the world that South America feared it and catered to it; it became the habit to send only white Brazilians, Bolivians, and Mexicans abroad to represent their countries; to encourage white immigration at all costs, even to loss of autonomy; to draw color lines in the management of industry dominated by Europe and in society where foreigners were entertained. In short, to pretend that South America hated and distrusted dark blood as much as the rest of the world, often even when the leaders of this policy were known themselves to be of Negro and Indian descent.

Thus the race problem of South and Central America, and especially of the islands of the Caribbean, became closely allied with European and North American practice. Only in the past few decades are there signs of an insurgent native culture, striking across the color line toward economic freedom, political self-rule, and more complete social equality between races.

There still is a residual sense of racial difference among parts of Europe; a certain contemptuous attitude toward Italy has been manifest for a long time, and the Balkans have been a byword for inefficiency and muddle. The pretensions of the Greeks to represent ancient Greek culture and of the Rumanians to be Roman have been laughed at by Western Europe. The remainder of the Balkans and Russia have been looked upon as Asiatic barbarism, aping civilization. As quasi-Asiatic, they have come in for the racial contempt poured upon the yellow peoples. This attitude greeted the Russian revolution and staged almost a race war to uphold tottering capitalism, built on racial contempt. But in Eastern Europe today are a mass of awakening men. They know and see what Russia has done for her debased masses in a single generation, cutting across race lines not only between Jew and Gentile but between White Russians, Ukrainians, Tartars, Turks, Kurds, and Kalmuks. As Sidney and Beatrice Webb declared:

All sections of the community—apart from those legally deprived of citizenship on grounds unconnected with either race or nationality—enjoy, throughout the USSR, according to law, equal rights and duties, equal privileges and equal opportunities. Nor is this merely a formal equality under the law and the federal constitution. Nowhere in the world do habit and custom and public opinion approach nearer to a like equality in fact. Over the whole area between the Arctic Ocean and the Black Sea and the Central Asian mountains, containing vastly differing races and nationalities, men and women, irrespective of conformation of skull or pigmentation of skin, even including the occasional African Negro admitted from the United States, may associate freely with whom they please; travel in the same public vehicles and frequent the same restaurants and hotels; sit next to each other in the same colleges and places of amusements; marry wherever there is mutual liking; engage on equal terms in any craft or profession for which they are qualified; join the same churches or other societies; pay the same taxes and be elected or appointed to any office or position without exception.

This, Eastern Europe knows, while Western Europe is still determined to build its culture on race discrimination and expects Russia to help her. But how far can Russia be depended upon to defend, in world war, British and American investments in Asia and Africa?

The attitude of America and Britain toward De Gaulle is puzzling until we remember that, since Gobineau, racial assumptions have entered into the relations between France and the Nordic world. During the first World War the United States was incensed at the social equality attitudes of the "frogs," while Britain as well as Germany resented the open dependence of France on her black colonial soldiers. One present great liberal statesman, Smuts, led a crusade against arming blacks in any future European war. Yet De Gaulle not only uses Senegalese soldiers but recognizes the Negro governor of a strategic French colonial province; while Burman, writing of the history of the Free French, exclaims: "I am witnessing a miracle, the rebirth of France in the jungles of Africa!" Racial caste and profitable investment after the war indicate a halt in our support of De Gaulle. France since the eighteenth century has insisted on recognizing the social equality of civilized men despite race. She has for this reason been regarded as traitor to the white colonial front, in government and in society, despite her investors who have supported British methods. Hitler is not the only modern statesman who has sneered at "mongrel" France.

These are some but by no means all of the race problems which face the world; yet they are not being discussed except indirectly. The Atlantic Charter as well as the agreements in Moscow and Teheran have been practically silent on the subject of race. It is assumed that certain fundamental matters and more immediate issues must be met and settled before this difficult question of race can be faced. Let us now ask ourselves if this is true. What *are* the fundamental questions before the world at war?

If we measure the important matters by current discussion, we may range them somewhat as follows: (1) defense against aggression; (2) full employment after the war; (3) eventual fair distribution of both raw materials and manufactured goods; (4) abolition of poverty; and (5) health.

To anyone giving thought to these problems, it must be clear that each of them, with all of its own peculiar difficulties, tends to break asunder along the lesions of race difference and race hate. Among the primary factors entering into the discussion is the folklore and superstition which lurks in the mind of modern men and makes them thoroughly believe, in accord with inherited prejudice and unconscious cerebration, that the peoples of the world are divided into fundamentally different groups with differences that are eternal and cannot be forgotten and cannot be removed. This philosophy says that the majority of the people of the world are impossible.

Therefore, when we discuss any of the listed problems, we usually see the solution within the frame of race and race difference. When we think of defense against aggression, we are thinking particularly of Europe, and the aggregation which we have in mind is not simply another Hitler but a vaster Japan, if not all Asia and the South Sea Islands. The "Yellow Peril" as envisaged by the German Emperor William II has by no means passed from the subconcious reactions of Western Europe. That is the meaning of world police and "our way of life."

When we think of the problem of unemployment, we mean especially unemployment in the developed countries of Western Europe and America. We do not have in mind any fundamental change so far as the labor of the darker world is concerned. We do not think of full employment and a living wage for the East Indian, the Chinese coolie, and the Negro of South Africa or even the Negro of our own South. We want the white laborer in England and in America to receive a living wage and economic security without periodic unemployment. In such case we can depend on the political power of white labor to maintain the present industrial organization. But we have little or no thought of colored labor, because it is disfranchised and kept in serfdom by the power of our present governments.

This means, of course, that the industrial organization of these countries must be standardized; they must not clog their own avenues of trade by tariff restrictions and cartels. But these plans have very seldom gone far enough to envisage any change in the relations of Europe and America to the raw material of Africa and Asia or to accepting any idea of so raising the prices of this raw material and the wages of the laborers who produce it that this mass of labor will begin to approach the level of white labor. In fact, any such prospect the white laborers with votes in their hands would in vast majorities oppose.

In both the United States and the Union of South Africa it has been the organized white laborers who have systematically by vote and mob opposed the training of the black worker and the provision of decent wages for him. In this respect they have ranged themselves with exploiting investors and disseminators of race hatred like Hitler. When recently in the United States the President's Fair Employment Practices Commission sought to secure some steps of elementary justice for black railway workers, the railway unions refused even to attend the hearings. Only the Communists and some of the C.I.O. unions have ignored the color line—a significant fact.

Our attitude toward poverty represents the constant lesion of race thinking. We have with difficulty reached a place in the modern white world where we can contemplate the abolition of poverty; where we can think of an industrial organization with no part of its essential co-operators deprived of income which will give them sufficient food and shelter, along with necessary education and some of the comforts of life. But this conception is confined almost entirely to the white race. Not only do we refuse to think of similar possibilities for the colored races but we are convinced that, even though it were possible, it would be a bad thing for the world. We must keep the Negroes, West Indians, and Indonesians poor. Otherwise they will get ambitious: they will seek strength and organization; they will demand to be treated as men, despite the fact that we know they are not men; and they will ask social equality for civilized human beings the world over.

There is a similar attitude with regard to health; we want white people to be well and strong, to "multiply and replenish the earth"; but we are interested in the health of colored people only in so far as it may threaten the health and wealth of whites. Thus in colonies where white men reside as masters, they segregate themselves in the most healthful parts of the country, provided with modern conveniences, and let the natives fester and die in the swamps and lowlands. It is for this reason that Englishmen and South Africans have seized the high land of Kenya and driven the most splendid of races of East Africa into the worst parts of the lowland, to the parts which are infested by the tsetse fly, where their cattle die and they are forced laborers on white farms.

Perhaps in no area of modern civilized endeavor is the matter of race revealed more startlingly than in the question of education. We have doubts as to the policy of so educating the colored races that they will be able to take part in modern civilization. We are willing to educate them so that they can help in our industrial development, and we want them to become good workmen so long as they are unorganized. But when it comes to a question of real acquaintance-ship with what the more advanced part of the world has done and is doing, we try to keep the backward races as ignorant as possible. We limit their schools, their travel, and their knowledge of modern tongues.

There are, of course, notable exceptions: the Negro colleges of the southern United States, the Indian universities, and some advance even in university training in South Africa and in East and West Africa. But this advance is hindered by the fact that popular education is so backward that the number of persons who can qualify for higher training is very small, especially the number who can enter the professions necessary to protect the economic status of the natives and to guide the natives in avoidance of disease. In all these matters race interferes with education.

Beyond this we have only to mention religion. There is no denying that certain missionaries have done fine work in ameliorating the lot of backward people, but at the same time there is not a ghost of a doubt that today the organized Christian church is unfavorable toward race equality. It is split into racial sections and is not disposed to disturb to any great degree the attitude of civilization toward the Chinese, the Indians, and the Negroes. The recent pronouncement of the Federation of Churches of Christ was a fine and forward-looking document, but it has aroused no attention, much less enthusiasm, among the mass of Christians and will not. The Catholic church never champions the political or economic rights of subject peoples.

This insistent clinging to the older patterns of race thought has had extraordinary influence upon modern life. In the first place, it has for years held back the progress of the social sciences. The social sciences from the beginning were deliberately used as instruments to prove the inferiority of the majority of the people of the world, who were being used as slaves for the comfort and culture of the masters. The social sciences long looked upon this as one of their major duties. History declared that the Negro had no history. Biology exaggerated the physical differences among men. Economics even today cannot talk straight on colonial imperialism. Psychology has not yet recovered from the shame of its "intelligence" tests and its record of "conclusions" during the first World War.

Granted, therefore, that this is the basic attitude of the majority of civilized people, despite exceptions and individual differences, what must we expect after this war? In the first place, the British Empire is going to continue, if Mr. Churchill has his way, without "liquidation"; and there is slight chance that the English Labour party or any other democratic elements in England are going to be able to get past the suspensory veto of the House of Lords and the overwhelming social power of the British aristocracy. In America the control of wealth over our democracy is going to be reinforced by the action of the oligarchic South. A war-weary nation is going to ignore reform and going to work to make money. If, of course, the greedy industrial machine breaks down in 1950 as it did in 1929, there will be trouble; but the Negroes will be its chief victims and sufferers. Belgium has held its Congo empire with rare profit during the war, and the home land will recoup its losses in Europe by more systematic rape of Africa. So Holland will batten down again upon the South Seas, unless the Japanese interlude forces some slight change of heart. South America will become an even more closely integrated part of British and American industry, and the West Indies will work cheaply or starve, while tourists throw them pennies.

The only large cause for disquiet on the part of Western Europe and North America is the case of Russia. There they are reassured as to the attitude of Stalin toward the working people of the Western world. Evidently he has decided that the Western European and American workers with votes in their hands are capable of deciding their own destiny; and, if they are not, it is their own fault. But what is going to be the attitude of Russia toward colonial peoples? How far and where and when is Russia going to protect and restore British and American investments and control in Asia and Africa? Certainly her attitude toward the Chinese has shown in the past and still shows that she has the greatest sympathy with coolie labor and no love for Chiang Kai-shek. Will she have a similar attitude toward the other peoples of Asia, of Africa, and of the South Seas? If so, smooth restoration of colonial imperialism is not going to be easy.

What now can be done by intelligent men who are aware of the continuing danger of present racial attitudes in the world? We may appeal to two groups of men: first, to those leaders of white culture who are willing to take action and, second, to the leaders of races which are victims of present conditions. White leaders and thinkers have a duty to perform in making known the conclusions of science on the subject of biological race. It takes science long to percolate to the mass unless definite effort is made. Public health is still handicapped by superstitions long disproved by science; and race fiction is still taught in schools, in newspapers, and in novels. This careless ignorance of the facts of race is precisely the refuge where antisocial economic reaction flourishes.

We must then, first, have wide dissemination of truth. But this is not all: we need deliberate and organized action on the front where race fiction is being used to prolong economic inequality and injustice in the world. Here is a chance for a modern missionary movement, not in the interest of religious dogma, but to dissipate the economic illiteracy which clouds modern thought. Organized industry has today made the teaching of the elementary principles of economic thought almost impossible in our schools and rare in our colleges; by outlawing "Communistic" propaganda, it has effectually in press and on platform almost stopped efforts at clear thinking on economic reform. Protest and revelation fall on deaf ears, because the public does not know the basic facts. We need a concerted and determined effort to make common knowledge of the facts of the distribution of property and income today among individuals; accurate details of the sources of income and conditions of production and distribution of goods and use of human services, in order that we may know who profits by investment in Asia and Africa as well as in America and Europe, and why and how they profit.

Next we need organized effort to release the colored laborer from the domination of the investor. This can best be accomplished by the organization of the labor of the world as consumers, replacing the producer attitude by knowledge of consumer needs. Here the victims of race prejudice can play their great role. They need no longer be confined to two paths: appeal to a white world ruled by investors in colored degradation or war and revolt. There is a third path: the extrication of the poverty-stricken, ignorant laborer and consumer from his bondage by his own efforts as a worker and consumer, united to increase the price of his toil and reduce the cost of the necessities of life. This is being done here and there, but the news of it is suppressed, the difficulties of united action deliberately increased, and law and government united in colonial areas to prevent organization, manipulate prices, and stifle thought by force. Here colored leaders must act; but, before they act, they must know. Today, naturally, they are for the most part as economically illiterate as their masters. Thus Indian moneylenders are the willing instruments of European economic oppression in India; and many

America and West Indian Negroes regard as economic progress the chance to share in the exploitation of their race by whites.

A union of economic liberals across the race line, with the object of driving exploiting investors from their hideout behind race discrimination, by freeing thought and action in colonial areas is the only realistic path to permanent peace today.

A great step toward this would be an international mandates commission with native representation, with power to investigate and report, and with jurisdiction over all areas where the natives have no effective voice in government.

Notes

Introduction

1. See for example, Elliott M. Rudwick, *W. E. B. Du Bois: A Study in Minority Group Leadership* (Philadelphia: University of Pennsylvania Press, 1960), p. 119; James Weldon Johnson, *Along this Way: The Autobiography of James Weldon Johnson* (New York: Viking Press, 1933), p. 203; Earl E. Thorpe, *Black Historians: A Critique* (New York: William Morrow and Co., 1971), p. 72; E. E. Embree, *Thirteen against the Odds* (New York: Viking Press, 1946), p. 153.

2. W. E. B. Du Bois, *The Autobiography of W. E. B. Du Bois* (New York: International Publishers, 1968), pp. 97–99.

3. Ibid., pp. 135–36.

4. Rebecca Chalmers Barton, *Witness for Freedom: Negro Americans in Autobiography* (New York: Harper and Brothers, 1948), p. 181.

5. W. E. B. Du Bois, Letter to Harvard faculty, undated, ca. April 1890. Harvard University Archives.

6. *Autobiography*, p. 199.

7. Ibid., p. 149.

8. Ibid.

9. Clark A. Elliott, assistant curator, Harvard University Archives. Personal communication, April 4, 1973.

10. Francis L. Broderick, *W. E. B. Du Bois: Negro Leader in a Time of Crisis* (Stanford: Stanford University Press, 1959), p. 27.

11. Wolfram Fisher, "Gustav Schmoller," *Encyclopedia of the Social Sciences* 14 (1968): 60–62.

12. W. E. B. Du Bois, "Schmoller U. Wagner Notebook," 1893–94, W. E. B. Du Bois papers, University of Massachusetts.

13. W. E. B. Du Bois, "A Program for a Sociological Society," 1897, Du Bois papers, University of Massachusetts.

14. Broderick, *W. E. B. Du Bois*, pp. 27–28.

15. W. E. B. Du Bois, *Dusk of Dawn: An Essay toward an Autobiography of a Race Concept* (1940; New York: Schocken, 1968), p. 47.

16. *Autobiography*, p. 160.

17. Herbert Aptheker, ed., *The Correspondence of W. E. B. Du Bois*, vol. 1 (Amherst: University of Massachusetts Press, 1973), pp. 26–29.

18. Francis L. Broderick, "The Academic Training of W. E. B. Du Bois," *Journal of Negro Education* 27 (Winter 1958): 10-16.

19. W. E. B. Du Bois, "The Talented Tenth," In *The Negro Problem*, ed. Booker T. Washington, et al. (1904; New York: Arno Press, 1969), pp. 31-75.

20. *Autobiography*, p. 184.

21. *W. E. B. Du Bois*, p. 29.

22. *Autobiography*, p. 194.

23. Ibid.

24. Du Bois, *Autobiography*, p. 194. See also Rudwick, *W. E. B. Du Bois*, p. 30; Samuel McCune Lindsay, Introduction to W. E. B. Du Bois, *The Philadelphia Negro: A Social Study* (1899; New York: Benjamin Blom, 1967), pp. vii-xv.

25. *Autobiography*, p. 195.

26. W. E. B. Du Bois, *The Philadelphia Negro: A Social Study* (1899; New York: Schocken, 1967), p. 194 (unless otherwise indicated, references are to this edition).

27. W. E. B. Du Bois, "The Negroes of Farmville, Virginia: A Social Study," *Bulletin of the Department of Labor* 3 (January 1898): 1-28 [165-95]. (Throughout the notes, page numbers in brackets refer to the present volume.)

28. *Autobiography*, p. 199.

29. Ernest Kaiser, Introduction to W. E. B. Du Bois, *The Atlanta University Publications* (New York: Arno Press, 1968), p. iv.

30. W. E. B. Du Bois, "The Laboratory in Sociology at Atlanta University," *Annals of the American Academy of Political and Social Science* 21 (May 1903): 503 [61].

31. W. E. B. Du Bois, "The Study of the Negro Problems," *Annals of the American Academy of Political and Social Science* 11 (January 1898): 22.

32. W. E. B. Du Bois, "My Evolving Program for Negro Freedom," in *What the Negro Wants*, ed. Rayford Logan (Chapel Hill: University of North Carolina Press, 1944), p. 46.

33. Ibid., p. 47.

34. "The Laboratory in Sociology at Atlanta University," p. 504 [63].

35. "My Evolving Program for Negro Freedom," p. 48.

36. *Dusk of Dawn*, p. 64.

37. W. E. B. Du Bois, "The Atlanta Conferences," *Voice of the Negro* 1 (March 1904): 86 [55].

38. Rudwick, *W. E. B. Du Bois*, p. 132.

39. W. E. B. Du Bois, *In Battle for Peace: The Story of My 83rd Birthday* (New York: Masses and Mainstream, 1952), p. 155.

40. Du Bois, "The Atlanta Conferences," p. 88.

41. Elliott M. Rudwick, "W. E. B. Du Bois and the Atlanta University Studies on the Negro," *Journal of Negro Education* 26 (Fall 1957): 473.

42. W. E. B. Du Bois, "The Negro in the Black Belt: Some Social Sketches," *Bulletin of the Department of Labor* 4 (May 1899): 401-17.

43. *Autobiography*, p. 213.

44. W. E. B. Du Bois, *The Souls of Black Folks: Essays and Sketches* (1903; New York: Fawcett, 1961).

45. Johnson, *Along this Way*, p. 203.

46. *W. E. B. Du Bois*, p. 46.

47. Rudwick, *W. E. B. Du Bois*, p. 298.

48. Aptheker, *The Correspondence of W. E. B. Du Bois*.

49. *Dusk of Dawn*, p. 222.

50. Ibid.

51. Ibid., p. 67.

52. "My Evolving Program for Negro Freedom," p. 59.

53. *Autobiography*, p. 258.

54. Rudwick, *W. E. B. Du Bois*, p. 150.

55. Broderick, *W. E. B. Du Bois*, p. 171; see also Raymond Wolters, *Negroes and the Great Depression* (Westport, Conn.: Greenwood Press, 1970), pp. 266-301.

56. Langston Hughes, Untitled tribute to Du Bois in *Freedomways* 5 (Winter 1965): 11.

57. W. E. B. Du Bois, "The Economics of Negro Emancipation in the United States," *Sociological Review*, October 1911, pp. 303-13.

58. *Dusk of Dawn*, p. 230.

59. Elliott M. Rudwick, "Du Bois versus Garvey: Race Propagandists at War," *Journal of Negro Education* 28 (Fall 1959): 428-29.

60. *Dusk of Dawn*, p. 317.

61. See Du Bois, *Autobiography*, p. 319.

62. Ibid., p. 323.

63. W. E. B. Du Bois, "Three Centuries of Discrimination against the Negro," *Crisis* 104 (December 1947): 262-64.

64. Du Bois, *Autobiography*, p. 349.

65. Ibid.

66. Ibid., p. 350.

67. Shirley Graham Du Bois, *His Day Is Marching On* (Philadelphia: J. B. Lippincott, 1971), pp. 127-28.

68. *Autobiography*, p. 379.

69. W. E. B. Du Bois, *The Ordeal of Mansart* (New York: Mainstream, 1957).

70. S. G. Du Bois, *His Day is Marching On*, p. 223.

71. Ibid., p. 323.

72. W. E. B. Du Bois, "On the Future of the American Negro," in "Some Unpublished Writings of W. E. B. Du Bois," ed. Herbert Aptheker, *Freedomways* 5 (Winter 1965): 123.

73. Herbert Aptheker, ed., *Afro-American History* (New York: Citadel, 1971), p. 263.

74. St. Clair Drake, Introduction to W. E. B. Du Bois, *The Black North in 1901: A Social Study* (1901; New York: Arno Press, 1969), pp. iii-xii.

75. *Autobiography*, p. 222.

76. Du Bois, "A Program for a Sociological Society," Du Bois Papers, University of Massachusetts (material used from notes by Francis Broderick, Schomburg Library, New York).

77. "The Study of the Negro Problems," p. 1 [70].

78. W. E. B. Du Bois, "Post Graduate Work in Sociology at Atlanta University," speech delivered in Athens, Georgia, ca. 1900, Du Bois papers, University of Massachusetts (material used from notes by Francis Broderick, Schomburg Library, New York).

79. "The Laboratory in Sociology at Atlanta University," p. 503 [61].

80. "The Study of the Negro Problems," p. 1 [70].

81. "The Atlanta Conferences," p. 85 [53].

82. W. E. B. Du Bois, "Sociology Hesitant," Du Bois papers, University of

Massachusetts (materials used from notes by Francis Broderick, Schomburg Library, New York).

83. W. E. B. Du Bois, "The Twelfth Census and the Negro Problems," *Southern Workman* 29 (May 1900): 306 [67].

84. "Sociology Hesitant."

85. Ibid.

86. "My Evolving Program for Negro Freedom," p. 58.

87. "Sociology Hesitant."

88. "The Atlanta Conferences," p. 85.

89. *Dusk of Dawn*, p. 64.

90. "The Study of the Negro Problems," pp. 16–17 [80].

91. "A Program for a Sociological Society."

92. Francis L. Broderick, "German Influence on the Scholarship of W. E. B. Du Bois," *Phylon* 19 (December 1958): 369.

93. "The Study of the Negro Problems," p. 12 [76].

94. W. E. B. Du Bois, "The Beginning of Slavery," *Voice of the Negro* 2 (February 1905): 104.

95. Du Bois, "My Evolving Program for Negro Freedom," p. 57.

96. W. E. B. Du Bois, "Race Relations in the United States, 1917–1947," *Phylon* 9 (third quarter 1948): 234.

97. *Autobiography*, p. 195.

98. Aptheker, *The Correspondence of W. E. B. Du Bois*, p. 75.

99. *Dusk of Dawn*, p. 51.

100. "The Atlanta Conferences," p. 85 [53].

101. "The Laboratory in Sociology at Atlanta University," p. 503 [61].

102. "The Atlanta Conferences," p. 85. See, for example, Robert Merton, *Social Theory and Social Structure*, rev. ed. (Glencoe, Ill.: Free Press, 1957), pp. 85–117.

103. In 1971 Oliver Cox became the first recipient of the American Sociological Association's Du Bois-Johnson-Frazier Award. The biannual award was presented to St. Clair Drake in 1973 at the presidential session of the sixty-eighth annual meeting of the American Sociological Association. This newly created award, which carries a stipend of $500 and bears Du Bois' name along with those of Johnson and Frazier, is evidence of an increasing recognition of Du Bois' sociological contributions. The award, formally specified by resolution from a caucus of black sociologists submitted to the American Sociological Association in 1970, was officially established in 1971 and was to be given either to a sociologist or to an institution whose work in the development of black sociologists was in the tradition of the three scholars.

The ASA award was established only a year after the creation of an annual W. E. B. Du Bois award by the predominently black Association of Social and Behavioral Sciences. Recipients of this award have been Oliver C. Cox, Lewis W. Jones, and Horace Mann Bond.

104. Dan S. Green, "The Truth Shall Make Ye Free: The Sociology of W. E. B. Du Bois" (Ph.D. dissertation, University of Massachusetts, 1973), pp. 486–545.

105. Howard Odum, *American Sociology: The Story of Sociology in the United States through 1950* (New York: Greenwood, 1969).

106. Allen Eaton and Shelby Harrison, *A Bibliography of Social Surveys* (New York: Russell Sage Foundation, 1930), pp. 231, 235–37.

107. Nathan Glazer, "The Rise of Social Research in Europe" in *The Human Meaning of the Social Sciences*, ed. Daniel Lerner (New York: Meridian Books, 1959), pp. 63–64.

108. Green, "The Truth Shall Make Ye Free," pp. 508-10.

109. E. Franklin Frazier, *The Negro in the United States*, rev. ed. (New York: MacMillan, 1957); Gunnar Myrdal, *An American Dilemma: The Negro Problem and Modern Democracy* (New York: Harper and Row, 1944).

110. Arnold Rose, *The Negro's Morale: Group Identification and Protest* (Minneapolis: University of Minnesota Press, 1949); Robert E. Park, *Race and Culture* (Glencoe, Ill.: Free Press, 1950); E. B. Reuter, *The American Race Problem* (New York: Thomas Crowell, 1938); H. A. Miller, *Races, Nations and Classes* (Philadelphia: Lippincott, 1924).

111. See John H. Bracey, Jr., August Meier, and Elliott Rudwick, eds., *The Black Sociologists: The First Half Century* (Belmont, Calif.: Wadsworth, 1971), p. 1.

112. W. E. B. Du Bois, "The Negro Race in the United States of America" (1911), in *Inter-Racial Problems: Papers from the First Universal Races Congress Held in London in 1911*, ed. G Spiller (New York: Citadel Press, 1970), p. 362 [108].

113. Du Bois, "The Economics of Negro Emancipation in the United States," p. 311.

114. Du Bois, "The Negro Race in the United States," p. 363.

115. Du Bois, "Race Relations in the United States," p. 236.

116. Bertram W. Doyle, *The Etiquette of Race Relations in the South: A Study in Social Control* (Chicago: University of Chicago Press, 1937).

117. W. E. B. Du Bois, "Problem of the 20th Century Is Problem of Color Line," *Pittsburgh Courier*, January 14, 1950.

118. W. E. B. Du Bois, "The Future of the Negro Race in America," *The East and the West* 2, no. 5 (1904): 11.

119. E. Digby Baltzell, Introduction to W. E. B. Du Bois, *The Philadelphia Negro: A Social Study* (1899; New York: Schocken, 1967), pp. xix, xvi, xviii; Aptheker, *The Correspondence of W. E. B. Du Bois*, p. 40, 43.

120. Shirley Graham Du Bois, Du Bois' second wife, verified this in a personal communication, September 19, 1975.

121. Du Bois, *Autobiography*, p. 199.

122. R. C. Key, "A Critical Analysis of Racism and Socialization in the Sociological Enterprise: The Sociology of Black Sociologists" (Ph.D. dissertation, University of Missouri, Columbia, 1975), p. 47.

123. G. Franklin Edwards, "E. Franklin Frazier," in *Black Sociologists: Historical and Contemporary Perspectives*, ed. J. G. Blackwell and M. Janowitz (Chicago: University of Chicago Press, 1974), p. 94.

124. Odum, *American Sociology*, pp. 235-36; Edwards, "E. Franklin Frazier," p. 112.

125. W. E. B. Du Bois, "The Negro Scientist," *American Scholar* 8 (Summer 1939): 318; Edwards, "E. Franklin Frazier," p. 112.

126. E. Franklin Frazier, "The Pathology of Race Prejudice," *Forum*, vol. 67 (June 1927).

127. H. Maus, *A Short History of Sociology* (London: Routledge and Kegan Paul, 1956), p. 63.

128. Odum, *American Sociology*, pp. 323, 325-26.

129. "A Critical Analysis of Racism," pp. 33-64.

130. *American Sociology*, pp. 327-28.

131. W. E. B. Du Bois, "Die Negerfrage in den Vereinigten Staaten," *Archiv fur Socialwissenschaft und Sozialpolitik* 22 (1906): 31-79.

6. THE PHILADELPHIA NEGRO

1. I shall throughout this study use the term "Negro," to designate all persons of Negro descent, although the appellation is to some extent illogical. I shall, moreover, capitalize the word, because I believe that eight million Americans are entitled to a capital letter.

2. "In the Fifth Ward only there are 171 small streets and courts; Fourth Ward, 88. Between Fifth and Sixth, South and Lombard streets, 15 courts and alleys." "First Annual Report College Settlement Kitchen," p. 6.

3. In a residence of eleven months in the centre of the slums, I never was once accosted or insulted. The ladies of the College Settlement report similar experience. I have seen, however, some strangers here roughly handled.

4. It is often asked why do so many Negroes persist in living in the slums. The answer is, they do not; the slum is continually scaling off emigrants for other sections, and receiving new accretions from without. Thus the efforts for social betterment put forth here have often their best results elsewhere, since the beneficiaries move away and others fill their places. There is, of course, a permanent nucleus of inhabitants, and these, in some cases, are really respectable and decent people. The forces that keep such a class in the slums are discussed further on.

5. Gulielma street, for instance, is a notorious nest for bad characters, with only one or two respectable families.

6. The almost universal and unsolicited testimony of better class Negroes was that the attempted clearing out of the slums of the Fifth Ward acted disastrously upon them; the prostitutes and gamblers emigrated to respectable Negro residence districts, and real estate agents, on the theory that all Negroes belong to the same general class, rented them houses. Streets like Rodman and Juniper were nearly ruined, and property which the thrifty Negroes had bought here greatly depreciated. It is not well to clean a cess-pool until one knows where the refuse can be disposed of without general harm.

7. The majority of these were brothels. A few, however, were homes of respectable people who resented the investigation as unwarranted and unnecessary.

8. Twenty-nine women and four men.

9. There may have been some duplication in the counting of servant girls who do not lodge where they work. Special pains was taken to count them only where they lodge, but there must have been some errors. Again, the Seventh Ward has a very large number of lodgers; some of these form a sort of floating population, and here were omissions; some were forgotten by landladies and others purposely omitted.

10. There is a wide margin of error in the matter of Negroes' ages, especially of those above fifty; even of those from thirty-five to fifty, the age is often unrecorded and is a matter of memory, and poor memory at that. Much pains was taken during the canvass to correct errors and to throw out obviously incorrect answers. The error in the ages under forty is probably not large enough to invalidate the general conclusions; those under thirty are as correct as is general in such statistics.

11. The chief source of error in the returns as to birthplace are the answers of those who do not desire to report their birthplace as in the South. Naturally there is considerable social distinction between recently arrived Southerners and old Philadelphians; consequently the tendency is to give a Northern birthplace. For this reason it is probable that even a smaller number than the few reported were really born in the city.

12. Compare "The Negroes of Farmville: A Social Study," in *Bulletin of U.S. Labor Bureau*, January, 1898.

13. In the case of lodgers not at home and sometimes of members of families answers could not be obtained to this question. There were in all 862 persons born outside the city from whom answers were not obtained.

14. "Condition," etc., 1848, p. 16.

15. Not taking into account sub-rent repaid by sub-tenants; subtracting this and the sum would be, perhaps, $1,000,000—see *infra*, p. 291. That paid by single lodgers ought not, of course, to be subtracted as it has not been added in.

16. Here, again, the proportion paid by single lodgers must not be subtracted as it has not been added in before.

17. The sentiment has greatly lessened in intensity during the last two decades, but it is still strong.

18. At the same time, from long custom and from competition, their wages for this work are not high.

19. One room under such circumstances may not by any means denote excessive poverty or indecency; the room is usually rented in a good locality and is well furnished.

9. The Negroes of Farmville, Virginia

1. Letters of introduction and some personal acquaintances among the people rendered intercourse easy. The information gathered in the schedules was supplemented by conversations with townspeople and school teachers, by general observation, and by the records in the county clerk's office.

2. The numbers involved in the Farmville inquiry were of course very small, and conclusions from percentages computed from them must consequently be made with due reservation. It is not intended in this or similar cases to push comparisons too far, but in all cases the conclusions stated are borne out by general observation here and elsewhere as well as by the figures.

3. Dancing, although indulged in somewhat, is frowned upon by the churches and is not a general amusement with the better classes.

Selected Bibliography of W.E.B. Du Bois

1896 *The Suppression of the African Slave Trade to the United States of America, 1638-1870*. New York: Longmans, Green.
       Atlanta University Publications, vol. 1, nos. 1-6 (editor). 1896-1901. Reprint New York: Octagon, 1968.
1897 "The Conservation of Races." In American Negro Academy, *Occasional Papers*, no. 2. Washington, D.C.
       "The Problem of Amusement." *Southern Workman* 27 (September): 181-84.
       "A Program for a Sociological Society." Ms. of speech given at Atlanta University. Du Bois Papers, University of Massachusetts.
       "Strivings of the Negro People." *Atlantic Monthly*, August, pp. 194-98.
1898 *Some Efforts of Negroes for Social Betterment* (editor). Atlanta University Study, no. 3. Atlanta: Atlanta University Press.
       "The Negroes of Farmville, Virginia: A Social Study." *Bulletin of the Department of Labor* 3 (January): 1-38.
       "The Study of the Negro Problems." *Annals of the American Academy of Political and Social Science* 11 (January): 1-23.
1899 "The Negro and Crime." *Independent*, May 18, pp. 1355-57.
       The Negro in Business (editor). Atlanta University Study, no. 4. Atlanta: Atlanta University Press.
       "The Negro in the Black Belt: Some Social Sketches." *Bulletin of the Department of Labor* 4 (May): 401-17.
       The Philadelphia Negro: A Social Study. Reprint New York: Schocken, 1967. New ed. New York: Benjamin Blom, 1967.
1900 *The College-bred Negro* (editor). Atlanta University Study, no. 5. Atlanta: Atlanta University Press.
       "Post Graduate Work in Sociology at Atlanta University." Ms. of speech delivered in Athens, Ga., ca. 1900. Du Bois Papers, University of Massachusetts.

"The Problem of Negro Crime." *Bulletin of Atlanta University,* February, p. 3.

"The Religion of the American Negro." *New World* 9 (December): 614–25.

"The Twelfth Census and the Negro Problems." *Southern Workman* 29 (May): 305–9.

1901   *The Negro Common School* (editor). Atlanta University Study, no. 6. Atlanta: Atlanta University Press.

The Black North in 1901: A Social Study. Reprint New York: Arno Press, 1969.

"The Negro Landholder of Georgia." *Bulletin of the Department of Labor* 6 (July): 647–777.

"The Problem of Housing the Negro." *Southern Workman* 30 (July, September, October, November, December 1901): 390–95, 486–93, 535–42, 601–4, 688–93; 31 (February 1902): 65–72.

"Results of Ten Tuskegee Conferences." *Harper's Weekly,* June 22, pp. 641–45.

"The Relation of the Negroes to the Whites in the South." *Annals of the American Academy of Political and Social Science* 18 (July): 121–40.

"The Social Training of the Negro." *Scroll* 6 (December): 19–23.

"The Spawn of Slavery: The Convict Lease System in the South." *Missionary Review of the World* 24 (October): 737–45.

"Testimony: General and Industrial Education." In Industrial Commission, *Report of the Industrial Commission on Education,* United States Industrial Commission Reports, 15:159–75. Washington, D.C.

1902   "Crime and Our Colored Population." *Nation,* December 25, p. 499.

The Negro Artisan (editor). Atlanta University Study, no. 7. Atlanta: Atlanta University Press.

Atlanta University Publications, vol. 2, nos. 7–11 (editor). 1902–6. New York: Octagon, 1968.

1903   "The Atlanta University Conferences." *Charities* 10 (May): 435–39.

"The Laboratory in Sociology at Atlanta University." *Annals of the American Academy of Political and Social Science* 21 (May): 502–5.

The Negro Church (editor). Atlanta University Study, no. 8. Atlanta: Atlanta University Press.

The Negro in the South (coauthor with Booker T. Washington et al.). Reprint New York: Citadel Press, 1970.

"Sociology Hesitant." Ms. ca. 1903–4. Du Bois Papers, University of Massachusetts.

"Some Notes on the Negroes in New York City." In *The Atlanta University Conference, Special Report,* pp. 1–5. Atlanta.

The Souls of Black Folk: Essays and Sketches. Reprint New York: Fawcett, 1961.

1904 "The Talented Tenth." In *The Negro Problem*, ed. Booker T. Washington et al. Reprint New York: Arno Press, 1969.

"The Atlanta Conferences." *Voice of the Negro* 1 (March): 85–89.

"The Development of a People." *International Journal of Ethics* 14 (April): 291–311.

"The Future of the Negro Race in America." *The East and the West* 2, no. 5 (January): 4–19.

"The Negro Farmer." Department of Commence and Labor, Bureau of the Census, *Bulletin*, no. 8, Washington, D.C., pp. 69–98.

"The Negro in America." In *The Encyclopedia Americana*, ed. Frederick C. Beach, vol. 11. New York.

Notes on Negro Crime: Particularly in Georgia (editor). Atlanta University Study, no. 9. Atlanta: Atlanta University Press.

"The Training of Negroes for Social Power." *The Colored American Magazine*, May, pp. 333–39.

1905 "Atlanta University." In *From Servitude to Service*, ed. Kelly Miller, et al. Boston: American Unitarian Association.

"The Beginning of Slavery." *Voice of the Negro* 2 (February): 104–6.

"The Black Vote of Philadelphia." *Charities* 15 (October 7): 31–35.

"The Negro South and North." *Bibliotheca Sacra* 62 (July): 500–13.

A Select Bibliography of the Negro American (editor). Atlanta University Study, no. 10. Atlanta: Atlanta University Press.

1906 "Die Negerfrage in den Vereinigten Staaten." *Archiv fur Social-wissenschaft und Socialpolitik* 22:21–79. (Written at request of journal's editor, Max Weber.)

"The Economic Future of the Negro." *Publications of American Economic Association* 7 (February): 219–242.

Health and Physique of the Negro American (editor). Atlanta University Study, no. 11. Atlanta: Atlanta University Press.

1907 *Economic Co-operation among Negro Americans* (editor). Atlanta University Study, no. 12. Atlanta: Atlanta University Press.

"The Negro in Large Cities." Speech reprinted in large part in the *New York Evening Post*, September 20.

"Sociology and Industry in Southern Education." *Voice of the Negro* 4 (May): 170–75.

1908 "Race Friction between Black and White." *American Journal of Sociology* 12 (May): 834–38.

1909 *Efforts for Social Betterment among Negro Americans* (editor). Atlanta University Study, no. 14. Atlanta: Atlanta University Press.

The Negro American Family (editor). Atlanta University Study, no. 13. Atlanta: Atlanta University Press.

1910 *The College-bred Negro American* (editor). Atlanta University Study, no. 15. Atlanta: Atlanta University Press.

"The Marrying of Black Folk," *Independent* 69 (October 13): 812–13.

"Post-graduate Work in Sociology," Ms. Du Bois Papers, ca. 1910.

"The Souls of White Folk," *Independent* 69 (August 18), 339–42.

1911 *The Common School and the Negro American* (editor). Atlanta University Study, no. 16. Atlanta: Atlanta University Press.

"The Economics of Negro Emancipation in the United States." *Sociological Review*, October, pp. 303–13.

"The Negro Race in the United States of America." Reprinted in *Inter-Racial Problems: Papers from the First Universal Races Congress Held in London in 1911*, ed. G. Spiller. New York: Citadel Press, 1970.

"The Social Evolution of the Black South." *American Negro Monographs* 1 (March): 3–12.

"A Symposium on Race Prejudice" (coauthor). *International* 4 (July): 29–31.

1912 *The Negro American Artisan* (editor). Atlanta University Study, no. 17. Atlanta: Atlanta University Press.

"The Rural South." *American Statistical Association Publications*, March, 80–84.

"The Upbuilding of Black Durham." *World's Work* 23 (January): 334–38.

1913 "Intermarriage." *Crisis* 4 (February): 180.

"The Social Effects of Emancipation." *Survey* 29 (February 1): 570–73.

1914 *Morals and Manners among Negro Americans* (editor). Atlanta University Study, no. 18. Atlanta: Atlanta University Press.

1915 "The Immediate Program of the American Negro." *Crisis* 9 (April): 310–12.

The Negro. Reprint New York: Oxford University Press, 1970.

1919 "An Essay toward a History of the Black Man in the Great War." *Crisis* 18 (June): 63–87.

1920 "Crime." *Crisis* 19 (February): 172.

Darkwater: Voices from within the Veil. Reprint New York: Schocken, 1969.

"Race Pride." *Crisis* 19 (January): 107.

1921 "Mixed Schools." *Crisis* 22 (August): 150–51.

1922 "Self-Help." *Crisis* 24 (June): 60.

"Social Equality and Racial Intermarriage." *World Tomorrow*, March, pp. 83–84.

1923 "The Superior Race." *Smart Set*, April, pp. 55–60.

1924 "The Dilemma of the Negro." *American Mercury*, October, pp. 179–85.

The Gift of Black Folk: The Negroes in the Making of America.
       Reprint New York: Washington Square Press, 1970.
1925 "Inter-Marriage." *Crisis* 29 (April): 251.
1926 "Crime." *Crisis* 32 (October): 286–87.
1927 "Negro Crime." *Crisis* 32 (May): 105.
1928 "Race Relations in the United States." *Annals of the American
       Academy of Political and Social Science* 140 (November): 6–10.
1930 "Classes among Negroes." *Crisis* 37 (June): 210.
1932 "Black America." In *America as Americans See It*, ed. F. J. Ringel.
       New York: Harcourt, Brace.
       "Crime." *Crisis* 39 (July): 234–35.
1934 "The Atlanta University Housing Project." *Crisis* 41 (June): 174–75.
       "Protest." *Crisis* 41 (June): 183.
       "Study of the Atlanta University Federal Housing Area." May. Ms.,
       Trevor Arnett Library, Atlanta University, Atlanta, Georgia.
1935 *Black Reconstruction in America 1860–1880.* Reprint New York:
       Atheneum, 1969.
1938 "A Pageant in Seven Decades, 1868–1938." Address delivered on his
       seventieth birthday at the University Convocation of Atlanta
       University, Morehouse College, and Spelman College, February 23,
       Atlanta, Georgia.
1939 *Black Folk Then and Now: An Essay in the History and Sociology
       of the Negro Race.* Reprint New York: Octagon, 1970.
       "The Negro Scientist." *American Scholar* 8 (Summer): 309–20.
       "The Position of the Negro in the American Social Order: Where Do
       We Go from Here." *Journal of Negro Education* 8 (July): 351–70.
1940 "The Atlanta University Studies of Social Conditions among Negroes,
       1896–1913." Ms., Du Bois Papers, University of Massachusetts.
       *Dusk of Dawn: An Essay toward an Autobiography of a Race
       Concept.* Reprint New York: Schocken, 1968.
1941 "Federal Action Programs and Community Action in the South."
       Social Forces 14 (March): 375–80.
1942 "Mr. Sorokin's Systems" (coauthor with Rushton Coulborn). *Journal
       of Modern History* 14 (December): 500–521.
1943 "The Negro Soldier in Service Abroad during the First World War."
       Journal of Negro Education 12 (Summer): 324–34.
       *Report of the First Conference of Negro Land-Grant Colleges for
       Coordinating a Program of Social Studies* (editor). Atlanta Uni-
       versity Study, no. 22. Atlanta: Atlanta University Press.
1944 "My Evolving Program for Negro Feedom." In *What the Negro
       Wants*, ed. Rayford Logan. Chapel Hill: University of North
       Carolina Press.
       Report of the Second Conference of Negro Land-Grant Colleges for

Coordinating a Program of Cooperative Social Studies (editor). Atlanta University Study, no. 23. Atlanta: Atlanta University Press.

1945 *Color and Democracy: Colonies and Peace.* New York: Harcourt, Brace.

Encyclopedia of the Negro: Preparatory Volume with Reference Lists and Reports (coeditor with Guy Johnson). New York: Phelps-Stokes Fund.

1947 "Three Centuries of Discrimination against the Negro." *Crisis* 54 (December): 262–64.

1948 "Race Relations in the United States, 1917–1947." *Phylon* 9 (Third Quarter): 234–47.

1952 *In Battle for Peace: The Story of My 83rd Birthday.* New York: Masses and Mainstream.

1957 "His Last Message to the World." (Written June 26, 1957; released when he died August 27, 1963). *Journal of Negro History* 49 (April 1964): 145.

The Ordeal of Mansart. New York: Mainstream.

1959 *Mansart Builds a School.* New York: Mainstream.

1961 "Letter of Application for Admission to Membership in the Communist Party of the United States." *Political Affairs* 40 (December): 347–52.

Worlds of Color. New York: Mainstream.

1963 *An ABC of Color.* New York: International.

"The Reminiscenses of William Edward Burghardt Du Bois." Oral History Research Office, Columbia University.

1968 *The Autobiography of W. E. B. Du Bois: A Soliloquy on Viewing My Life from the Last Decade of Its First Century.* New York: International Publishers.

Index

Acheson, Dean, 27
Adler, Felix, 23
African slave trade, 5
Aldridge, Ira, 108
American Academy of Political and
  Social Science, 36
American Communist Party, 30
American Economic Association,
  39, 102
American Historical Association, 5
American Negro Academy, 246,
  247, 248
American Sociological Association,
  45, 46, 47, 312
American Sociological Society, 39
*Annals of the American Academy of
  Political and Social Science*, 47
Aptheker, Herbert, 30
Association of Social and Behavioral
  Sciences, 312
Atlanta Exposition, 110
Atlanta Studies, 13, 14, 15, 16, 19,
  20, 31
Atlanta University, 11, 12, 13, 14,
  16, 20, 24, 25, 39, 44, 49, 50,
  55, 57, 59, 61, 62, 63, 64, 99, 200
Atlanta University Conferences, 11,
  24, 25, 58, 62, 63
Atlanta University Publications, 12

Baltzell, E. Digby, 113

Banneker, Benjamin, 90, 108
Berlin, University of, 6
Black self-sufficiency, 21
Boas, Franz, 23
Bond, Horace Mann, 312
Booth, Charles, 40
Broderick, Francis L., 17
Brown University, 44
Bulletin of the United States De-
  partment of Labor, 16, 63, 165
Burgess, Ernest, 45

Census Bureau, 64
Chattanooga Tradesman, 60
Chestnutt, Charles W., 109
Chicago, University of, 44, 45, 47
China, 28
Chivers, Walter, 24
Cole, William Earle, 25
Columbia University, 44, 45
Comte, August, 34
Consciousness of kind, 34, 38, 47
Cook, Will, 109
Council on African Affairs, 26
Cox, Oliver, 312
Crisis, 21, 22, 23, 39, 41
Cultural and Scientific Conference
  for World Peace, 27
Cummings, Edward, 6

Darwin, Charles, 43, 45, 46, 239

Diggs, James R., 45
Dill, Augustus G., 20
Dorantes, Stephan, 89
Douglass, Frederick, 91, 93, 108
Drake, St. Claire, 30
Du Bois, Alfred, 1
Du Bois, Mary Burghardt, 1
Du Bois, W. E. B.: Atlanta University, 11–16, 24–25; Award,
W. E. B. Du Bois, 312; conception of sociology, 32, 49; critical
of sociological peers, 31; discovery of truth, 31, 35, 80;
empirical orientation, 1, 31, 37;
Fisk University, 4; Harvard University, 4–6; NAACP, 20–24, 25–
26; neglect in sociology, 39–41;
Niagara Movement, 18–20; Pennsylvania, University of, 9–11;
science of human action, 53;
science of sociology, 14, 35; social
action, 39; sociological conferences, annual, 11, 15; study in
Europe, 6–8, 36; study of the
Negro, 80, 81; training in social
science, 8; training in sociology,
6, 8; veil of color, 222; Wilberforce University, 8, 9
Du Bois-Johnson-Frazier Award,
312
Dunbar, Paul L., 109
Durkheim, Emile, 31

Encyclopedia Africana, 29, 30

First Modern Pan-African Conference, 23
Fisk University, 3, 4, 99
Fitzhugh, George, 45
Frazier, E. Franklin, 25, 39, 41, 45
Freedman's Bureau, 92

Garvey, Marcus, 23
Georgia, Dougherty County, 154–
64, 201

Ghana, 29, 30
Giddings, Franklin, 34, 37, 46, 47
Glazer, Nathan, 40, 41
Great Barrington, Massachusetts,
1, 3

Hall, Gus, 30
Hampton University, 99, 230
Harrison, C. C., 44
Hart, Albert Bushnell, 5
Harvard Historical Series, 8, 40
Harvard University, 2, 3, 4, 5, 8,
11, 18, 44
Haynes, George Edward, 45
Haynes, Lemuel, 108
Hill, Mozell, 39
Horizon, 17
Howard University, 25, 99
Hughes, Henry, 45
Hughes, Langston, 22

Illinois Wesleyan University, 44, 45
Industrial Commission, U.S., 154
Israel Hill, 188

Johnson, Charles S., 25
Johnson, Rosamond, 109
Jones, Lewis W., 312
Justice, Department of, 28

Key, R. C., 46

Labor, Bureau of, 59
Labor, Department of, 64
Laboratory in sociology, 11, 61–64
Le Suicide, 31

McClurg, A. C., 17
Manchester Guardian, 23
Manifest Destiny, 43, 44, 45, 47
Marx, Karl, 24
Maus, Heinz, 45
Mayo-Smith, Richmond, 62
Michigan, University of, 44
Miller, H. A., 41

Miller, Kelly, 109
Moon, 16
Myrdal, Gunnar, 41, 113

NAACP, 20, 21, 22, 24, 25, 26, 284
National Negro Business League, 64
Negro crimes, 105, 149, 181
Negro criminals, 193
Negro problem, 14, 63, 66, 67, 71,
   75, 117, 140, 222, 288. *See also*
   Race problem
Negroes' problems, 12, 19, 32, 36,
   37, 73, 74, 79, 105, 115, 118, 152
New School for Social Research, 28
New York Age, 12
New York Globe, 2
New York Independent, 5
New York Times, 27
Niagara Movement, 18, 19, 20, 284
Nkrumah, Kwame, 29

Odum, Howard W., 25, 40

Pan-African Conferences, 23
Pan-African Movement, 26
Park, Robert Ezra, 41
Peace Information Center, 26, 27,
   28
Pennsylvania, University of, 9, 11,
   44, 45, 115, 231
Philadelphia, 7, 10, 11, 15, 36, 37,
   65, 229, 232
Phildelphia College Settlement, 44
Philadelphia Negro, 10, 31, 36, 40,
   113
Phylon, 25, 39

Race, 239, 240, 296; differences,
   243, 294, 296; organizations, 245;
   problem, 7, 31, 293, 294 (*See also*
   Negro problem)
Racial separation, 23
Randolph, John, 188
Reid, Ira De A., 24, 39
Reuter, E. B., 25, 41

Rose, Arnold, 41
Ross, Edward A., 46
Rudwick, Elliott M., 10, 15

Schmoller, Gustav, 6, 36
Schurz, Carl, 92, 93
Second Pan-African Conference, 23
Slater Fund, 6, 8
Small, Albion, 46
Smith, Adam, 240
Smith, T. Lynn, 25
Social Darwinism, 43, 44, 45, 47
Social problems, 71, 72, 118
Social reform, 20, 35
Social study, 33, 50, 67, 68, 79
Sociological Laboratory, 11
Sociological measurement, 37, 39
Sociological Society in England, 22
Sociological study, development of,
   70
Sociologist: car-window, 37; ideal
   of the twentieth century, 54
Sociology, 20, 32, 33, 34, 35, 36,
   38, 39, 61, 80, 83; laboratory in,
   11, 61-64
Sociology for the South, 45
Souls of Black Folks, 17, 22
South Carolina, University of, 44
Southern Workman, 63
Soviet Union, 27, 29
Spencer, Herbert, 34, 37, 38, 39,
   43, 45, 54
*Springfield, Massachusetts,
   Republican*, 2
State Department, 29
Stockholm Appeal, 27
Stowe, Harriet Beecher, 91
Strong, Hersey, 24
Sumner, William Graham, 46, 47

Talented Tenth, 9, 17
Tanner, H. D., 108
Thomas, W. I., 46
Thomas Jefferson School, 29
Thompson, Edgar T., 25, 40

Toennies, Ferdinand, 23
Toussaint, L'Ouverture, 90, 243
Treatise on Sociology, 45
Turner, Nat, 91
Tuskegee Institute, 9, 99

Uncle Tom's Cabin, 17, 91
United Nations, 26
United Negro Improvement Association, 23
Universal Races Congress, 22, 85

Virginia, Farmville, 16, 154, 165–95

Ward, Lester, 46
Washington, Booker T., 9, 14, 17, 18, 19, 20, 21, 109, 111, 284
Weber, Max, 48

Wharton, Susan P., 44
Wharton School, 11, 44
Wheatley, Phillis, 90, 108
White, Walter, 26
Wilberforce University, 8, 9
Willcox, Walter, 37
Wirth, Louis, 43
Wisconsin, University of, 44
Woods, Granville, 109
Woofter, Thomas J., 40
World Council for Peace, 29
Wright, Richard R., 45

Yale University, 44
Young, Donald, 25

Zangwill, Israel, 23